SOUL
CRISIS

SOUL CRISIS

ONE WOMAN'S JOURNEY
THROUGH
ABORTION TO RENEWAL

SUE NATHANSON, Ph.D.

NAL BOOKS

NEW AMERICAN LIBRARY

A DIVISION OF PENGUIN BOOKS USA INC., NEW YORK
PUBLISHED IN CANADA BY
PENGUIN BOOKS CANADA LIMITED, MARKHAM, ONTARIO

In telling my story, I have changed some minor details and the names of many of the people mentioned; other than that, this is a true story.

ACKNOWLEDGMENTS

"Slow Buffalo's Prayer" from THE SACRED PIPE: BLACK ELK'S ACCOUNT OF THE SEVEN RITES OF THE OGALA SIOUX, Recorded and Edited by Joseph Epes Brown. Copyright © 1953 by the University of Oklahoma Press.

"The Lost Baby Poem" by Lucille Clifton. Copyright © 1972 by Lucille Clifton. Originally published in GOOD NEWS ABOUT THE EARTH by Random House, Inc. Reprinted by permission of Curtis Brown, Ltd.

Reprinted by permission of the publishers and the Trustees of Amherst College from THE POEMS OF EMILY DICKINSON, edited by Thomas H. Johnson, Cambridge, Mass.: The Belknap Press of Harvard University Press, Copyright 1951, © 1955, 1979, 1983, by The President and Fellows of Harvard College.

From SELECTED POEMS AND LETTERS OF EMILY DICKINSON, Robert N. Linscott, ed. Copyright © 1959 by Robert N. Linscott. Reprinted by permission of Doubleday, a division of Bantam, Doubleday, Dell Publishing Group, Inc.

From "Singing for Life: The Mescalero Apache Girls' Puberty Ceremony," by Claire R. Farrer. Reprinted from BETWIXT AND BETWEEN, Louise Mahdi, ed., by permission of Open Court Publishing Co., La Salle, Illinois. Copyright © 1987 by Open Court Publishing Company.

Reprinted from THE QUEEN OF SWORDS by Judy Grahn. Copyright © 1987 by Judith Grahn. Reprinted by permission of Beacon Press.

From WOMAN AND NATURE by Susan Griffin. Copyright © 1978 by Susan Griffin. Reprinted by permission of Harper & Row Publishers, Inc., United States, Canada, Philippines, Open Market.

From THE WAY OF ALL WOMEN by Esther Harding. Copyright © 1970 by the C. G. Jung Foundation for Analytical Psychology, Inc. Reprinted by permission of the C. G. Jung Foundation for Analytical Psychology, Inc.

From WOMEN'S MYSTERIES: ANCIENT AND MODERN by Esther Harding. Copyright © 1971 by the C. G. Jung Foundation for Analytical Psychology, Inc. Reprinted by permission of the C. G. Jung Foundation for Analytical Psychology, Inc.

From C. G. Jung and C. Kerényi, ESSAYS ON A SCIENCE OF MYTHOLOGY: THE MYTH OF THE DIVINE CHILD AND THE MYSTERIES OF ELEUSIS. Bollingen Series XXII, trans. by R.F.C. Hull. Copyright 1949, © 1959 by Bollingen Foundation, New York, N.Y. New material copyright © 1963 by Bollingen Foundation; published by Princeton University Press, Princeton, N.J.

(The following pages constitute an extension of this copyright page.)

Library of Congress Cataloging-in-Publication Data

Nathanson, Sue.
  Soul crisis: one woman's journey through abortion to renewal / by Sue
Nathanson.
    p.   cm.
  ISBN 0-453-00657-4
    1. Abortion—United States—Psychological aspects—Case studies.
  I. Title.
  HQ767.5.U5N365   1989
  155.9'3—dc19   88-27228
                                                                      CIP

Designed by Leonard Telesca

First Printing, June, 1989

1   2   3   4   5   6   7   8   9

PRINTED IN THE UNITED STATES OF AMERICA

For my parents, my children, and my husband.
Each of you will always be a part of me,
even as we go our separate ways.

Contents

Author's Note

I have recorded the events and personal experiences in this book as accurately as possible. However, to protect the privacy of my family, friends, colleagues, and clients, I have altered the names and identifying characteristics of everyone, other than myself, attempting, nonetheless, to preserve the psychological truth of our lives. I suspect that readers will recognize aspects of themselves and of their own experiences in the individuals who appear in the book, for, paradoxically, we are as similar as we are different.

In the course of creating this manuscript, I have learned that the boundary between fiction and nonfiction is not as discrete as I once believed. We continually shape and reshape the raw material of our personal experience; as though it were a lump of wet clay that never hardens, we sculpt it into new forms, each a valid manifestation of the eternally indissoluble blend of subjective truth and objective reality. The story told in this manuscript is one such personal sculpture.

SOUL
CRISIS

Prologue

What would happen if one woman told the truth about her life?
The world would split open.

—MURIEL RUKEYSER[1]
From *"Käthe Kollwitz"*

What began as the private record of a very personal story
has become a book. To set this personal story in its
larger context, I must say a bit about who I am and how this
book came into being.

I began my life forty-four years ago as the daughter and
only child of parents to whom I was extremely precious.
After my birth, my parents, who had hoped to have a large
family, lost two male children who were born too prematurely to survive. My mother was advised not to attempt
additional pregnancies, and consequently both of my parents
went on to devote all their parental energy to me. In the
process, they imparted to me their own deeply embedded
moral values—to honor, above all, family, education, and
service to others. For as long as I can remember, I expected
that my adult life would include a husband and children, as
well as some form of work that would be satisfying to me
while contributing something of worth to others.

I worked hard to make this vision a reality for myself. By

1

the time I was twenty-three, I had met and married my
husband, Michael, whose vision of life and values matched
my own. By the time I reached the ripe age of twenty-seven,
I had earned a doctorate in psychology and was in the process
of developing what would become a successful private psychotherapy practice. During the intervening four years, Michael worked to establish his own law practice. By the time I
arrived at my thirty-third year, Michael and I had become the
proud and devoted parents of three children: Jill, Rebecca,
and Benjamin. Michael had by this time established a successful law firm, and I was now respected in the local professional
community as a psychotherapist.

When I look back with gratitude at the fullness of this life
from my present vantage point, my belief never wavers that
the experience of bearing and rearing our three children—an
ongoing and complicated mixture of inexplicable joy and heart-
rending pain—remains its center, its heart and soul. No matter what the future may hold, I cannot imagine that my
outlook will change. To me, childbirth and parenting—assisting
at the natural unfolding of unique, individual beings—is the
peak of the mountain, and no other mountaintop I reach or
climb can ever stand as high.

Five years ago my life took an unanticipated and extraordi-
narily difficult turn. When Ben, our youngest child, was five
years old, I unexpectedly became pregnant with a fourth
child through the failure of our method of birth control. Like
many women of different ages and situations in life, I had to
decide whether to bear or to abort this unplanned child. Once
a new life has been conceived, there is no turning back; an
unalterable event—physical and psychological—has occurred.
Ultimately, given the context of my life and the needs of
everyone involved, I chose to have an abortion, knowing with
my rational mind that either choice would be difficult for me
and for the members of my family.

I believed then, and still believe, that the choice of an
abortion was essential for the well-being of everyone in my
family, though I wished then, and still wish with every ounce
of my being, that I could have chosen otherwise. I would

have given anything to be able to climb one last time to the unparalleled peak of that mountain. But I made the best choice I could make with my rational mind. I did not antici- pate how profoundly I would suffer emotionally, or how long my suffering would endure.

Two months after my abortion I made another difficult decision that also involved an irreversible change: I decided to have a tubal ligation in order to avoid another unplanned pregnancy. This choice, like that of the abortion, made sense in rational terms. In addition to my worry that I might become pregnant by accident, I was fearful that the awesome, primal power of the longing to have a baby would combine with a yearning to fill the void created by the loss of my fourth child. Together these forces might lead me to become pregnant again—if not by conscious choice, then by accident. I knew that if I were to become pregnant again, I could not choose to bear again the suffering that accompanied my abor- tion. Yet the compelling reasons that led me to choose an abortion would become only more pressing with the passage of time. My husband was advised not to undergo a vasectomy because research at that time indicated he would be at higher risk of having a stroke. Thus the safest available protection against another pregnancy was sterilization, the closing off of my fallopian tubes. Tubal ligation was not a procedure that I had ever expected to elect voluntarily, but I did not feel that I could take the risk of less drastic, but less secure, methods of birth control. Once more I made the best, most rational choice I could—but again, I could not foresee the anguish to which the sudden, surgical loss of my fertility would give rise.

I am normally a very private person, accustomed to keeping my thoughts and feelings to myself. I first wrote to describe my experiences of the abortion and tubal-ligation surgery because I felt as if I would burst from the pressure of the painful and conflicting feelings I carried inside me. I discov- ered that writing about them not only helped me place this internal turmoil outside of myself, relieving the pressure, but it also enabled me to put my inner discord to positive use. Like a tangled skein of yarn that can be woven into cloth when disentangled, these discordant thoughts and feelings, once sorted out, could be understood and given meaning. I had no plan to do anything with the written manuscript; I had only the unformed notion that some distant day when my children were grown I might share it with them so that they could come to an understanding of what I had been grappling with during a portion of their childhood years.

For the first two years after my abortion and tubal ligation, the manuscript collected dust on a shelf. But as pressure to challenge the Supreme Court *Roe v. Wade* decision affirming the legal right of women to choose abortion began to mount during the second term of the Reagan administration, I found myself assaulted by an unending series of media reports. I read accounts of the bombings of Planned Parenthood clinics and the picketing of women attempting to enter them, in tandem with reports of the continuing debates among politicians as to whether the precedent established by *Roe v. Wade* should be overturned. Other articles, on the controversy over the management of teenage pregnancies, appeared; laws were passed in some states requiring that pregnant teenagers seeking abortion either notify their parents or appeal to a judge for permission. Debates in California continued on the issue of allocating medical funds for abortion procedures. Nationally, an effort was underway to prohibit federal funding for family-planning clinics that inform pregnant women about the option of abortion. On a more personal level, I continued to hear stories, from women friends and psychotherapy clients, of women who, like me, had been catapulted into whirlpools of emotional pain as a consequence of their abortions. I began to pay more attention to stories of equally painful reactions to other experiences that, like abortion, are unique to women (though male partners may also participate): miscarriage, infertility, or the decision to bear an unplanned and unwanted child.

The stories lingered in my mind, and I found that I could no longer leave my manuscript on the shelf. Contemplating the bitter and emotional polarization in our country between the Pro-Choice and Right to Life advocates, I found that I could not remain silent. I saw that the war between the two opposing sides was consuming so much energy and attention that none was left to meet the special needs of the individual women who must face this dilemma, no matter which choice they might make. At the time of my own crisis, I had searched unsuccessfully for some reflection of my inner experience in the written words of others, knowing that such an account would help me. I unearthed abstract ideas and concepts that fit the form of my experience and concise poetic renderings of my feelings, but nowhere did I find a full description of my experience. I hope that by sharing my story, I will provide others with the all-encompassing mirror that had been missing for me.

Although I know that individual women vary tremendously in the amount of conflict they experience over the choice to continue or to end a pregnancy, as well as in how much distress they experience in both the short and the long term, the choice is nonetheless a difficult one. It is also a choice that women, because of their biological capacity to bear children, will inevitably continue to confront. As long as unplanned pregnancies continue to occur, some women will choose abortion, no matter what abortion laws our country passes, no matter what conclusions scholars reach concerning the ethical, religious, and moral standing of abortion. The choice that women make to bear or to abort a child arises in the end from a complicated and not always fully conscious weighing of their own needs, as well as those of the father, the unborn child, and other family members. The choice can only be made in the context of the woman's life situation, itself a complicated distillation of past experiences, present outlook, and future plans. Because the needs of everyone involved may conflict, often in an irreconcilable way, no perfect choice exists, and *any* choice may result in suffering. I found that my own suffering persisted, even though I believe my decision was necessary and even though I was fortunate in having had the right to make the choice that was best for me, given the context of my life.

The psychological tasks I faced in working with my suffering at first seemed overwhelming. For me, mothering, like hunger, is a primordial instinct that begins to function automatically at conception; consequently I felt the abstract potentiality of the fetus as a tangible reality. Central to the mothering instinct within me is a predisposition to recognize and meet the needs of my children, voluntarily sacrificing my own at times when there is a conflict. The abrupt severing of the powerful mothering energy that surged forth in response to my fourth pregnancy resulted in nearly unendurable emotional pain. I had found my best self in the exquisite harmony of loving children, who need love above all else (infants whose physical needs are fully met fail to thrive without an attachment to a mothering person). Committed to life, not death, having always celebrated my fertility and joy in giving birth, I fell into an abyss of despair from which I could see no exit. How would I find a way to accept the loss of my unborn child, to bear the sudden excising of my fertility, and to live with myself after choosing to deny life to the fourth child I had already begun to protect and nurture?

These necessary yet inconceivable tasks precipitated a crisis at the deepest center of my being—a crisis of soul—unlike any other experience of suffering I have encountered. "Soul-crisis" is my name for an experience that consists of much more than an intense emotional reaction to loss and trauma. It involves the shattering of one's beliefs about oneself and one's life into fragments that cannot be put back together again in exactly the same way. It is an experience that forces an assessment of one's basic mode of being in the world, that compels the examination of familiar assumptions, that requires the loss of innocence and a simple worldview, that demands the rebuilding of one's basic foundations.

Just as all the king's horses and all the king's men could not put Humpty Dumpty together again, the efforts of others who cared about me could not by themselves restore to me a sense of wholeness and peace. The work of restoration was essentially mine; completing it successfully took years of psychological effort on my part, combined with the active support and assistance of others. The bigger the soul-crisis, the stronger the support that is required; my crisis required the assistance of my husband, family, and friends, a guide found in an unexpected place, every iota of knowledge gleaned from my years of work and study as a psychologist, and the help of myth and ritual.

As a result of my quest for healing, I came to understand that individuals who are grappling with a crisis of soul need a strong "holding environment," a "container" that can hold them securely until their intense emotional reactions subside and the sense of self that was shattered by the crisis can be reconstituted in a new way. One layer of the holding environment to which I refer metaphorically can be composed of human relationships within which the person in crisis feels understood empathically. A second layer may be provided by the culture, if the culture recognizes the crisis as warranting concern; in our culture, abortion is a controversial issue, with the focus primarily upon whether women have the right to choose it. Little attention remains to address the psychological needs of those women who exercise their right. A third layer of the holding environment may be provided by the archetypal or universal realm of wisdom available to each of us; this archetypal realm surfaces in the form of myths, images, and dreams and can be evoked by rituals. We are accustomed to drawing upon this archetypal realm for losses that are a natural part of the human condition, such as death or illness. Most of us are less inclined to avail ourselves of it for help in bearing the emotional anguish that may arise from abortion, as well as for less controversial but equally painful losses related to childbearing, such as infertility and miscarriage.

I know that other human beings will inevitably confront personal crises of this magnitude, whether such soul-crises are brought about through life choices or through the kinds of difficulties that life can bring to us unbidden. Trials of life inevitably lie in wait for each of us, regardless of our age or gender. They vary only in intensity and in the circumstances that precipitate them. As human beings who are both gifted with and saddled by consciousness, we share the common tasks of surviving our difficult times as well as making meaning of them, a process that requires us to allow the transformation of our consciousness. I believe we have much of value to contribute to one another in relating our solitary efforts to wrest meaning from suffering. I am hopeful that telling the story of my personal soul-crisis and of the creation of a multi-layered holding environment within which I could reorient and heal will help others in their efforts to withstand and to make meaning of what my young son Ben named, at the early age of eight, "the hard parts of life." However we may differ from one another, we are nonetheless fellow travelers on the same road, each of us hoping to surmount with dignity and courage the obstacles before us in order to live satisfying and meaningful lives. In the spirit of our common humanity, I offer my story.

ONE

Pregnancy

Many women sense dimly that in the experience of childbirth more happens than they are entirely conscious of. They know intuitively that the significance of childbearing is deeper than the production of the actual physical child. The infant means to them far more than they can explain. . . .

If the woman is not chiefly concerned during this process with the discomforts and limitations pregnancy imposes but is willing to allow life to be lived through her, she may experience an entirely new phase of consciousness, for she becomes complete in herself, independent of man. She is all mother and offspring . . . she is one of "the Mothers. . . ."

Then when her hour comes she must give herself up to be merely the medium for this new life . . . the distinguishing marks of her personality, of her social grade, of her race, are stripped off, until she like her remote ancestress of old is revealed only as woman—as female creature engaged in her most fundamental task. . . .

To those whose natures are more profound, it brings a knowledge of the significance of life which is seldom found in any other way. Hence, in spite of the pain, childbearing is most deeply desired by many women because of the contact with the deepest meaning of life which has come to them by this road and by it alone.

—Esther Harding
The Way of All Women[1]
1970

There are some griefs so loud
They could bring down the sky,
And there are griefs so still
None knows how deep they lie,
Endured, never expended.

—MAY SARTON[2]
From *"Of Grief"*

My period is five days late, which is very unusual. My menstrual cycle has been as regular as the phases of the moon, recurring every twenty-eight days ever since I gave birth to my third child, Ben. It is evening, an ordinary Monday night in May, and I am lying on my bed reading a book. The thought bursts upon me—a sudden explosion of awareness from an unknown place: I am *pregnant*. There is an intense and brief moment in which I experience an odd combination of horror and joy. I flee from this mixture of feeling and run downstairs to tell my husband.

Michael is sitting in his favorite chair in our family room reading a newspaper and is slow to look up at me over the top of his horn-rimmed reading glasses as I bound down the steps into the room. Our three children have already gone to bed, and I am free to speak my news aloud.

"Michael! I am *pregnant*!" I announce. He looks at me without comprehension, an utterly blank expression on his face. What is the matter with him? Why doesn't he react? My heart is pounding with a physical urgency that I cannot control.

"How can that be?" he asks finally. We have been careful to use birth control ever since Ben was born five years ago. Truth be told, however, in a silent, secret part of me, a pregnancy would not be altogether unwanted. My three pregnancies, the births, and the subsequent mothering of my children as infants and babies have been the best part of my entire thirty-eight years. I do not know why this is so, only that I have neither before nor after felt so much in harmony with my body, with my self, and with life. In fact, after Ben was born and I knew I would not have other children—we had struggled hard with the very decision to have a third child—I went through a year-long period of mourning for the end of my childbearing, a period during which I felt that the best part of my life was over.

"I don't know *how*," I tell Michael impatiently. "I just know I *am*." Michael, who I can see is hoping I am wrong, encourages me to wait until I find out for sure. We do not talk further, not wanting to grapple with a problem that may not be real. But he comes right up to bed with me, and we lie silently together, he on his back with his arm around me; I nestle into his body, my legs curled under his knees and my head in the hollow of his neck. Soothed, myself an infant encircled in his physical warmth, I let thoughts and memories arise and pass away like ocean waves.

I ponder my profound attachment to pregnancy, birth, and mothering. The strength of my attachment feels so rooted in my body that I wonder whether it is instinctive, carried in my genes. Yet I know that not all women are as drawn to the experience of childbearing as I am; could their female genetic heritage be different from mine? I have never understood why some women are so invested in their childbearing and mothering capacities and others are not. My friend Julia, for example, who is twenty years older than I am, had only one child. And it was her husband, Stephan, who was the more nurturing parent, caring for their son when he was sick or in distress. Even when she had a hysterectomy, at age forty-two, she did not mourn the loss of her reproductive organs. It was a relief to her not to have her period anymore, whereas I imagine that I will miss its rhythmic appearance, despite the discomforts. Katherine, on the other hand, who is only a few months older than I am, would give anything to have a child. Her prospects are now growing slimmer as her fortieth birthday approaches and there is no man in her life. The notion of a life without children is unthinkable to her and equally unimaginable to me, knowing as I do what a wonderful mother she would be; yet childlessness is a real possibility that she must face. Fortunately she is not entirely without hope. She has recently met and begun to date Chris, who seems to be a very loving man. Not wanting to let myself feel hopeful about the future of their relationship too quickly, I shut off further thoughts about the two of them.

A picture comes into focus of Michael and me when we

were trying to decide whether to have a third child. We are watching Jill and Becky play in the bathtub together, with Jill, the older, occupying her privileged place at the "deep" end by the faucet. In my parental role of lifeguard, I am sitting on top of the closed toilet seat cover, hunched over. Michael has come in to join us and is standing in the doorway. With their freshly washed chestnut-colored hair plastered to their faces, pink cheeks, and sparkling eyes, our daughters are the picture of glowing health. Momentarily lost in heart-bursting pride and love, Michael and I forget the seemingly endless hours spent holding hair dryers to their wet heads, picking up toys, folding their miniature-size laundry, struggling to control our outrage in response to endless provocations, and drying tears—theirs and ours.

Michael looks at me and shakes his head; he knows what I am thinking. "Look," he says, keeping his voice low so that Becky and Jill won't hear us. "We have our family life under control now. I'm so happy with my daughters, and you and I finally have time for each other and for ourselves. It's such a sunny time in our lives—we can have lunch together, take Jill and Becky on outings, read books at night! If we have a third child, we'll be disrupting all this, going back to changing diapers, night feedings, doctor's visits, the whole works."

"I know, but Jill and Becky are doing so well! It's *because* things are under control now that we could handle a third! And the diaper stage is finite—it only lasts a few years. We'd be back to a sunny place in no time," I reply, nearly overcome with a deep yearning for another baby, another child, another member of my family.

"You're only picturing us *having* a baby, not the years that come after that," Michael answers. "I'm thirty-eight now. If we have another child, I'll be nearly forty years old. That means I'll be raising children until I'm sixty. You'll be fifty-four! You've learned to set aside your own needs, to take care of others instead of yourself. Don't you want to have time for yourself? Time for us to be together?"

I look at Michael's face and watch the intensity of his feelings etch a frown on his forehead; I hear the passion fueling his words. I know he is trying to be an advocate for me, for us. No wonder he is such a good lawyer! His words ring true. While I can be acutely sensitive to the needs of others, I am often blind to my own. But my wish for another child seems to be in complete harmony with the needs that I do see clearly; I cannot perceive a conflict. I tell him, "Of course I want time for myself and time for us! But children grow up so fast! They go off and live their own lives even before they're eighteen. I just can't see time for myself or for us as being a problem!"

"It isn't just a matter of time," Michael answers, patiently and persistently arguing his case. "It's the responsibility, the expense. We want to give our kids every opportunity— lessons, education, good child care. I have to think about our income and being able to support a big family."

"I work, too, you know," I tell him, but my words sound unconvincing even to me. Michael, like both of our fathers, has assumed the role of the primary financial provider for the family. He takes his responsibility very seriously; this quality, along with his capacity for absolute loyalty to our relationship, met similar needs and proclivities in me and was partly what attracted us to each other. His concerns about disrupting our stability and about diverting energy from each other and from ourselves are completely understandable; I have them, too. Having reached the impasse we always encounter when we discuss the possibility of enlarging our family, I turn my attention to our girls. "Okay, time to let the water out!" I tell them, having discovered serendipitously that they will emerge from the bathtub without complaint, or at least without blaming me for spoiling their fun, when the last of the water disappears. Another Dr. Spock guideline bites the dust; so much for the worry that children will fear being sucked down the drain. Enjoying this memory now, I stifle a laugh, not wanting to awaken Michael, who has the enviable ability to fall asleep effortlessly.

Warmed by Michael's body, my thoughts return to our present predicament. I remember the way we obsessed over our decision to have Ben. Fragments of the conversations we used to have with our closest friends, none of whom has a large family, float past. "Why would you want to have any more children? Why don't you nurture yourselves instead?" they would ask when we confided in them that we were thinking of having another child. My mind comes to rest upon Jonathan Chester, a therapist in my professional circle and our friend, the only person in our confidence who encouraged us to have another child. "In big families I've known, the older children help," he told us when we worried about the amount of work it would be to have three offspring. "Parents can have fun, too, you know," he countered when we worried about our lives being all work and no play. "There's just as great a probability that things will go well," he'd remind us when our anxieties would create catastrophic scenarios of disaster. "Other families with three children seem to survive. Besides, you two really *enjoy* being parents! You're good at it!" Did he sense intuitively that we were less ambivalent about a third child than fearful that something terrible would happen if we yielded to our deepest wishes?

For a long time, equal arguments on both sides of the question kept us immobilized. Then something shifted inside Michael and he moved firmly over to the side of wanting to have another child, pulling me, without resistance, along with him. "What's happened to you?" I asked him, baffled by this change in his attitude. "What's made you feel okay about having another child?" But Michael couldn't really answer me. "I just feel more confident about my life, about being able to manage another child without losing ground. I realized that having another child can bring us closer together— it doesn't have to take us away from each other. I don't know if I'm actually on more solid footing, or if my feeling about myself and my life is what's different. Are you sure *you* want to go ahead with it now that I've changed my mind?" he asked me with a smile, sensing that his certainty would leave more room for me to have doubts. "Absolutely," I replied. "I'm nervous, but more with excitement than with doubt."

How happy we were when Ben arrived! When we agonized over the decision to have a third child, we were not motivated by gender; we were not trying to have a son after two daughters. "Are *you* sure you won't mind if we have another daughter?" I would ask Michael during the pregnancy, worrying how he might feel surrounded by four females. "Actually," he would reassure me, "I'd be relieved if we had another daughter! If we had a son, I'd feel more responsible for him. I mean, I'd have to teach him how to work with tools, play baseball, football. I don't know if I could do it. I'm sort of used to having daughters!" I laugh fondly at this memory; the day after Ben arrived, Michael went out and bought child-size baseball gloves and baseballs for Jill and Becky. "I thought to myself, why shouldn't I teach my *daughters* how to catch a ball?" he explained, displaying his new purchases proudly. We didn't even know then that Becky would turn out to be left-handed and wouldn't be able to use the right-handed mitt Michael had automatically selected.

I reflect upon our decision-making process when we thought about having Ben. In the end, all our rational considerations seemed to fade into the background and we simply felt right about having another child. And even though I did not have doubts about our decision, going ahead with our plan required no small amount of courage. I felt as if I were taking a deep breath, closing my eyes, and jumping off a big cliff into an opaque pool of unknown water far below. At that moment, it didn't matter how certain I felt, how clear about all my reasons. In the end, I still had to leave familiar ground. My decisions to marry Michael and to have Jill and Becky had been made in exactly the same way: Compelling rationale had yielded to intuition.

We conceived Ben immediately, but we would not have changed our minds about wanting him even if it had taken us longer to create that miraculous opening in the firmament through which he emerged into our waiting arms. Contemplating the miracle of Ben sends a wave of panic through me: What do we choose now? Do I keep that miraculous opening closed to our fourth child? I know I would love this child as wholeheartedly as I love Jill, Becky, and Ben. And if I keep the aperture sealed, will I then have to mourn not only the loss of this child but also the ending of my childbearing yet again? It was so hard to let go after Ben was born. Could I go through this mourning process again?

I remember how I felt in the months after Ben's birth. I was relieved to know I would no longer have to bear the anxiety of wondering if I would survive a pregnancy and delivery, if my baby would be healthy, if we would be spared additional problems that could arise. No more terrifying night-time fantasies of the umbilical cord being wrapped around the fetus's neck, of the placenta detaching, of toxemia developing, of a breech birth or a last-minute cesarean section. But at the same time I had difficulty assimilating the fact that my child-bearing experiences were actually over. For so many years of my life, having children was a goal that I mentally located first in my future and then in my present life. With Ben's lusty emergence from my body, this experience had abruptly relocated itself squarely in my past. I could not get used to this new vantage point. When I sought support for my sor-row, I was met with genuine puzzlement: Aren't you relieved to be finished with having children? Aren't three children enough? I remember with a frown how I had finally put myself on a stringent diet to lose the extra weight of preg-nancy. Though I had not known it at the time, my fierce willpower was fueled in part by the grief of mourning this ending: Of what use now are the womanly curves of my body?

Michael takes a deep breath and sighs in his sleep, inter-rupting my reverie. I wait to see if he will wake up, and when his breathing settles into an even rhythm, I return to my thoughts. I picture myself sitting in the rocking chair in Ben's bedroom late at night. Ben, nearing eighteen months of age, is ready to wean himself away from the comforting warmth of the milk in my breasts. Now he wants to hold his own bottle at night and to drink from a cup in the daytime like his older sisters. This is how it should be, I think to myself, trying to ease my sorrow at the finality of this ending. Children should have their parents there for them until they are ready to move away. I feel pleasure in having been able to let Ben wean himself away from me at his own pace, but this does not allow me to bypass the special sorrow of a final parting. This night is the last time I will ever nurse an infant. Knowing this, I pay attention to the smallest physical sensations, as if to engrave them forever in my mind: the tingling of the milk letting down in response to Ben's sucking, the strength and pressure of his mouth and tongue so skillfully draining the reservoir of milk, the relief that comes as the milk empties from my breast, even though there is so much less available now, since Ben is nearly weaned. I hold him in my arms for a minute, watching him sleep. Then I put him down, slowly, gently, in his crib, laying to rest this night not only my son but also myself as mother of a baby.

Michael, still asleep, rolls over onto his side. Instinctively I press myself backward, pushing as far into the curve of his body as it is possible to go. Without awakening, he wraps his arm tightly around my stomach, clinging to me as if to a giant teddy bear. Finally I sleep.

Tuesday morning in the ten minutes between clients I stand at the desk in my office and call my doctor's office. An impersonal woman's voice answers the phone, and I am forced to tell her my problem. Embarrassed and reluctant to talk to a stranger—how will she know that I am basically a responsible person, that I do not take pregnancy lightly, that I am not a reckless person or an inadequate mother, even if I sometimes feel like one—I haltingly blurt out my problem.

"I think I may be pregnant, and, uh, I already have three children, so I don't think . . . I can't really . . . we can't have another one. I don't know what I should do."

Her voice immediately acquires warmth, and I am overcome with gratitude; I must have been expecting a judgmental response. She instructs me to go for a pregnancy test, telling me that if I go right away, they will have the results that afternoon. But my heart sinks when she tells me that Dr. Hodge, the obstetrician who cared for me through all three pregnancies and delivered two of my children, is out of town. The only doctor with whom I can schedule an immediate appointment, should the results be positive and should I

choose to have an abortion, is young and new. He has not yet
filled his practice with patients and has free time. The receptionist tells me his name: Dr. Rhodes. I repeat the name to
myself, as if to make him as familiar and real to me as Dr.
Hodge. Much as I have complained at times that Dr. Hodge
is too paternal and been irritated by his ingenuous brand of
antifeminism—why, he would query, would women want to
join clubs that are for men only?—I now yearn for his presence. He would surely understand what a pregnancy means
to me.

I decide to schedule an appointment with the new young
doctor as soon as possible, just in case. The receptionist gives
me one on Thursday morning, in the time when I usually
swim, so I will not have to cancel any appointments with my
own clients. As a psychoanalytic patient with four sessions a
week myself, I know firsthand how important the hours with
one's therapist are. Only for emergencies would I ever cancel
their appointments.

I have blood drawn as soon as possible that morning in a
small laboratory near the hospital in which I gave birth to my
children. The lab is next to a kidney dialysis unit, and I can
see the complex medical equipment clearly through the large
glass windows. What am I doing here, I think to myself; this
cannot be happening to me. But the chair in which I sit while
I hold out my arm for the rubber tourniquet is very real, and
the blood that I watch fill the small glass tube comes directly
from my arm. I stare at it, as if by staring I will be able to see
the mysterious hormone that signals the fact that my body
has begun to adjust to a new presence inside. The young
technician tells me I must wait until the afternoon to find out
the results. But I know the results already, in my body, my
heart, my soul. I know that I am physically and psychologically merged with another life. The scientific blood test is not
needed for the diagnosis, and there is nothing science can
offer me that will help me cope with what cannot now be
changed.

After the blood test I go off to see Dr. Ross, my therapist.
He is the psychoanalyst whom I have been seeing for nearly

three years now. I began to see him primarily as a result of my interest in doing long-term, in-depth psychotherapy with my own clients. Like most psychotherapists with this interest, I believe that the more I continue to grow and develop, the better I will be able to work with my own clients. Because I sought analysis more out of a wish to understand my personal issues than out of any pressing life crisis or internal turmoil, I have not yet presented Dr. Ross with any urgent needs or complicated problems. I am sure that he would describe me as an interesting, undemanding client, a capable and competent therapist and mother, with a strong ego and a good capacity for self-reflection.

I wonder to myself how he will react to the news of my pregnancy. Over the past two years Dr. Ross has proved to be a very reliable, conscientious person. He generally remains rather quiet in my sessions, and I enjoy the freedom to use the time talking about whatever I want. Perhaps because he is such a quiet and introverted man, I have never seen any evidence of his needs to receive attention and admiration, to make clever interpretations, or to offer his opinions. Although I sometimes wish he would be more forthcoming, and I miss comments from him that would help me make connections between my early history and current experiences or that would clarify the transference nature of my relationship to him—the ways I relate to him that reflect patterns established in relation to my parents—this lack has not been particularly distressing. I have always been self-reliant and able to manage my life; it's hard for me to imagine myself needing to rely upon interpretations from him. His obvious high regard for me and his ability to let me occupy the entire hour have up until now enabled me to blossom. My interest in my work has expanded enormously; I have been reading widely in my field and have enjoyed discussing my ideas with him. His interest in my stories about my children has left me feeling happily effective as a mother, and my relationship to my family has flourished.

I park my car on the street in front of the two-story brick building in which he has his office and climb up the staircase to the second-floor waiting room. In fact, I think to myself, it must have been this very blossoming that led me to my current plight. My zest for life, my energy and vitality, have increased dramatically since the beginning of my analysis with Dr. Ross. Along with this energy, my libido had increased, too, and, instead of being exhausted and ready for sleep at night, Michael and I have had renewed sexual energy. The thought of sexual energy brings me back to the reality of this pregnancy, to the reality of a potential fourth child.

I will not let myself think about it now, but I know exactly when I conceived this child-not-to-be. It was that Tuesday night three weeks ago when there was an open house at our children's elementary school. I was also scheduled to attend an evening seminar, but I regretfully planned to miss it because the back-to-school night was particularly special; this year was the last one when all three of our children would be located at the same school. But the back-to-school meeting had ended unexpectedly early, and I had gone off cheerfully to my class. I had been happy to be able to attend both events and had returned home energized by them. Listening to Jill's teacher make such perceptive comments about her, reading Becky's well-written essays in the neat red folder on her desk, and seeing my small son's work displayed on the bulletin board along with his classmates' efforts had filled me with pride. The seminar discussion, an unexpected treat, had been both challenging and lively. Michael, who always waits up for me when I am out at night, had opened the door between the house and the garage when he heard me pull my car in. The sight of his familiar smile as he gave me his standard mock salute increased my sense of joy at being alive, at having so much in my life. Even though it was a work night, and late, we made love.

Lost in these thoughts, I sit in silence in the familiar waiting room at Dr. Ross's office. The man who has a Tuesday morning appointment with another doctor at the same time as I do is there, too, and his presence is comforting, though we have never exchanged a single word. He is engrossed in an old magazine, and, oblivious to my gaze, doesn't look up even when I realize I have been staring at him and imagine that he must sense my presence. I reach for a worn and outdated *Sports Illustrated* on the corner table next to the couch and turn the pages automatically.

Dr. Ross appears in the open doorway. He is a short man, rather chubby, who reminds me of a teddy bear. The teddy bear image is reinforced by the color of his clothing: He always dresses in dark brown slacks, a plain shirt, and a tan sweater. I can count on him to appear in the waiting room promptly at 11:30 A.M., the exact time of my appointment. He keeps a precise schedule of fifty-five-minute appointments, beginning at 8:30 in the morning and stopping promptly at 4:00 in the afternoon. As usual, he says nothing when he come to get me; he just looks at me expectantly and then steps aside with his eyes lowered when I stand up to walk down the newly carpeted hallway to his office.

I sit down in the black leather chair, and he sits in a larger one that he turns at right angles to me, so that I talk to the side of his face. Sometimes he will turn his head and look directly at me; then I know that I have captured his full attention. Now I cannot find words to express myself, and a few moments pass in silence. Finally I blurt out, "I think I am pregnant," and my throat immediately constricts with tears. This is the first moment I have experienced any feelings.

I generally cry only when I am by myself. I envy my friends Margaret and Katherine, whose feelings surface easily in my presence. I once believed that I couldn't reach my feelings, but I have come to understand that they surface when I am alone. In the presence of others, I automatically monitor their reactions to me and rarely notice my own emotional state. Perhaps for this reason, I have not yet cried in Dr. Ross's presence either, despite my steadily growing feeling of safety. He is looking directly at me now.

I explain, "I didn't realize I was going to cry. It's just that I think I am pregnant. I had a blood test right before I came here, and I'll get the results this afternoon."

"You must be upset," he comments. I can see that he is

concerned, that he is making a concerted effort to digest my news and to empathize with me.

I tell him, "No, I'm not upset. I haven't really had any feelings about the pregnancy yet, even though I know I choked up just now. It feels more like I'm on an airplane, when you can't really do anything but pass the time until you land. These few hours feel like a time out for me, the only freedom I will have. When I get the results, when the reality of this pregnancy is confirmed, that's when I'll have the feelings."

The rest of the session drags by; each minute passes in an agonizing slow motion. I cannot bear to talk about being pregnant, and yet I cannot think about anything else. My mind is locked solidly in this stalemate, its gears frozen and unable to move. I apologize to Dr. Ross. "It must be hard for you just to sit here, but I can't find anything to talk about."

Finally the time is over, and I proceed to my regular Tuesday lunch with Katherine. We have been friends for more than twenty years, ever since we met in graduate school. Now we are both therapists in private practice. We meet at a small restaurant that we haven't tried before. It's an old-fashioned diner, and it has cottage cheese and fruit on the menu. I find myself ordering it, as if already eating properly to nourish my child.

"You're all dressed up!" Katherine comments. I look down at myself and see that I have put on that beige cotton suit that I rarely wear. Only when I adopt my professional-woman persona do I wear this suit. Without realizing, I must have chosen this outfit for the blood test, wanting to draw upon all my competence in order to handle the experience.

"I have something big to tell you," I announce. "I think I'm pregnant!" Inexplicably I feel enormous pride wash over me as I make my announcement. I also envision the feelings my news will evoke in Katherine, who wishes more than anything that she could be pregnant.

"Oh, Sue," Katherine intones, her voice a mixture of compassion and concern. For the first time, I begin to talk aloud about the consequences.

"I had a blood test, and I'll get the results this afternoon, but I just know I'm pregnant. I had all the symptoms of getting my period—swollen breasts, congestion in my pelvis, cramps—and then they just evaporated, but my period didn't come. That's exactly what happened the other three times. I don't know what I'm going to do. I don't think I can have this baby. Michael doesn't want to be responsible for a fourth child. It was all he could do to have Ben, and then he was only forty years old. If we have a child now, he'll be forty-six; he'll be parenting most of his life. And he has high blood pressure and high cholesterol; he's so worried he'll have a stroke, like his father did. I can't make him have this baby. And yet we would be such good parents! We have a functioning family, good help, I have a job with flexible hours. Why shouldn't I have the baby? Once it arrived, I know Michael would love it, and so would I. We'd adjust to include it."

I begin to feel literally split in two with this conflict and abruptly stop talking. "Let's talk about something else. I'm not going to think about this until I have to. But whatever happens with this pregnancy, like it or not, I'm going to have to have a tubal ligation. I just can't risk another unplanned pregnancy again."

"I don't blame you," Katherine says. "No risk, even a small one, is worth this kind of pain."

Katherine and I set aside my plight and talk about everything else we can think of to divert our attention. After our lunch I am able to stop at home and check on Ben—the girls are still in school—and go on to my office to see my afternoon clients.

It is just before five o'clock, and I am standing at my telephone, in the exact same position that I was only seven hours ago. I dial the number of the doctor's office. When the receptionist answers, I give her my name and then take a deep breath so that I can ask the question that has been hovering on my mind all day like a heavy storm cloud. "I'm calling to get the results of a pregnancy test that I had this morning at the Abbott Laboratory."

"Just a moment, let me check the slips. . . ." The secretary puts me on hold, and I stand immobilized, butterflies in my stomach, trying to focus upon the calendar hanging on my wall above the phone. The picture for May is a field of wildflowers, a peaceful scene that is now totally at odds with my state of mind.

There is a faint click as she comes back on the line. "Well, Sue, your slip says positive," she tells me in a neutral voice. For an instant I wonder if she has been instructed to react in a neutral way, not knowing the import of the news she is imparting.

"Oh no," I moan, my heart sinking. "Oh no." But, at the same time, I feel a rush of pleasure and pride in my body, in my fertility, in the miracle of conception. I cannot recall any other time in my life when I have felt two completely opposite feelings simultaneously.

"I'll be keeping my Thursday morning appointment with Dr. Rhodes, then," I tell her, and I hang up the phone. Not allowing myself to think or feel anything, not until I get home, not until I see Michael, I gather my belongings and lock up my office for the night. I have two days to wait until the appointment with Dr. Rhodes.

I find I have a capacity for compartmentalization that I never knew existed. When I make dinner for the family, I focus upon nothing else. I listen to the children's conversation as if nothing else matters. In fact, nothing else is on my mind. For once, the routine complaints about the food, questions about how much each child has to eat in order to have dessert, and the constant rivalry for Michael's and my attention are a welcome distraction. Ordinarily these dinnertime rituals leave me feeling either ready to explode with irritation or that I have failed totally as a mother.

Later that evening Michael and I finally talk.

"I am absolutely clear that I do not want a fourth child under any circumstances," he announces, taking the lead. "It's enough dealing with three. I'm forty-six years old. I'd be sixty years old when the child is thirteen. I don't want to spend my sixties raising children. The law firm isn't all that stable right now, and I don't want any additional economic worries. It's me who is primarily responsible for supporting the family. Besides, I have my high blood pressure and high cholesterol to deal with. I feel like it will literally kill me to take care of another child."

The word *kill* chills me to my bones and brings home to me the extent of Michael's worry about himself. Even though he is careful of his diet, and even though he jogs long distances regularly for exercise, his blood pressure and cholesterol levels have been elevated ever since his father had a stroke nearly one year ago. Our internist informed us that high blood pressure and high cholesterol levels interact to increase the risk of a heart attack or stroke, and Michael has been working with doctors to reduce these risks. In fact, I have been very proud of his determination to take good care of himself, even when the factors that put him at risk are absolutely invisible, silent dangers. Leaving no stone unturned, Michael has also learned biofeedback techniques and recently, in an effort to redirect his life, he began psychotherapy. Just now, when he is beginning to pay attention to his own needs for perhaps the first time in his life, he is confronted with the dilemma of having fathered a fourth child. My heart aches for him, and for myself, but we are not talking about the choice of whether to conceive a child; this child is a reality, taking shape already deep within my body.

"I know about all that," I reply. "But if we had this child, I also know that we would love it as much as we love Jill, Becky, and Ben. And we can't foresee the future. Maybe it wouldn't be as hard to manage four children as we think."

Michael answers immediately. "I don't have any doubt that we would love a fourth child. But I'll be sixty years old when this child is thirteen. I'll have worked so hard all my life. We're already worrying about providing for the three we have. Do you realize what it will cost to have three children in college ten years from now? It isn't just a matter of money. What about our physical and emotional limits? Is it fair to them to split even further the emotional, physical, and economic supplies we have available?"

"I don't know what's fair. But we aren't just contemplating

conceiving another child. This fourth child exists, it's here, it's a reality. It's the fate of this child that we have to decide. Maybe it's meant to be born, or it wouldn't have gotten conceived, and we're interfering with fate in a way that will doom us all. Or maybe I should bring it into the world and give it up for adoption." But I know as I utter the words that I could never give my baby up. And my heart literally stands still as I try to imagine choosing to terminate this pregnancy. I gulp for air.

Michael, who I know shares my feelings, continues to play the devil's advocate. "You could just as easily argue that it is our fate to make an incredibly difficult decision. We're only limited human beings. We don't have perfect control over our lives, even though we like to think we do. Accidental pregnancies happen; it isn't as if we were completely irresponsible. Our birth control method wasn't infallible, just as we aren't infallible. We also aren't capable of unlimited physical and psychological nurturing. I'm not a superman, and even though you don't like to think about it, you aren't superwoman either. We have limits, and they have to be accepted. Can't you see that we're being very responsible to ourselves and to our living children by making the difficult choice not to have a child?"

Michael is persuasive, but I cannot be convinced. "But what else is important in life besides caring for children? When we retire, we aren't going to feel best about our jobs; we'll feel best about having participated in raising the next generation. Maybe we should make whatever sacrifices are necessary to bring this child forth."

Michael pauses for a moment's thought. "We could go around and around on this forever. The problem is we're trying to see what is impossible to see. We can't know the answers to the questions you're asking. We can only do the best we can now, without having seen all the cards in the deck. And I know now, for certain, without any doubts at all, that I do not want to have to provide and care for this fourth child. I'm trying to take care of myself! I have high blood pressure, high cholesterol, my father had his stroke one year

ago and has been suffering ever since with terrible impair-
ment. I'm in absolutely no position to think about nurturing
an infant. You know how much I love the kids! If I try, I can
picture our fourth child too. I could never give it up for
adoption either. But I don't want to picture that fourth child.
I can't let myself!"

I am split in half, experiencing absolutely conflicting feelings simultaneously. Hate swells inside me toward this man
who is pressuring me to give up my fourth child, and yet I
am also awash in love for him, for his staunch devotion to all
of us, his willingness to shoulder total responsibility for us,
for his efforts to care for himself that are so long overdue.
How can I weigh the life of my unborn child against the life
of my husband? And he is not alone in feeling that he cannot
care for yet another child. I felt compelled to devote myself
exclusively to my children in the first two years of their lives.
I nursed all three children around the clock until they weaned
themselves. Michael and I have rarely spent even a single
vacation night away from them since they were born. We
have no family nearby to help us raise and care for them or to
give us a temporary respite from our responsibilities. I don't
know if I have the physical stamina it would require to care
for a new baby in this way. I don't even know if I could bear
to go through another pregnancy, having worked so hard after
Ben was born to renounce forever that cherished part of my
life. But I also cannot escape the certainty that I would adjust
to and enjoy the pregnancy and the baby once I made a
commitment to that path. How could I once have been so
naive as to think that if I were to get pregnant, I would
"simply" have an abortion! Now my simplistic moralistic
position on abortion—that it is fine for other women to have a
choice but that the choice to have an abortion is one I could
not make—seems light-years away.

Then Michael shatters the quiet lull in our discussion by
uttering the words that permanently silence me. His voice is
very quiet and sad.

"If you don't choose to abort this child, I will push you to
do it."

It is at this moment that I know that *I* will take responsibility for the decision that must be made and that I will have an abortion, even though Michael and I will repeat this discussion over the next few days with no variation in our positions. I do not want to enter into a life-and-death battle with this man whom I love and who shares my life. I do not want to push him to father this child, and I do not want him to push me to end its potential for life. If that opening in the heavens is to be kept closed to this new life inside me, I want to be the one responsible for keeping it shut. If I had chosen to become pregnant, I would have done everything in my power to bring my child through that miraculous opening into the world. It seems fitting to me that I also be the one to block its entrance, if this must be our choice.

Visions of my three living children swim in vivid color in my mind. I see Jill, so like a young fawn with her long and lean limbs and her loving brown eyes, always so happy to melt into my arms. I picture Becky, so deceptively small and cuddly that she could have been a model for a line of little dolls, but too fiercely stubborn and autonomous to allow me near enough to catch and cuddle her. I see Ben, small like Becky, but sturdily built and so filled with an infectious, mischievous spirit that embraces life with an unquenchable delight. My unborn child has its place in my vision, too, but not in the vivid colors of the other three. Hard as I try to pierce through it to the unique and surely beloved form of the child that has not emerged from it, all I can see is a dense swirl of mist. My wish to have this unborn, though very alive, fourth child is so strong it is palpable. When I see this misty vision and experience in full force my wish to make it manifest in this lifetime, nothing else matters. But when I put it in the context of my life in this world, when I balance it against the overwhelming reality of the needs of my husband, the needs of my three living children, and my own ability to care for everyone, myself included, my wish alone is not enough to tip the scale. I cannot block out existing realities and act upon my wish alone.

Nevertheless, the final responsibility for the choice clearly

rests with me alone. The baby is growing in my body, not
Michael's. Somehow, no matter how equal a participant Michael has been in its creation, this physical fact makes a
difference that cannot be circumvented. This physical fact
renders me all at once the judge, the jury, and the lawyers
representing both sides. And no matter which perspective I
adopt, the balance scale appears the same. I will keep that
window in the firmament closed to my fourth child; I will not
let it enter this world. And even though my decision is clear,
I know inside that I will need to muster all my courage and
strength to carry it out. I am going to have to jump off that
cliff yet again, not knowing how or where I will land.

TWO

Abortion

*This incident [referring to a case example] of a successfully termi-
nated pregnancy furnishes a most striking example of the importance of the inner aspect of the experience. Inasmuch as there were
no external results, it might be supposed that nothing of importance could be happening within. Yet even where the external
situation has been passed over merely as a disagreeable necessity,
much like an illness, its inner effects do not so pass. Any other
minor operation is an experience which can be accepted at its face
value, and after the pain, anxiety and convalescence are over it
falls into the background, leaving no long train of inner consequences. But an interference with pregnancy does not act this way,
for pregnancy involves more than physical changes. The bearing of
children is a biological task. The roots of the maternal instinct
reach back into the deepest layers of a woman's nature, touching
forces of which she may be profoundly unconscious. When a woman
becomes pregnant these ancient powers stir within her, whether she
knows it or not, and she disregards them only at her peril.*

—ESTHER HARDING
The Way of All Women[1]
1970

The Lost Baby Poem

the time i dropped your almost body down
down to meet the waters under the city
and run one with the sewage to the sea
what did i know about waters rushing back
what did i know about drowning
or being drowned

you would have been born into winter
in the year of the disconnected gas
and no car   we would have made the thin
walk of Genesee Hill into Canada wind
to watch you slip like ice into strangers' hands
you would have fallen naked as snow into winter
if you were here i could tell you these
and some other things

if i am ever less than a mountain
for your definite brothers and sisters
let the rivers pour over my head
let the sea take me for a spiller
of seas   let black men call me stranger
always   for your never named sake

—*Lucille Cliffton*[2]

Several days before the abortion, I had the following dream. I call it my farewell dream:

I am riding in our family's brown Dodge van. The curtains that Suzanne, our last baby-sitter, made for the windows are drawn shut. The children had pleaded with her for months to make them, but she always complained that they never gave her enough time to sew. Then she left them for us as a surprise gift on the day she departed for college. We discovered them only after we had said a tearful good-bye to her.

The curtains are a warm toast color, dotted with small brown and yellow flowers. When they close over the window, as they do in this dream, they give a cozy and secure feeling to the interior of the van. In my dream the van becomes a small, safe enclosure, completely removed from the outer world. I am not alone; with me is Ginger, our very first baby-sitter, who came to live with us when Jill was two years old and Becky only six months. She has stayed in close contact with our family for the past eight years, though she now lives one thousand miles away and we are unable to see her often. She is still, eight years after our first meeting, the same stable, calm, loving presence that she was then, when she was so patient and ever-present for Michael, Jill, Becky, and me.

My fourth child is in the car, too. The child is a boy, but he appears not as a baby but as a miniature old and wise man. I try to speak to him in another language that sounds like German. The word I try to pronounce is Müller. (Later I will learn that this word in German means "miller," as in a "miller of wheat." I discover that grain and wheat are associated with the Goddess Demeter, the "Grain-Mother" who caused an enormous drought over the entire earth because of her grief at losing her daughter Persephone to the Underworld.) In my dream I repeat this word over and over, but I cannot manage to say it with the correct accent. Finally I stop trying to speak with words. I reach over for my child and hug him. He hugs me

back. For a brief moment we cling to each other. I can feel the
pressure of his tiny but strong arms encircling my neck, and I savor
the pleasure of this physical bond with all the intensity of concentra-
tion I can muster. Then I must let go. We have both understood,
even as we hugged each other, that this embrace is the only contact we
will ever have.

I treasure this dream, even though I cry each time I recall
the hug, my only meeting with my lost fourth child.

Thursday morning Michael and I arrive together for an
appointment with the new doctor. We park our car in the rear
of the building and take the elevator to the fifth floor in
silence. This building has a long history for us; not only have
I made many pre- and post-natal visits to the obstetrician,
but our pediatrician's office is two floors below. I think of this
building as a place of beginnings, a place for nurturing young
lives. I cannot believe that I am coming here to explore the
option of ending the infinitesimal essence of new life that has
taken hold within me.

We sit in the waiting room, which was remodeled just after
Ben's birth. I am not used to this large room and prefer the
worn and familiar couches to these smart mauve and peach
chairs. The receptionists are now separated from me by a
glass window; there is a telephone on the wall through which
patients can communicate. This new procedure creates a feeling of terrible isolation in me, though perhaps I could not
have avoided this feeling under any circumstances. I am thank-
ful that the waiting room is empty of pregnant women; I
think I could not bear the experience of sitting with happy
mothers-to-be.

Michael and I are not kept waiting at all, a very unusual
occurrence. I had come prepared for a long wait, accustomed
to sitting for up to an hour for my appointments when I was
pregnant. I remember how irritating it was to wait then,
when I was eager to see the doctor. Now I would be happy to
be kept waiting; this is not a visit I want to be having. A
nurse I recognize from former days smiles at me and ushers

us into a small examining room. Dr. Rhodes comes in after a moment and greets us. He is a large man with a thick neck and ruddy complexion, blond hair, and pale blue eyes; for a brief moment he makes eye contact with me and then he glances off to the side. This nervous gesture makes him seem a bit insecure to me, but his greeting is friendly. My first thought is, "Oh, he's so young!" and then I shake my head at the sudden awareness of the passage of time. I would not have had this thought had I been seeing him as a young mother for my first pregnancy.

He examines me quickly while he asks me questions: when my last period occurred, what symptoms I have experienced. When he is finished with the brief physical examination, he tells me to get dressed and says he will talk with us in his office. Michael waits while I quickly put on my clothes—the beige suit again, this time with a different blouse—and we cross the hall to Dr. Rhodes's office.

He looks older and more in charge sitting behind his mahogany desk. I see a framed picture of a toddler on it and again have the odd feeling of being older, more experienced, than this man who is to be responsible for my medical care. What can he know of my inner turmoil? Is this simply a routine procedure to him? I tell him immediately that I have decided to have an abortion. "I want the abortion right away; it's too painful for me to be pregnant, knowing I'm going to terminate the pregnancy," I add in a matter-of-fact tone. This is a business meeting, and there is no room for tears.

"Well," he says seriously, his elbows resting on his desk, hands held with fingertips touching, as if in prayer, "you should know that there are more risks involved if you have the abortion now. You're only about three to four weeks pregnant, and your uterus hasn't had a chance to soften. Generally it's safer to wait until the seventh or eighth week, at least."

"What can happen to me if you do the abortion right away?" I ask. I have another choice to weigh now: my emotional need to terminate the pregnancy immediately, unable to bear the state of being pregnant knowing I must end it, versus my own physical well-being. I am responsible for myself, my husband, and my children, and I cannot take unnecessary risks.

"It's possible that we might perforate the uterus, because it's still hard, or that we might not be able to remove all the contents," he replies.

I do not allow myself to dwell on the meaning of the word *contents* and continue my questions. "What would happen if you did perforate the uterus, or if you didn't remove everything?"

"It would mean that you'd take longer to recover. We might have to go back in and repeat the procedure, and that would be very uncomfortable and unpleasant for you," he answers.

"Would I be unnecessarily endangering my life?" I ask. This is the only issue that I care about. Any amount of physical pain would be preferable to the emotional anguish that having to make this decision is causing me.

"No, not in my opinion," Dr. Rhodes says with emphasis.

"I have another question for you," I tell him. "I'm thinking of getting a tubal ligation to prevent my being put in this situation ever again. Can you do this procedure at the same time?"

"Not if we go ahead with the abortion immediately. You'll need to sign a release in advance for permanent sterilization— that's to prevent impulsive decisions, since it's an irreversible procedure. Also, I don't recommend undergoing two emotionally stressful procedures at the same time," Dr. Rhodes replies.

While one part of me wishes I could get both procedures over with at once, another part of me is relieved. I appreciate Dr. Rhodes's recognition that the procedures are in fact emotionally stressful, and I am glad to postpone the tubal ligation for now.

"Let's go ahead with the abortion, then, as soon as possible," I say with a sigh. I have done it. These are the words that will become the deed.

"How about tomorrow?" he says brusquely, standing up

behind his desk and preparing to leave the room. "I'll have the desk call and make sure that the outpatient surgery department of the hospital has a room available. We won't be using a general anesthetic, so you should only be there for a few hours. The procedure will take about fifteen to twenty minutes, and then you'll be in a recovery room until you feel up to going home."

While we wait, I feel an urgent need to know this man as a human being, to shift my contact with him away from the clinical details to a more human plane. When he returns to the office and tells us that the surgery is scheduled for 10:00 A.M. the next day, I ask him, "Do you have children?" though I know what his answer will be from the photograph on his desk.

"Yes, I have a little boy who is eighteen months old," he answers, pleasure showing on his face.

"What is it like for you, performing abortions?" I inquire, rather shocked at what feels like a bold inquiry. I am ordinarily so careful to maintain an appropriate distance from doctors. But I have nothing to lose that matters to me now, and his answer is important.

He takes my question seriously, and I like him for that. "Before I had my son, I didn't think about it very much. I just learned how to perform them and carried out the procedure. But now that I have my son, it's gotten harder for me. The unborn child seems more real. But my job is to help my patient, and it's the woman who is my patient."

I feel a rush of gratitude for him, for his willingness to help me, even if this means carrying out an act that clearly is not easy for him. What would I do if there were no one willing to stand up for me, no one on my side? I am glad I asked my question; his answer has given me a human connection to him, and that counts more at this moment than any amount of clinical expertise he might have.

Michael and I leave the office in a somber mood. We go off in our separate directions to clear our commitments for the next day. Dr. Rhodes has told me that I should be able to work on the following Monday, so I need to cancel only my appointments for only one day. For Jill, Becky, and Ben, it will be an ordinary school day; I won't even need to arrange for a babysitter. Such a huge event in my inner world is ironically only a minor inconvenience in the ordinary outer world.

I go from my appointment with Dr. Rhodes to my therapy session with Dr. Ross, where I announce that I am going to have an abortion the next day and will have to cancel my appointment with him. Dr. Ross does not question my decision to have the abortion and accepts the cancellation readily. He generously offers to see me on Saturday, the day after the abortion, a weekend day, when he would not ordinarily work. I accept this offer, more because of my intellectual awareness that I always avoid depending upon others and insist on being self-sufficient and the thought that I should try to let in whatever help I am offered, than because I am certain that I will want or need the session. I am glad that Michael has his own therapist with whom he can share his feelings, a place where he can find the support he needs. I know that I will be leaning heavily on him, and I will have little to offer in return.

Later that afternoon I call my Friday clients: "I am going to have to cancel our appointment for tomorrow. I need to have a minor medical procedure. It isn't serious, but it does need doing. I will be able to meet at our regular time next week." This is the best compromise I can make; to cancel clients at the last minute without offering them any explanation seems unnecessarily cruel, yet the only explanation I feel I can offer in my role of therapist wounds me simply in the saying of it. An abortion is not a "minor medical procedure" except from a medical point of view. For me, it is a major emotional event. But tolerating such wounding and the voluntary sacrifice of needs, an integral part of the task of parenting, is also part of being a psychotherapist.

Only three friends know of my plight. Katherine knows because I told her at lunch, and I call to keep her up to date on my plans. Margaret knows because I call her specifically to tell her. Like Katherine and myself, she is a therapist in private practice, though we have known each other for only ten years. Katherine and I first met Margaret in a leaderless women's group we participated in during the early 1970s. Because the group was a place where the most intimate thoughts and feelings could be safely shared, we became good friends. Margaret has a college-age daughter from a first marriage that ended in divorce and is now remarried with a three-year-old son. Having spent all of her adult life mothering (she had her daughter when she was only twenty), she does not want any more children. In fact, she had a tubal ligation shortly after Andy's birth. From her perspective, she is relieved to be able to pursue her own life and interests; consequently, she does not question my choice.

"Oh, Sue, I'm so sorry this happened to you," she says. But I am afraid to receive too much sympathy. I need to stay above my feelings now. If I permit myself to feel my wishes for this child, I will not be able to go through with the abortion.

"I know," I answer, "but I'll be okay." And in fact, I expect to be all right. I have had women friends and clients who have had abortions, and all of them have not only been able to put the experience behind them but have been relieved at having terminated the pregnancy. Why should I be any different?

I also call Julia to tell her. These three women are my closest friends; I see them regularly for lunch, and we keep track of each other every few days by telephone. Julia's response to me is similar to Margaret's, and, as with Margaret, I ward off any mention of my feelings. "It'll be good to have it over with," she tells me. "I'll call you tomorrow night to see how you are."

Having created a solid floor, with my feelings trapped securely beneath it, I am able to work that afternoon, as well as to care for my family. Dinner is painfully ordinary that night. The five of us take our regular places at the white Formica table in our kitchen. Ben sits silent, as usual, his way of keeping out of trouble and avoiding the scorn of his two older sisters. Becky picks at her food; she is petite (where did she come from, this tiny child in a family of ordinary size?) and eats very little. We bargain over how many green beans she must consume, by now a well established routine. Jill eats rapidly, making sure to finish enough of everything so that she won't have to bother fighting with us. Tonight we do not keep her from leaving the table before everyone else is finished. Every time I find myself wondering what they would think about having a little brother or sister, where the new baby would fit at our small table, I try to stop myself and think about other things. This territory is too painful, and there is nothing to be gained from entering it. But the awareness I have of the new life inside me, an awareness my three small children do not have, creates a gulf between us that leaves me feeling isolated and alone, even in the midst of my family. This family, which until now had seemed to me to be a fixed unit, now has had its boundaries opened suddenly to include a new member, a ghostlike presence. After everyone is finished eating, the children go off, Jill and Becky to watch television and Ben to play in his room. Michael and I clean up after our offspring, both of us heavy with the awareness that for us a potential child has also been present at this evening meal.

"How are you doing?" Michael asks, but I am not yet ready to put the burgeoning mass of emotions inside me into ordinary language. "I'm okay," I tell him, uncomfortable with the attention. "How about you?"

"I'm mostly worrying about you, wanting to be there to help you get through this. The baby doesn't have much reality to me. I guess I feel sort of sad all over," Michael replies thoughtfully. He understands my need to be by myself and doesn't press me to talk any further.

It is not until now, when all my commitments for the day have been met, my responsibilities carried out efficiently and with dispatch, that I permit myself some solitude, a chance to be alone with my feelings.

It is nearly eight o'clock on this Thursday night, the last evening of the last pregnancy I will experience in my life on this earth. It is a clear night, as is usual in May, and I sit alone upstairs in my bedroom, huddled in the small armchair, which I swivel around in order to look out the large window at the hills beyond our house. I watch the colors in the sky shift as the sun sets, and I watch the stars emerge against the darker background of the night sky. But mostly I sit with the life of my fourth child growing inside me, trying to contemplate this ending, and I grieve and grieve and grieve and grieve. The experience of this grief is entirely physical, manifested in the lump in my throat, the ache in my heart (so this is why we say "heartache" and "broken-hearted," I think); it is a state without words, without coherent thought, even without images. In the most simple and apt terms, I am laden with sorrow.

I sit weighted down with this wordless grief, feeling no urge to action, no impulse of energy, no will or motivation to alter the choice I have made. I have seen the balance of the scale; I have seen that my commitments to my living family and to myself outweigh my longing to give birth and life and care to the miraculous combination of cells that rests without awareness in my womb. Oh, child of mine, child of my heart, child I cherish, oh my child, oh my child, would that I could bring you forth, would that I could know you, love you, would that you could know me, oh my child. . . .

In the morning I am up at dawn. I take myself for an early-morning swim at the pool we have joined for exercise. It is located near the hospital in which my 10:00 A.M. appointment awaits me. Fueled by my grief, I try to exhaust myself physically, to lose myself in this rhythmic, repetitive, mindless physical activity. I swim more than a mile in record time. In the locker room I stare at my naked body in the full-length mirror, savoring the satisfaction of knowing there is a healthy life growing in me, relishing my body's ability to perform this miracle, enjoying the fullness of my breasts—the only observable sign of pregnancy at this stage upon which I can focus.

Less than one hour later I am in the impersonal hospital lobby, sitting on a couch next to Michael. I put my head on his shoulder. "Michael, why am I doing this? Why am I here? I don't want to be doing this."

He answers me, "You don't have to do this. You can cancel the procedure." Why is he giving me this permission now, after being so adamant all along that his life will be in danger if he has to care for another child? Is he serious in telling me I can call off the abortion, or is he simply putting the total responsibility for the decision in my lap as if he has had no part in it? What would he do if I really did call the whole thing off? I decide that his statement is not meant to be taken seriously, that it is Michael's way of divesting himself of responsibility for causing me anguish. Even though I understand that he cannot bear to be causing me pain by having needs that conflict with mine, I feel a flash of anger. But the weight of my sorrow deadens it for now. The anger will come later. In this lifetime, in this reality, as a thirty-nine-year-old woman with three children and a forty-six-year-old husband with medical problems and a huge financial responsibility on his shoulders, I cannot make any other choice. Having this baby might spare me the grief and anguish of mourning its loss, but it would also create anxieties and problems for Michael and for me with which I am equally unsure of being able to cope. The decision that has felt best, the decision to have the abortion, still feels like the only choice available to me. I cannot cancel the procedure.

Finally, as the scheduled time approaches, Michael and I walk slowly over to the outpatient surgery department. While waiting at the counter, I see a slim, brown-haired woman standing nearby who looks familiar. I realize that it's Susan, who once took an exercise class with me. We befriended one another upon discovering that we shared the same name. She recognizes me and comes over to us.

"Sue! Hi! What are you doing here?" she asks me with a friendly smile. I cannot find words to say, I cannot tell her, "I am here for an abortion." Instead, I mumble, feeling embarrassed and awkward, "I'd rather not say, if you don't mind." Skilled as most women are in covering over such awkward moments, Susan nods as if I have given her a comprehensible reason and says, "Oh. I'm here to have a mole removed. It's nothing serious, they're only removing it to prevent any problems from developing." Politely she moves away from us.

When it is my turn, I stand at the counter and watch the receptionist type "unwanted pregnancy" as the reason for my admission. I scream to her silently that "it is *not* an unwanted pregnancy," but the scream only echoes within the boundaries of my body, and she can neither see nor hear my anguish. To her, and to Michael, I must appear to be an ordinary woman; inside I feel a mounting despair and panic.

In minutes I am taken to an operating room, brightly lit and filled with gleaming medical instruments and neatly packaged supplies. These are the tools of modern science. Where are the tools that will help my soul? The nurses are compassionate and sensitive; they instruct me to undress and to lie down upon the table. Always controlled, cooperative, compliant, an excellent patient, automatically responsive to the needs and feelings of others, I am shocked that my grief erupts and breaks through my normally strong controls. Naked now, I sob quietly and climb upon the cold and narrow table. The nurses are upset when they notice that they have forgotten to put out a pillow for my head and a sheet-covered pad to warm and soften the table. But I have not noticed; I am oblivious to these minor physical discomforts. My pain has nothing to do with the external, physical, world.

The locus of my awareness shifts, and I notice the presence of Dr. Rhodes. Now he has a white jacket on and seems to me to be an impersonal presence. At least in his office he wore an ordinary suit. He greets me rather distantly and walks over to a sink to wash his hands. He is bantering with the two nurses, and I feel invisible, filled with pain that they cannot see, in another world from these three professionals who are merely doing a routine morning's work.

I look away from them because their lighthearted repartee clashes with my emotional state, but there is nothing I can focus attention upon that is not a source of pain. I see the vacuum aspirator. It looks just like the one in the women's health manual I read in my effort to prepare myself for this experience. Some people prefer simply to turn themselves over to doctors, but I need to be as informed as I can about what will happen to me. Unexpected events feel too shocking and make it harder to cope. The picture of the machine in the manual had been upsetting enough; the actual machine is even worse. Who could build this machine of destruction? Don't look at it, I instruct myself, and I turn my head away.

I see the nurse coming toward me with an I.V. stand. She reaches for my arm. This is an unexpected occurrence. What are they doing? "What's that for?" I ask her.

"Oh, that's some Valium and Demerol that we're going to give you to make you more comfortable." It's Dr. Rhodes who answers me.

"I don't want any anesthetic," I tell him, in a panic. "You didn't tell me that you were going to give me an anesthetic." Even now, I know that I am struggling to take whatever control I can of a situation where events have gone beyond my control; it is really the unwanted abortion, not the unexpected medication that is a problem.

"We're not giving you enough to put you to sleep. The medication is just to help relax the uterus," Dr. Rhodes tells me, "and that will make the procedure safer."

"The" uterus, "the" procedure. . . . Such neutral words do not help me remove myself from the experience. It is *my* uterus, *my* baby, *my* abortion, and I am *not* removed from the scene. With one small observing part of my mind I see myself passively spread-eagled upon the operating table, allowing these monstrous attackers to come and take my baby without my even trying to defend it. How can I be doing this? Why don't I assert myself, get up from this bare table, tell them to stop? What kind of mother am I?

I feel the warmth from the I.V., and then the medication takes over. I remain conscious but, as if in a dream, see the bright lights, the white forms of the doctor and the nurses. Through a haze I feel the cramping and pain, as if it is happening to another body that my mind is only watching from an unfathomable distance.

Somehow I find myself in a bed in a recovery room, alone with my husband. For the first time, I feel the emptiness, and worse, the raw and bleeding edges of my empty womb, and I know that there is no bandage that human beings can apply, no medicine for this open boundary, for my wounded soul. I am lost in an anguish that I never imagined I could possibly feel. I know Michael is sitting close to me, trying to hold my hand, but I barely feel his presence. I am lost in a chaotic realm of multicolored pain washing over me in gulping waves, hot and burning. This realm is all there is; the observer-self is gone. I do not know how long I remain at the hospital, nor do I have any awareness of being removed and driven home.

Later I find myself at home in my own bed, alone in the room. I feel crazed as never before in my life. I scream aloud into my pillow to muffle the sound, afraid to frighten my children or anyone else who might hear, afraid to hear myself. I scream and scream, an inhuman sound rasping across my throat, carving grooves in it. I grip the headboard with all my might to prevent myself from acting upon my overwhelming impulse to claw my stomach. I want to tear my skin and rip out my insides. I will strew them across the bed, scratching and clawing, ripping away until there is no life left within. But I grip the headboard instead, because I know deep within me that I cannot create a physical pain that will be as unbearable as my soul-agony, that no amount of physical pain can divert me from such anguish. I am frightened by the intensity of my impulses and by the thin thread that enables me to control them. The strength with which I grip the headboard feels superhuman to me, as if it would lift a car.

"Mommy isn't feeling well; she has to stay in bed today, but she'll be better tomorrow." I hear Michael talking to the children downstairs in the family room. I know they will be worried about me, so I try to pull myself together and join them for dinner. But the sight of their anxious and loving faces, their small and healthy bodies, simply their aliveness, is too painful for me, too much of a contrast with their now-obliterated sibling. I return to my bedroom and try to find sources of comfort for myself. I have known so many women who have had abortions, both clients and friends, and not one of them has had as intense a reaction as mine. Even though I recognize that these women, even if conflicted, did not want their unborn child more than they wanted it, and that more of me wanted to have this child than didn't, I cannot understand the magnitude of my anguish. Only later will I realize that I am grieving at more than the loss of my baby. I am raging at my human limits—my age, Michael's age, the passage of time, the finality of my having ended my capacity to become a mother. In the words of Dylan Thomas, I am not going gentle into that good night.

Becky and Jill come into my bedroom to say good-night to me so I won't have to go down the stairs to their rooms. I hug and kiss them with special care. Somehow, in the face of their lost sibling, they have become more precious than ever. I take pleasure in singing "Good-night, Sweetheart," to Ben, our bedtime ritual now just as it once was Jill's and Becky's; my own father once sang this song to me, and I feel the comfort of being part of a chain of generations for the brief time I sit in his room. Michael is already in bed when I finish tucking Ben in, and as he did the night I first realized I was pregnant, he cradles me in his arms.

On Saturday morning I get myself up and dressed. If nothing else, the scheduled 11:00 A.M. appointment with Dr. Ross gives me a reason to function. Though I put on worn and comfortable jeans and an old sweater, I do not yet feel at home in my body. The unfamiliar sanitary napkin I must wear feels bulky and uncomfortable, a reminder of the loss of the child, so different from the normal bleeding that persisted after the births of Jill, then Becky, then Ben.

It feels strange to be returning to Dr. Ross's familiar brick building on a weekend. I have never before needed an extra session. The normally busy street in front of the building is devoid of cars, and I have my pick of parking spaces. Dr. Ross has unlocked the door for me, which feels welcoming, but the waiting room is cold and empty. Even though I am a

few minutes early, Dr. Ross comes quickly to get me, and I
follow him into his office. Oh, how I wish this were an
ordinary appointment on an ordinary workday! The deserted
street, the soundless building, the flat scent in the air because
it has been closed up for the weekend, together mirror the
inner emptiness I feel in my abdomen.

I look squarely at Dr. Ross and immediately register the
enormous contrast in our physical conditions. I remember
now that he mentioned to me some weeks ago when we were
talking about exercise that he had taken up jogging. Although
he is dressed in a white shirt and his usual dark brown slacks,
he clearly has just come from a good run; he has that relaxed
demeanor and freshly showered look that I, too, have after
strenuous exercise. I, on the other hand, still in the process of
reclaiming my body, am unable even to walk freely, let alone
exercise.

Dr. Ross greets me pleasantly and beckons me to sit in the
patient's chair, which I do automatically. Looking down beside me, I see that the wastebasket has not yet been emptied;
there are a number of crumpled tissues in it that I know must
belong to another patient. What did my imaginary comrade-
in-sorrow have to cry about, I wonder. I envy that person's
ability to come to Dr. Ross and simply cry. My grief feels
huge, heavy, as if it has congealed into a solid ball; I am afraid
it is so tightly packed that I will never be able to release it into
a flow of tears. At this moment I feel as if I will have to carry
it around with me for the remainder of my life, that I am
doomed to be weighted down forever by my personal iron
ball and chain.

"There is no room big enough, or hour long enough, to
contain all my tears, even if I could let myself cry," I say to
him, after a moment of silence. "Besides, I can cry on my
own," I add, hearing myself sound like a defiant little girl
who insists on pushing her parent away. Underneath, I yearn
for him to comfort me, to tell me, "Go right ahead and cry.
This is really a difficult time for you." These are words I am
certain I would say to a client of mine, and I feel an odd
mixture of anger and deprivation at this awareness. But Dr.

Ross and I have quite firmly established another pattern of relating, around ideas rather than feelings, and I realize it will not be easy for either one of us to shift to a different plane. I am becoming all too well aware of my fear that if I start to cry, I will be unable to stop when the hour ends. Then, for only an instant, I am terrified at my sudden sense of the extent of my pain; it seems so enormous to me that I am afraid it will overwhelm both of us if I even try to approach it. I cannot even put these fears into words, cannot name them to Dr. Ross out loud, at least not now, not today, maybe never.

In the odd way that thoughts float to the surface unexpectedly when one is a psychotherapy patient, a memory of my very first hour with Dr. Ross floats into my mind. I hear myself utter the very first words I spoke to him then, on a September day more than two years ago: "Don't be taken in by my competence and my ability to cope. I want to be able to have my vulnerabilities be visible, too." I repeat these words again in my mind, unable to say them aloud, and then I wait for Dr. Ross somehow to hear this plea for help. But I am communicating on an inaudible wavelength; he sits silently across the room in his leather chair, and I remain silent and far away in mine.

With the pathway of venting feelings blocked for now, I try instead to make meaning of my loss. Armed as if for a final exam, I have brought two books with me to this session. Searching for comfort, for some reflection of my inner state, for some written words that might meet my unarticulated needs, I spent last night looking through my library and found some useful passages in these. I read them aloud to Dr. Ross, beginning with Harry Guntrip's book, *Psychoanalytic Theory, Therapy, and the Self*. I pick a section that describes Guntrip's emotional involvement with patients, his human compassion and concern for them, because it describes the level of relating with Dr. Ross to which I now need to shift. I can no longer remain on our former comfortable plane of ideas, of the intellect:

One cannot practice a stereotyped technique on patients: one can only be a real person for and with the patient. I am sure that this is why so much effort is put into trying to find impersonal scientific techniques, or pills or what not that will make some kind of difference to the patient that he will accept as a cure. It is a far more exacting thing having to be a real person for another human being . . . persons who are able to be just what is needed by the patient who may say, "I can't reach you. If you can't reach me, I'm lost."[3]

The last line is the key and carries my unspoken cry to Dr. Ross across the distance between us: I am lost, I am lost. Please, find me! Immobilized, choked by the solid ball of grief, I cannot speak directly for myself; I can only read the words and hope Dr. Ross will see that I am talking to him through them. I can see that he is a willing and attentive audience, but he cannot hear the plea in the words I have chosen; he cannot hear my inaudible wish for him to respond to me as Guntrip might have responded to his clients and as Guntrip urges other therapists to do. I have always been so competent, so in control with Dr. Ross; how could he ever imagine how very lost I am?

I try again. I read to Dr. Ross from a Jungian book, *The Symbolic Quest*, about the feminine yin and yang principles. These opposites—masculine and feminine—are both essential for human growth. The feminine tendency to create life and to allow death endlessly, in cycle after cycle, requires the complementary active, masculine intervention of consciousness to check this mindless and unending pattern of nurturing and decay. Perhaps I can find some justification for my choice of the abortion in the words written by Linda Fierz-David, a woman and Jungian analyst:

Just as outer nature, without man's intervention, ceaselessly creates and destroys in unconcerned and senseless continuation, allowing fruits to ripen and decay and an-

imals to live and die, so the feminine without the active
intervention of the conscious mind proceeds on an un-
disciplined and ever life-productive way.[4]

Perhaps, I explain to Dr. Ross without waiting for his response, it is necessary for me to use my active consciousness,
the masculine "yang" energy, to balance the static feminine
"yin" energy.

Dr. Ross listens intently and, accustomed to our usual
discussions of psychological theory, tells me how interesting
this idea is: "I hadn't thought about that before!" How can he
be so deaf to the resounding clashes of these opposites as they
battle within me? I slowly begin to realize that the tremendous upheaval I feel is an invisible one; I know that I have
been drastically, permanently altered by the abortion, but
this alteration, huge as it is seems to me, has not altered my
outer appearance. Dr. Ross cannot see inside me, cannot see
through to my emotional state, is oblivious of the dynamics
between us, of my efforts to express my needs and vulnerability as best I can. And I am no more able to articulate these
feelings in words than I was able to encompass and communicate the totality of my grief. My forty-five-minute session is
passing, and I feel no comfort from my hard work, only an
increasing pressure from all these feelings that are locked
inside.

As I bid good-bye to Dr. Ross and leave the empty building all alone, I wonder if I will ever be able to let myself fall
into anyone's comforting arms and cry. I wonder if I will ever
find a receptive person who is strong enough to hold my
sorrow, wise enough to help me bear my indescribable pain.

Michael spends the rest of the weekend close at hand, and I
can see reflected in his familiar brown eyes his concern for
me, his worry, as well as his relief that the procedure is over.
I know that he expects the worst to be over; for him the
medical procedure would have been the hardest part. Neither
of us can find much to say, so we do not talk much with
words; but we manage to communicate with the intuition we

have developed by traversing together the hills and valleys of our fifteen-year marriage. His pats on my shoulder, his silences, the times I catch him in postures of silent repose gazing at the floor, all tell me that he is sorry, sorry for our loss, sorry for my agony, but vastly relieved as well.

I try to behave normally with Jill, Becky, and Ben. Michael and I had decided not to tell them about the abortion. They are too young to grasp the complexity of this decision, and we do not want them to be frightened by the power we have exercised in ending the life of their potential sibling. We worried that we might trigger primitive fears in them, that they could imagine we might do away with them too. We have told them only that I am not feeling well and need to rest this weekend. But I lose myself in endless rumination, imagining their simplistic yet distinctly individual responses if we had told them: "Why didn't you just have the baby if it makes you so sad?" Becky would reason sensibly. Jill would be silent, wondering, since I could decide to take the life of a potential sibling, how I might decide to harm her. Ben, the youngest, would have thought primarily of himself: "I *wanted* a baby brother! How could you do that?" Will they ever be able to understand all the dimensions, the different facets with which I struggled, the limitations of age, of health, of life energy that I had to weigh along with my own needs and desires? I hope I can find a way to explain to them someday that it was like looking into a kaleidoscope where every pattern formed by the individual colored stones gave way to yet another. Will I ever be able to talk to them about the suffering, the internal havoc wrought by this momentous, shattering event? I heave hugh sighs to end these thoughts and try to engage myself in the present, in their activities, in the never-ending daily chores of keeping them fed, clothed, and happily occupied.

My three closest women friends—Katherine, Margaret, and Julia—check in by telephone to see how I am faring. But how can I describe my anguish to Julia, who is twenty years older than I, so far past her childbearing years that even if she had been as invested in nurturing children as I am, her memories of the intensity of the bond between mother and unborn child would long since have faded? How can I grieve for the loss of my fourth child with Katherine, who yearns so deeply for just one child of her own and fears that she may be too old to make her lifelong dreams a reality? As for Margaret, I have known her long enough to be well acquainted with her absolute dislike of talking on the telephone at all; for me to have received even a single brief call from her is a mark of her recognition of the importance of the abortion to me. All three of these good friends wish for me to turn my nurturing energy toward myself and have long felt that three children are more than enough. In the end I ignore that gnarled ball of grief inside and assure them that I am doing well.

On Monday, only two days after my Saturday appointment with Dr. Ross, I am back at work. My patients know nothing of the major transformation my body and heart have undergone, and consequently they treat me as if I am the same person they saw the week before. This is a mixed experience for me; on the one hand, it is a relief to have one place where business proceeds as usual, but on the other, I am left feeling isolated and alone with the loss that feels so enormous to me, that stubbornly refuses to diminish.

And the physical loss is not yet over. My body must take over on its own the process that was initiated by the cold metal instruments of the medical profession. The bleeding that had subsided the day after the abortion begins again on Monday night. This was one of the risks I had been warned about: When abortions are performed very early, it is sometimes impossible to remove all the tissue. This has happened to me, and my body is rejecting whatever remains. I call Dr. Rhodes's office, as he has instructed me to do in the event anything untoward occurs. The answering service puts me through to him. In a reassuring voice, he tells me, "Your body is just rejecting whatever tissue we did not remove. We'll give you some medication to help the process along. I'm going to prescribe some pills for you to take, and I'd like you to lie with your hips elevated and rest. You'll experience some cramping, which the pills induce."

I lie awake all night on my back, pelvis elevated, knees up, as the doctor instructed me, in a kind of labor, delivering not a healthy infant but the shredded physical remains of my child. Michael sleeps next to me, and I know I could awaken him and ask for comfort, but I choose to be alone with the pain, just as I lay awake next to him nearly eleven years ago, when I was in labor for the first time with Jill. This child, too, its destiny and my fate, in this moment seem mine alone to bear. Yet I feel a small spark of anger toward Michael, too. Why is he free to sleep while I must carry this burden? But I do not know how to set down even a small part of the load I carry.

And still the pregnancy goes on. Dr. Rhodes sends me to have a blood test to check the hormone level in my blood; if the pregnancy was in the fallopian tube, the hormones will remain high. "It's an unlikely possibility, but one that we are better off ruling out," he says. I am certain that the pregnancy was a normal one, but the hormone level in my blood somehow remains high, and I have to return for more blood tests, day after day, until finally the hormone levels subside. Dr. Rhodes is then reassured of what I have known from the beginning—the pregnancy was a normal one. A tiny wisp of anger, as small as the one toward Michael, surfaces toward him, too. I imagine him prescribing these interminable blood tests not because he is concerned about my welfare but because he is fearful of a malpractice suit. But the worst consequence of these repetitive blood tests is not anger. As long as I am informed that the hormone level in my bloodstream is high, it is impossible for me to escape the fantasy that my pregnancy has somehow been magically restored to me. Oh, how I wish, how I will it to be true. The final blood test, which shows that the hormone level has dropped, brings me no relief, because it dashes my irrational hope with its impersonal statistical account.

One more impersonal laboratory report is to come my way. One week after the abortion I stand in my office, the telephone receiver at my ear. I wait for the receptionist in the doctor's office to come back on the line and give me the results of the pathology report on the tissue removed from my uterus during the abortion procedure. I hear her voice say, "The pathologist found living tissue. . . ." and I am flooded with a torrent of horror that virtually lifts me off the floor and sweeps me into a dark fog of nausea. Alone, I sob for myself, my child, the remains, the child smeared into bits by the vacuum aspirator, sucked from the warmth of my womb in a violent moment of death. I am a shriek of horror and anguish, straining with all my might somehow to reverse what cannot be reversed, what is irrevocable. I do not know, I cannot imagine, how I will be able to live with the horror of what *is*, the horror that I alone have caused.

THREE

Aftershocks

"On the abortion issue, what would you do if either of your daughters came to you and said she was going to have an abortion and it was not for reasons of health?"

"I would do everything in the world I could to be supportive of her and to help her, and I would have to urge that she not resort to that. When I was governor, [abortion] legislation came up in California. This was the first time I had ever faced the issue, and I realized I didn't have any position on it. I did soul-searching and studying and talking to people in the medical field, the clergy, every kind of person. I came to the conclusion that you are taking a human life, and the only way we could justify that is in self-defense. Unless someone can prove that this is not a living entity, then I feel that we have to oppose abortion on demand."

"You said you would support your daughter. What if she said, 'I disagree with you'? Then what would you do?"

"In this instance, they are both of age and they are both married, and I probably wouldn't have any authority over them. All I could do is be persuasive."

> —From an interview with President Ronald Reagan,
> reported in *People* magazine, February 4, 1985

The Moon Goddess was thus giver of life and of all that promotes fertility, and at the same time she was the wielder of the destructive powers of nature. To the ancients her contradictory character was an essential factor, frankly recognized. But viewed from our rational and standpoint a deity can be either friendly or malicious, but cannot be both. From the Christian point of view it is well-nigh impossible to conceive of a god who is at once kind and cruel, who creates and destroys. For God is conceived of as good: evil is always the work of the devil. But to the worshippers of the Moon Goddess there was no contradiction. Their supreme deity was like the moon, not like the sun. She was dual in her very nature.

—ESTHER HARDING
Women's Mysteries: Ancient and Modern[1]

It is Tuesday, ten days after my Saturday session with Dr. Ross, one week after the nightmarish second labor in which my body completed the abortion the doctor had begun, and one day after the phone call from the doctor's office with the pathology report. I have been managing to function in all my tasks, trying in whatever spare time I can muster to find comfort in reading, searching for some reflection of myself and my struggle in written words. It seems to me that Michael, my friends, and Dr. Ross expect me to be fully recovered; after all, the physical ordeal is now complete, and there should be nothing to keep me from resuming my ordinary life. But I find that the abortion is not over for me and that I need someplace where I can safely experience my feelings.

Today, with no warning, I wake up in a state of despair so overwhelming that I am rendered incapable of pretending to myself or to anyone else that nothing is wrong. Internally something has shifted, and all meaning seems lost; I have never felt such hopelessness, such complete inability to carry on with my life. In this unfamiliar state of immobilization, I remain numb. I experience no emotional distress, only a rather distant awareness that I am less resilient in coping with life than I had thought I would be. I appear alarmingly deadened to Michael, who is so frightened by this utter lassitude in me that he takes the morning off from work and waits at home with me until my 12:30 P.M. appointment with Dr. Ross. I have a free morning without work commitments; this is the first weekday block of time in which I have not had any commitments to care for clients or children. Only later will I realize that this Tuesday morning is the first opportunity I have had to allow my own feelings to surface, without needing to push them aside in order to care for someone else.

Michael drives me to Dr. Ross's office and waits for me in the car. From within my numbed and retracted physical self,

57

I can see that Dr. Ross is shocked and alarmed at my appearance. There is a frown on his forehead, and anxiety shows in his eyes. In the two years he has known me, I have never been like this, so lacking in my customary energy and vitality. I am surprised to notice a glimmer of feeling in myself, the first sign of inner life since I awakened in the morning: it is a feeling of hope. I am hoping that Dr. Ross will help me. I do not know exactly what "help" might be, cannot define a specific response that I need. But as my fifty-five precious minutes relentlessly tick past, I know only that this essential help is not there. Dr. Ross sits silently, watching me, as if he can think of nothing to say. Surely there is some center of wisdom inside him from which he can draw words! I wait expectantly as phrases that I might utter to myself if I were my own client drift across the surface of my mind: "It will take a long time for us to be with your feelings of loss around this child," or, "You've had to make an unthinkable choice, one that has completely shattered your sense of yourself. This is a crisis of soul, one that cannot be overcome easily," or "I know you are in terrible pain, and we'll meet as frequently as we can so I can try to share it with you," or, "Try to tell me what you are feeling." But Dr. Ross does not utter these words or any comparable ones; he has withdrawn into silence and seems completely immobilized by my despair.

In the face of his utter blankness, I begin to feel a mounting panic. This is the one place where I had felt certain I could bring my agony. Other feelings follow in the wake of my panic: anger rapidly masked by disappointment in Dr. Ross and utter disbelief that he can find nothing to say to me; fright that if a psychoanalyst is unable to help me, no one can; worry for myself, for what seems to me to be an abnormal reaction to an event that I know other women have experienced without this level of anguish. These feelings continue to mount as the session with Dr. Ross passes inexorably by. Finally I experience myself actually receding physically from Dr. Ross until I am only a small dot on a distant horizon about to disappear beneath its edge. In the last minutes of our session, Dr. Ross speaks: "You seem very tired. I think you need some rest. Let me prescribe some sleeping medication for you."

A surge of anger momentarily energizes me, and I reject his offer emphatically. "I don't want sleeping pills. I need to have my feelings, not to mute them. Not being able to have my feelings is what's wearing me down." How can he, a psycho-analyst, be offering me medication to numb my feelings? Surely my feelings are understandable, natural. Dr. Ross backs off, immediately retreating into his former cautious silence. He appears uncertain of what to say and fearful of making a mistake or of making me angry. His caution and timidity weigh like a stone upon my heart. A lump of grief begins to swell in my throat; how can I describe the inner experience of not receiving a safety rope, the feeling of slip-ping away, terrified, over the edge of that distant horizon?

As I stand up and walk toward the door, feeling even worse than when I came to the session, Dr. Ross urges me to go to my regular meeting with my friends, saying, "Go to Margaret and Katherine! I know how much they care for you." I cannot believe that he is not saying the words that I would simply know to say to a client in my situation. I cannot believe that he is not saying words that would at least help me endure his inability to respond with empathy for me: "I can see I'm not reaching you," or "I'll keep trying to help, to find a way." Sending me off to my friends feels like a total abandonment, an abnegation of his role. I am completely unprepared for his inability to help me. I have never before needed so urgently to lean on him—or on anyone—and the shattering of my illusions of his wisdom, of his ability to be a steadfast presence in the face of my despair, comes as a total surprise and shock.

I go out to the parking lot and tell Michael, "Dr. Ross told me I should go to my meeting with Katherine and Margaret. I don't really feel up to it, but I'll at least stop by to tell them I can't stay. Otherwise they'd worry about me. But I feel like an automaton following instructions."

Michael is silent, and I see how worried he is; he realizes that Dr. Ross has not come through for me. Finally he says,

"I don't know what else to do for you. It's awful that Dr. Ross isn't being helpful. Are you going to be okay?" I assure him that I will manage and he takes me to my car. He waits until I start the engine of my car before he goes on his way to work; this small protective gesture comforts me.

I carry out my plan and go to the familiar restaurant where Katherine, Margaret, and I meet every other week, alternating with sessions in Margaret's office, when we bring bag lunches. As therapists who have great respect for one another's work, in addition to our friendship, we have had an ongoing peer-consultation group for a number of years. We take turns presenting our most challenging cases to one another. An enormous sense of safety over these years has developed, and we know one another well; our strengths and vulnerabilities are both visible and valued. Ironically it is my week to present a case to them.

When I arrive, my friends are already seated at the private window table that we always occupy so that our confidential discussions cannot be overheard. They look up at me expectantly.

"I only came here to tell you that I'm not going to stay. I didn't want you to worry about me," I announce.

"Don't go!" says Margaret with exuberant concern. Her colorful red hair and bright blue eyes fit her personality; she is full of feelings, which she is quick to express, unafraid of how the other person might react to them.

"What's the matter?" Katherine asks me, worry for me evident on her face. More similar to me than Margaret, both physically and in her introverted manner, Katherine is my oldest friend. Our relationship dates back to that ancient time when we both arrived at graduate school as psychology students, eager and apprehensive. Eventually we came to share an apartment, along with the assorted triumphs and defeats that are inherent in academic life. Together we have lived through many major life events: my marriage to Michael, the death of her father, the birth of my children, the ending for her of significant relationships with various men, and her newly developing relationship with Chris. Now we are about to live through yet another.

I try to respond to them. "I am in such despair about the abortion that I don't know what to do. I don't think I'm going to be able to find a way to live with having made this choice. I went to see Dr. Ross, but he just sat there with nothing to say. Not that it really matters, because I don't think there is anything that anyone can do. It's simply an unsolvable problem."

My friends focus intense and compassionate energy on me, helping me as best they can. "It does matter that Dr. Ross doesn't have anything to say!" Margaret says. She's the freest of the three of us to be openly critical and angry. "It isn't an unsolvable problem; you need your therapist to withstand your feelings of loss until you can shoulder them yourself!"

"You're really having to face the shadow side of the mother archetype," Katherine adds. She is a Jungian analyst, as is Margaret, and I have become familiar with this language from them. "Mothers are destructive and devouring, too, not just nurturing."

Margaret tells me I must face the murderous, destroying side of me, the dark and death-dealing half of the mother archetype. "We all have that side in us. You aren't alone."

I try to cling to this idea as a way of encompassing my despair, a way of making it manageable so that I will not stay lost in these dark, gray clouds of hopelessness. I so much want a sturdy, unfrayable rope to grasp. I will pass hand over hand along its length until I emerge from the dark, gray clouds, back into the ordinary world in which I once had a place. I try to believe that I have a finite task I can accomplish, a way back: If I can face and accept my own dark side, then I can live again in the world of light. I leave this meeting with my good friends trying to believe that I have been helped.

Later that afternoon Dr. Ross calls to check up on me. This is a very unusual event. I know that I have worried him and that perhaps he feels some guilt at not having been helpful. I don't want to cause problems for him or for my friends. I am not all right, but I also believe that there is nothing they can do that will make a difference. So I reassure Dr. Ross.

"I feel much better. It's so nice of you to call and check up on me. Margaret and Katherine were very helpful and gave me a lot of support. I'll just see you at my next appointment."

"Good!" says Dr. Ross heartily. "I'm glad to hear that you're doing better."

My heart sinks at his response, even though it is my reassurance that has brought it about. If I had amputated an arm or a leg, would I have been expected to feel better the next day? He, of all the people in my life, should know the meaning to me of ending this pregnancy, should realize that I am not doing better, should understand by this time that I am taking care of him and not myself in reassuring him. He, as my therapist, ought to be able to tolerate my pain. I know that I am not doing better, that I need to feel my grief in some way that will enable me to heal, to find a way to live with what I have done, with my loss. But I do not know where to turn for this source of healing. I can see that Dr. Ross, Michael, even my women friends, have limits; no one should have to face the degree of anguish I feel. No one made me have this abortion—I am responsible for the choice, and for picking up the pieces of myself that remain. This is my problem, I created it, and now I have to handle it. I stand alone by the telephone, lost in these thoughts, the dead receiver in my hand.

Finally I take a deep breath and tell myself that I will simply have to pull myself together and function, setting aside my despair. Slowly I begin to feel a certain sense of elation, a sense of moral superiority that I do not recognize as a flight from a terrible fear of my own depths. I have an opportunity to become a more "complete" woman, having faced directly a dark side of my nature that many women never confront. Then I can use my experience to help raise the consciousness of other women. But unpleasant questions keep nagging at me: How could Dr. Ross really believe that I have recovered so rapidly from the state of utter despair I was in only this morning in his office? I am beginning to understand that I will need to go elsewhere for help.

Two days later in the next session with Dr. Ross, I tell him that I am terrified. "My normal defenses aren't operating. They seem to have crumbled, and I'm afraid that there's something wrong with me, that I'm crazy. What do you think?" I ask him directly. "Do you think I'm going crazy?"

Dr. Ross pauses, cautious. Then he says quietly, "No, I don't think you're crazy. If it weren't for the abortion, you wouldn't act this way." Neither of us is aware that his frightened, closed response to my emotional pain, his flight from my grief into a state of withdrawn silence, have contributed to my sense of feeling out of control. I have not yet grasped that I am struggling against experiencing a psychological descent into my despair, a descent that, if adequately contained, could become a positive, transformative time. I have not yet shaped my yearning for someone to be with me in my pain into the clear understanding that an empathic human relationship can literally function to embrace a person who is suffering intense anguish until the person can manage for herself. More important, I have not yet found that empathic person.

I bury my despair and continue to function because I have no other choice. No one in my life is available to sit with me in my despair, and I have yet another hurdle ahead of me, the crossing of which will take all the energy and determination I can mobilize: the tubal ligation. Of my four pregnancies, two were unplanned, the result of the failure of different and less drastic birth control methods than sterilization. I am adamant, certain that I must not delay taking steps to ensure that I won't become pregnant again. We have ruled out the option of a vasectomy for Michael because we have read that studies with mice indicate that an increased risk of stroke accompanies vasectomies. Since we are already dealing with two risk factors for Michael—elevated blood pressure and cholesterol—we don't feel secure in adding a third. I plan to discuss the tubal-ligation procedure with Dr. Hodge when I have my postabortion checkup.

The three weeks left until the time of this appointment pass by slowly. On a sunny day in early June, I find myself sitting for a second time on the peach-and-mauve-striped couch that matches the new wallpaper in the redecorated waiting room at the obstetrician's office. Michael is with me as before, though this time we are waiting for Dr. Hodge, who has returned from his vacation, instead of for young Dr. Rhodes. The checkup is included in the total flat fee—a convenient package deal.

"Oh, I really missed you," I tell Dr. Hodge, who is looking dapper and relaxed in his crisp white coat when he enters the tiny examining room where Michael and I have been told to wait. Dr. Hodge is one of those men who never seems to change in appearance, as if time will never wreak its havoc upon him. This apparent immortality is fertile ground for the projections of godlike competence that I, along with other female patients, gratefully cast upon him. Although my words of greeting are indeed genuine, I have also learned how to please him. Dr. Hodge clearly enjoys the unconditional positive regard of his women clients, and given his capability as a surgeon and physician, he deserves it. In any case, his broad face beams at me with pleasure.

"I'm so sorry I was away, but it looks to me as if you've done just fine. Dr. Rhodes did a good job. Nice to see you, too, Michael. Are you having any problems, Sue?"

"Not physical ones, no," I say, leaving the emotional ones aside. "But I want to talk to you about having a tubal ligation. I don't think I could go through this experience again."

I do not want to end my fertility, any more than I wanted to have an abortion. But I am terrified not only that I will become pregnant again through another failure of birth control but also that I will deliberately have a child because the loss, the empty hole, left by my missing fourth child will remain intolerable. And were I to act on these feelings, I know I would feel even worse, not better. I would feel worse because I would still have ended the life of my fourth baby. No subsequent new life could ever replace or restore this particular child to me. My fourth child was a distinct, unique being and consequently irreplaceable. Having a child now would only mean that our decision to have the abortion was a dreadful mistake, that Michael and I could in fact have managed to care for another life. And ever since the abortion, I have had no interest in a sexual relationship at all. From feeling vital, alive, proud of my womanhood, I have come to feel like a dead and decaying piece of meat, worthless flesh, its usefulness over. I am hopeful that a tubal ligation will be freeing, will help me restore a positive connection to my own body.

"Too bad I can't take your fertility and bottle it so that I could give it to some of my infertility patients!" Dr. Hodge comments. His words bring a surge of tears, because I treasure my fertility, too, and I do not want to end it. Only later, as I make meaning of my experience, when I am able to retrieve the lost connection to my feminine essence, will I understand that my tears carry more than my feelings at the impending loss of my fertility. They carry, silently and without words, my recognition that my fertility is a sacred gift and not a commodity. It is Dr. Hodge's loss, as well as my own, that neither of us can know this as we plan the tubal ligation.

Michael, who is so caught up in his own reactions to the idea of sterilization that he is completely unaware of my feelings, starts explaining to Dr. Hodge why he is allowing me to go through a riskier medical procedure instead of his having a vasectomy. He tells Dr. Hodge, "I have borderline hypertension and high cholesterol, and my doctor has told me that there is some research that shows that mice who are sterilized are at greater risk of stroke and heart attack."

Dr. Hodge nods his head, a frown creasing his forehead. "Yes, I do know about that research. Such a connection has in fact been made. Personally I prefer to do tubal ligations on women anyway. After all, it's the woman who can get pregnant, not the man! Even if a urologist does a vasectomy on you, Michael, Sue could still become pregnant!" He chortles at what to him is a little joke. Only later will I feel outraged at his unconscious masculine attitude. Only later will these research data be discredited; they apply to sterilized mice, not to human men. Now I am focused on the ordeal I will have to face, and I am too dependent on Dr. Hodge for medical care to risk incurring his disfavor. I am only too well aware that the medical procedure I face in order to be permanently sterilized involves much greater risk than a vasectomy. I face general anesthesia and an invasion of my internal organs. I have not forgotten the recent newspaper article describing the death of a young mother as a consequence of having been given the wrong medication during elective surgery to remove a benign cyst. Choosing to submit to this procedure is as traumatic a decision for me as the abortion; both are irreversible, emotionally and physically.

"I feel the same way about the tubal ligation as I did about having the abortion. If I'm going to do it, if I have to do it, I want to get it over with as soon as possible. I can't bear to put it off." I make this announcement with a determination that convinces both men. Only later will I grieve for myself, grieve that neither of them could stop me, could say to me, "You've had to make one irrevocable choice to sacrifice something precious. It's too soon for you to make another one," and, in the end, grieve that I could not stop myself.

"Well," Dr. Hodge considers my request with his usual thoughtfulness. "It usually takes six to eight weeks for a woman's body to resume normal functioning after an abortion. Assuming that your body is back on track, we could schedule the operation for mid-July. That will make it about ten weeks postabortion."

We have planned our annual summer vacation for August. This means our timing will be rather close, but I certainly do not want this operation facing me upon my return from vacation. "Let's schedule it," I say with finality, uttering more words that will soon become an unchangeable deed. "My body will work fine."

Dr. Hodge checks his schedule, and I sign the release forms that indicate I understand I am submitting to an irreversible procedure. How I wish I could sign a form that reads instead, "I, Sue Nathanson, agree to undergo an operation I in no way wish to have, because I believe right now that I have no other choice. My husband will not take the risk of having a vasectomy, and I cannot bear the possibility that I might become pregnant again. Even though right now I would much prefer never to have a sexual relationship again, this alternative would undoubtedly be unacceptable to my husband, and I am not yet brave enough to assert my own needs at the expense of others', nor do I expect at this moment that I ever will be. I do not want to have this surgery looming over me and consequently do not want to postpone it. I would prefer to put it behind me as quickly as possible. I do take full responsibility for this nonchoice, and I do agree not to sue the doctors, but I wish it to be on public record that I am choosing it only because I see no other viable alternative for myself."

But instead I quietly sign the printed form, and Michael and I leave the office building together. As we drive home, I share these sardonic thoughts and feelings with my husband. I am silently grateful to him because he accepts my bitter words with compassion; he is somehow able to withstand my bitterness, even if there is nothing he can do to alter it.

"I wish I could go ahead and have a vasectomy. If it weren't for the risk, I would. I don't have the same feelings about my fertility that you do about yours," he tells me. I am caught again with a confusing mixture of conflicting feelings: appreciation for Michael's recognition of the magnitude of my sacrifice and anger that I have to take the greater risk.

With the doctor's appointment behind me, there is nothing for me to do but wait for the scheduled surgery date in July. I have confidence in my body, the same body that produced three healthy children. I know it will resume its functioning, miraculous natural machine that it is. This is no time to feel my grief; that will have to wait until later, until I can find the right time and place.

My parents, who live about four hundred miles away from us, come for a visit several weeks after our appointment with the doctor. They want to see our family before we leave for vacation. I am preoccupied during the entire weekend they are with us, wanting to tell them about my abortion. The main reason I want them to know is not so that I can be the recipient of their sympathy, compassion, or sorrow. It does not occur to me that they might disapprove of my choice, so accustomed am I to their support and affirmation of my decisions and so careful have I always been to make decisions that would not distress them. No, I wish to tell them about the abortion because of the concrete reality my lost fourth child has to me. I want the existence of my lost baby to be made manifest; I want my unborn baby to have its special place in the genealogy of my family. I need my parents to know that there was a fourth grandchild, need them to know there is now an empty place that is separate, distinct, and different from the endless stretch of an infinite number of potential grandchildren. Without being able to acknowledge the loss of this child within the healing circle of my family, I am left alone to carry the burden of loss, the awareness of the empty place. If only there could be an open ceremony in our family, a ritual to mourn this lost child, a way of acknowledging that we are unable to welcome it into our lives. For now, this is not a shared loss, and I must carry its weight by myself.

In the back corner of my mind, too, is a wish to let them know about the impending tubal-ligation surgery. I have considered not telling them about it at all, especially since it is such personal surgery. But what if something goes wrong during the general anesthesia? I do not feel comfortable keeping them in the dark, especially since I have asked them to let me know if they have any medical problems. I have told them that I do not want to learn of such problems after the fact; such "protection" does not seem truly protective to me. But each time an opportunity arises to bring the subject up with them, the words stick in my throat; I gag upon them, choking, unable to make the event real simply by saying the words. Finally, on the last evening of their visit, the entire family goes to a local Chinese restaurant for dinner, the only kind of food the children enjoy eating out. After dinner, my parents will depart in their own car for the motel where they will stay overnight, so they can get a headstart on their long drive home. Since the children are with us, I am convinced that any chance of a private moment with either one of them is now lost to me.

of clear perception of another human being. I also comprehend instantaneously that she has not grasped that the pregnancy was unplanned and consequently was an ambivalent
rather than a joyous event for Michael and me. So I find
myself in the uncomfortable position of giving rational reasons to explain what was such an inexplicable choice:

"We're too old to raise a fourth child; Michael is under too
much stress as it is in his work. We're stretched thin caring
for the three we have. . . ." All these words ring hollow, and
I am appalled at the pleading tone I hear in my voice.

My mother immediately becomes firmly and completely
supportive; the content of her words barely register in me. It
is her reassuring tone I absorb, much as an infant is comforted not by words but by the murmurs and repetitive
sounds of a loving parent. For this moment, I rest at peace,
held firmly in the symbolic arms of my mother. Later, in
trying to reconstruct her words, I imagine her to have told me
not to be sentimental, that she has managed to survive the
losses of two stillborn children after my birth, that life moves
on, that I have made a good decision. In any case, there is
really no time to talk further, because the children, Michael,
and my father come bursting out of the restaurant on a wave
of shouts, laughter, and the total physical energy of their
beings. I apologize to my mother for bringing such a distressing subject up at the last minute when there is no time to talk
more, and I ask her to share the information with my father.

As I cram myself into the over-full car, I wonder what it
means that I have managed to select my mother alone as the
parent to tell, rather than my father alone or both my parents
together. Do I wish for the understanding, the empathy, of
my mother, a woman, or is it her forgiveness that I seek?
These possibilities do not seem convincing to me. But I am
also certain that it is not simply a matter of chance that I have
managed to speak first to my mother and not to my father. I
have an intuitive sense that my choice stems from my unexplored but nonetheless living connection to the feminine archetype, to the female mysteries that are related to the biological
capacity to bear children. It is this capacity that anchors all

women solidly to the realm of life and death, to the realm of earth and matter, and to one another. Even though my mother and I have never overtly acknowledged this powerful shared connection, even though it has remained buried, hidden in the unconscious, nevertheless I know that it exists. It is this connection that lends a sense of safety, of feeling known by my mother and of knowing her.

The next evening something unprecedented in my experience occurs, an event that for others might seem quite ordinary and unexceptional: My father calls me on the telephone. He wants to speak to me by himself; my mother is not present. I am accustomed to my mother's phone calls, or to both of them calling me together. My father has not initiated any separate contact with me for as long as I can remember.

Rather awkwardly (or is it I who feels awkward without my mother's presence?), he tells me, "Your mother has told me what happened." I am certain he is unable to speak the word *abortion* aloud and imagine that he can refer to it only obliquely. Abortion is a part of the realm of female mystery, a realm not ordinarily intended as a meeting ground for father and daughter. *Abortion*—an unspeakable word for an unspeakable deed—word and deed with a stigma attached. "I want you to know that I feel you have made the right decision," he continues, his voice stalwart and firm.

Over and over, in different ways while I listen silently, unable to respond in words, he repeats the same message, "You made the right choice." Tears come at his unconditional support of me, at his unfailing confidence in my judgment. But I also long to cry, to tell him, "Oh, Daddy, I am so sad," to be held in his arms while I sob to him, "I miss my baby so, I want my baby back." Inside I am weeping because in my heart I know that my abortion cannot only be reduced to a choice that is right or wrong. It is an occasion for grief, for tears, as well as for judgment and principles. But I have always prided myself on my self-reliance, on my ability to manage my own problems, and crying to my father is too far removed from our way of relating to each other. I understand that he is reaching out to me on his own, he is offering me his to live with it. Sacrifices cannot be made without the pain of renunciation." I can only wonder why this quality of empathy is absent and whether I will ever find another human being who can offer it to me. I do not yet feel that I am on secure enough ground to be able to ask for the empathic responses I need.

The next day my mother telephones me again, this time without my father. "I called because I think it would be a good idea for you to explore in your analysis the effect that your guilt over my second miscarriage may be having on your reaction to the abortion." My mother has always had a psychological attitude toward her own experience and an interest in psychoanalysis, though when I was growing up, I often disagreed with her interpretations. Whenever I had a cold, she would ask me, "Why are you crying on the inside?" and I would insist, "I'm just *sick!*" But now I am genuinely interested in her information.

Despite an excellent memory for the significant life events of others that I have cultivated through my years as a psychotherapist, I have had difficulty remembering some of the stories my mother has told me about my own early life experiences. I frequently need her to tell me the entire story anew, as if it simply never becomes stored in the memory traces of my brain. I ask my mother, "Tell me again what happened. I know you've told me before, but it was probably a long time ago, and besides, I can never remember it!"

My mother willingly tells me the story again. "When you were three and a half years old, we took you to New York City to a progressive hospital for a tonsillectomy. In this hospital parents were allowed to sleep in the room with children who were having any kind of surgery. This was a very progressive hospital for the 1940s; now it's much more common to let parents stay overnight with hospitalized children. So I was with you when the nurse carried you into the operating room; they didn't even put you on a hospital gurney, knowing this would be frightening for a young child. And I was standing with you when you awoke from the anesthesia. I was at the edge of your crib. You were calling for the book

Madeline, the one about the little girl who has her appendix taken out. We had gotten it for you before the surgery, and you liked to hear me read it over and over. Just at that very moment I began to lose the baby; I was four months pregnant. I had already lost the other baby boy when you were two and a half years old."

My mother drifts off into her own reverie. "I managed to carry that first baby boy for seven months. He was stillborn, and came with a caul around him. I had an Irish nurse, who told me that meant he was a special child, blessed. . . ." With a sigh that conveys the comfort this nurse provided her, she picks up the thread of the story. "Anyway, they took me immediately into intensive care, and I had to leave you. You were sent home from the hospital, to Aunt Rose's house since we were too far away to go home, and I had to stay in the hospital. I came back to Aunt Rose's two days later—the bed rest had kept me from losing the baby. But then all of a sudden I lost the baby for good—it just slipped out of me all of a sudden—and I had to go back to the hospital. So that time you had me and lost me not just once, but two times. I'm sure you must have overheard the family talking about how I lost the baby because I was so worried about you having your tonsils out. You might've felt guilty for causing me to be under such stress that I lost the baby, even though you never behaved as if you did. I think that's why you feel so guilty now."

I am touched by my mother's concern and realize how my own interest in psychology and my capacity to reflect upon the meaning of my past experiences must have been nurtured in my relationship with her. Her speculation about the guilt I felt about her miscarriage makes sense: At four, children live in an egocentric world, creating magical causal connections between their behavior and the events occurring around them. My tonsillectomy, traumatic enough for my three-and-a-half-year-old self to endure, surely would have seemed powerful enough to incapacitate my mother and to kill my unborn brother.

My mother continues, "And don't forget, you had already

had the experience of losing me when the first baby was stillborn. . . . Remember?" Without waiting for my answer, my mother tells the story of her first lost child. "As soon as your father came home from the Army after World War Two ended, I became pregnant. We always wanted to have lots of children! You were only two years old then. When I was seven months pregnant, I went into labor prematurely and was taken to the hospital. Unfortunately I had to leave while you were asleep for your afternoon nap. So when you woke up, I was gone, with no warning, no good-byes. After a few days, Daddy took you to Grandmother's house because he couldn't work, take care of you, and visit me in the hospital. Your grandmother kept you for about three weeks. Even though I had been released from the hospital, I didn't have enough energy to take care of you. Finally my friends told me that I absolutely had to bring you back, that you had been away from me for too long and that they would come and help me care for you. So your daddy went and got you. When you came home, you took one look at me, turned white as a sheet, and burst into tears. You were just hysterical—no one could comfort you. I realized that you were upset like that because I was wearing a nightgown, just as I had been when you took that nap when I disappeared. You were terrified that I would disappear again. So I went to my bedroom and got dressed in regular clothes. After that you calmed down and were all right. And you know, you were so good at Grandmother's house. You never even asked anyone where I was!"

How long those three weeks must have seemed to my two-and-a-half-year-old self! From the perspective of a child, three weeks would have seemed an eternity. I must have felt that I had lost my mother forever, perhaps even that I had caused her to disappear by being cranky or difficult. Did I sense that another child was on the way and dread the appearance of a competitor? Have I been carrying with me throughout my life an unconscious sense of responsibility for the deaths of my younger brothers? No wonder I tried so hard to be a good child at my grandmother's house; how fearful I must have been of destroying her, too. The seeds of a lifelong habit of keeping my needs from pressing upon those around me, of fearing their awesome power to destroy, may have begun to blossom during these early experiences of loss.

As they do each time I hear them, these stories evoke a deep sadness in me for that little girl who was separated so traumatically from her mother too early, for that little girl who had to become self-reliant too early. Now, pondering the stories again, I find in them some understanding of the source and depth of my pain at the impossibility of mothering my own lost baby and of my anguish over Dr. Ross's failure to empathize with and bear my intense feelings. Because mothers and children are—paradoxically—both separate beings and part of one another at the same time, I know that I must feel completely identified with my own unborn baby, whose mother is as lost to it as my own mother was once lost to me. And simultaneously I must feel identified with my own mother, who was unable to care for me on those critical occasions that, I can now intuit, were cumulatively traumatic for me. Not only was the separation from my mother on those occasions traumatic, but an additional trauma also occurred: For whatever reason, I could not release whatever feelings I was experiencing and have them received by those who cared for me. Unable to yield to my primitive terror or pain and be soothed and comforted in the arms of a loving person, I kept my feelings inside and tried to calm myself. By the time I was four, I apparently had formed a fixed belief that I had to take care of myself. No matter whether this belief was accurate or distorted—once formed, it acted like a filter that let through only affirming perceptions and kept out any information that might have altered the filter itself.

My inability to retain my mother's stories, apart from their important content, is a clear signal that they are indeed significant, directly relevant to the impact the abortion has had on me. My mother's suggestion that I work on them in my analysis pushes me to remember that I had in fact shared them with Dr. Ross early in my therapy. I realize now that he never referred to them again, despite the fact that they were pivotal events in my childhood. My inability to keep them in consciousness meant that I could not bring them up myself. Despite my theoretical knowledge of repression, I am astonished to experience its power so directly. Considering that I have no difficulty storing and recalling a multitude of facts about all my clients, my inability to remain conscious of the pivotal events in my own life is remarkable. But, I wonder to myself, why hasn't Dr. Ross helped me to make the connection between these early experiences and my reaction to the abortion. Isn't that his job? Just as a parent carries a sustaining image of the wholeness of a child as the child proceeds through the various developmental stages, I know that an analyst must hold a comprehensive vision of the client as the client navigates the different phases of analysis. I begin to doubt whether Dr. Ross carries an accurate vision of me. Acknowledging his limitations as my therapist, facing my anger and disappointment, and moving on from this relationship represents yet another hurdle I will have to face. But it will have to wait until I survive the tubal ligation.

I am sobered by the reminder that my mother has had to bear her own special suffering in childbirth. She lost two sons, one at seven months and one at four months. She, too, continues to carry the weight of the dark side of the female connection to birth and death. She, too, carries the weight of this dark side without any external supporting structures, structures that are beginning to seem conspicuously absent for women in our time and place.

Beyond relaying this important information and concern to me, I can see that my mother is primarily concerned with giving me a psychological boost. She, like my father, literally orders me to get on with the business of living. "It's all right to feel sad momentarily, but you must let the sadness pass and move on to other things. Otherwise, you're only wasting time, wasting your life. Don't get bogged down in it. There's no reason to be overly sentimental."

"I'm trying," I tell her. "It's just that I'm dealing with what to me is a huge loss."

I think about her advice, wondering if these are the words

she told herself after she lost her baby sons. Somehow, knowing that she has had to struggle with her own grief around childbearing helps me to feel our womanly connection, and for a time I feel more energized. The unexpected tightening of the bond with my mother and with my father through their efforts to reach out to me in telephone calls enables me to cope more effectively for the time being.

But the bond with my parents around the abortion is not to be renewed. My mother's phone call is the last communication my parents and I ever have on the subject. As my tubal ligation approaches, it pushes the abortion aside and takes over, in this way coming to occupy center stage in my consciousness.

FOUR

Tubal Ligation: Anticipation

TUBE CUTTING, HIS AND HERS

Apparently, on the principle that occasionally it pays to remind doctors of what they already know, the American Journal of Public Health *this month published a large-scale review of the costs and risks of male and female sterilizations.*

The male operation, vasectomy, costs one-third to one-fourth as much as the tubal ligation done in women.

The procedures are equally reliable.

And here's the clincher: The authors were unable to find any record of an American man dying of a vasectomy. A mortality rate of zero is remarkable for any procedure.

By contrast, at least 14 American women die each year of complications of sterilization, according to the report. And that's a conservative estimate.

Newton [spokesperson in the Journal *review] fears that much of the continued popularity of tubal ligation must be attributed to a particularly lethal version of male chauvinist piggishness.*

—Clipping from a local newspaper, April 11, 1985

Like Ishtar [the Babylonian moon goddess], moon goddesses from whatever region were regarded as guardians of the waters, rivers, brooks, and springs which, gushing forth out of the ground, were usually held sacred to the goddess of fertility; probably because they so aptly symbolize that invisible hidden power of "bringing forth from within" which is the peculiar characteristic of feminine creation.

—ESTHER HARDING
Women's Mysteries: Ancient and Modern[1]

It is several days before my surgery. Although the abortion took place in May, only eight weeks ago, the seasonal shift from spring to the summer heat of July has created a clear boundary between the two events. The surgery is scheduled for 7:00 A.M. on Saturday. Dr. Hodge has agreed to perform the surgery on a Saturday because he will be on call and in the hospital anyway. Even though I know rationally that he is not inconveniencing himself in order to accommodate me, I have a need to feel like his special patient and prefer to feel that he has offered me an exceptional time. My need to feel special meshes perfectly with his need to be appreciated and admired by his women patients. In exchange for offering gratitude, I am granted the much-needed illusion of feeling safe and cared for by him. In practical terms, Saturday is the most convenient time for me as well. I will not need to miss even one day of work, nor will Michael. With a bitter cynicism born of despair, I think to myself, how wonderful that modern medical technology can enable me to dispose of my fertility in mere minutes, without even skipping a beat!

My anxiety is not focused specifically upon the sterilization, but upon the idea of having any surgery at all. I have never had general anesthesia, except when my tonsils were removed when I was a child. My only direct memories of that experience are the hazy visual image of myself lying on my back in a crib (I can see the bars) while someone pricks my middle finger (for a blood test) and makes it bleed. My other visual image is of my father, who is seated in a chair positioned between my crib and a hospital bed located opposite my crib. He is asleep sitting up. But I know from my recent telephone call from my mother that this hospitalization had its traumatic aspects, not only because of the physical trauma and discomfort from the surgery itself, but also because I lost

81

my connection to her at the same time. Now even the idea of being rendered unconscious is terrifying to me.

I think back to my office visit with Dr. Hodge, when he, Michael, and I made arrangements for the surgery. I recall asking Dr. Hodge, "Is there any way I could have a local anesthetic instead?" He took my question very seriously; he has always responded with equal care to every question I have ever had, whether large or small. This quality of attention is one of the characteristics that I have found most endearing and that I have always valued highly. He had replied thoughtfully to this question as well: "I think that a general anesthetic would be better. There's likely to be considerable discomfort from the gas that we use to inflate the abdominal cavity. I don't know how easy it would be to tolerate that discomfort." Caught between two alarming choices—to be rendered unconscious and risk not waking up or to be inflated like a balloon to the point where I might fear bursting open—I choose the general anesthetic, in spite of my knowledge that it might increase the risk of complications. Only later will I learn from my friend Judith that she had much the same procedure performed, not to destroy her fallopian tubes as I am planning to do to prevent pregnancy, but to repair and open them to facilitate a pregnancy. Beset with the same fear of a general anesthetic I struggle with now, she chose to have a local anesthetic; with the support of her physician and her anesthesiologist, she tolerated the surgery well.

Having made my choice between two unpleasant alternatives, I try to help myself handle my apprehension about the anesthesia. I know that I am frightened about the general anesthetic because I do not want to relinquish my conscious experience of life—the fragile thread that links me to existence, that I rely upon to take care of myself. I do not want this fragile thread held in the hands of strangers who do not know, value, or care for me. I would have preferred to embrace the physical discomfort related to the local anesthetic willingly, as I had embraced those of pregnancy and childbirth, if Dr. Hodge had offered any support for this choice, if I had not been left alone to cope with it. Yet I can understand that Dr. Hodge might not want to put himself in the treacherous position of performing surgery on a panic-stricken woman. I am certainly in no position to reassure him that I will be able to tolerate any amount of physical pain. Meanwhile, the idea of an unknown anesthesiologist assaulting me with drugs becomes blurred in my mind with a picture of me being gassed in a concentration camp by Nazis. That dehumanization and the absence of human empathy and compassion that I imagine will occur in the sterile operating-room theater, feel the same to me.

I discuss my decision to have the surgery with Dr. Ross. "You don't have to do this," he tells me, when I talk about the difficulty of the decision, my dread of the surgery, my regret at losing my fertility in this way. His words eerily echo Michael's when we sat in the hospital lobby before the abortion. Does he, too, wish to absolve himself of any participation in my decision? Is he telling me he doesn't want to hear how awful I feel? I respond irritably, feeling misunderstood: "I know that I'm choosing to have this surgery, that nobody is making me go through with it. But under the circumstances, I don't feel as if I have any other choice. Any form of birth control other than tubal ligation leaves me at some risk of another pregnancy, and any risk at all is unacceptable from my point of view. Besides, making the choice has absolutely nothing to do with the feelings I have about it. I'm going to try to make the best of the situation and focus on the freedom from worry about pregnancy that I'll have. But right now I'd give anything to be able to choose the worry instead." I wish Dr. Ross could simply acknowledge my sorrow at feeling compelled to make such a decision.

Time seems to pass slowly from my original visit to Dr. Hodge when we planned the surgery, but finally the procedure is only a few days away. My anxiety has slowly mounted to an internal state of panic and dread that stays with me all the time, as if it were my normal condition. I find myself filtering it out in muted degrees to the people in my life. As with the abortion, no one in my life seems to appreciate the magnitude of the terror I feel. Perhaps this is because I can communicate only through ordinary language, channeling my terror into coherent words, forming complete sentences, which I utter in a normal tone of voice. Perhaps it is because my body remains normal in appearance and continues to work, dress itself, exercise, and perform chores efficiently even though internally I feel so altered. Even the words I manage to speak that do contain my terror are only a small portion of the total number of words that race around inside me. They are a minuscule part of the many dialogues, discussions, and casual conversations with others in my daily life. How odd that this intense inner terror does not distort the boundaries of my body, changing me into a misshapen, quivering, fluid form of shifting colors.

The panic and terror about what I will undergo is contained within the boundaries of my physical body. Large, opaque clouds balloon around inside me until I fear I will suffocate. These internal clouds force the air from my lungs so that I can scarcely breathe. My skin is stretched taut from straining to contain them. It is worse when I am alone. Then I cannot ignore their rhythmic motion as they expand and contract throughout what now feels like the hollow and empty shell of me. I have lost my child, I am losing my fertility—I was once filled with joy and vitality, but now I am empty. The panic clouds bump and shove around inside this shell at will.

On the Wednesday before the surgery I sit with my friend Julia in the sunlight of the outdoor patio of a local restaurant. While savoring bites of the vegetarian salad that is a house specialty, Julia tells me about her own experience with general anesthesia for the hysterectomy she had sixteen years ago at age forty-two. "I had a wonderful nurse who told me exactly what to expect. She had me count backward from one hundred, and I remember getting only to ninety-nine. Then the next thing I knew, I was awake! It was amazingly quick."

I know Julia is trying to help me cope with my anxiety by telling me what to expect and by reassuring me that what will happen is not terrible. This is in fact helpful information that has not been offered by any of the doctors or nurses.

My mind wanders as I sit with her, not tasting my own lunch at all, because I, too, remember Julia's hysterectomy. . . .

I was a beginning graduate student in psychology. Julia was my first supervisor, a wonderful, supportive person who had a knack for finding whatever was competent in me and reflecting that capacity back in a validating and reinforcing manner. The day after she had her hysterectomy, I went to visit her in the hospital with Florence, another supervisor, who was also a personal friend of Julia's. I rode in the front seat of Florence's car, a casual yet intimate setting at odds with our customary formal contact in Room 2131 of Haller Hall across the boundary of Florence's desk. I was only twenty-two years old, still unmarried. The experiences of pregnancy and childbirth were years ahead of me, not yet possibilities that held any reality for me. I was unable to understand, then, Florence's confession to me that she went through an early menopause when she was only thirty-nine years old and that she was relieved that this part of life was over for her. Hearing her self-disclosure had left me feeling entirely out of place, inappropriately present as a visitor to the hospital, to Julia. I was only a student, an entire generation removed from these two women, with no context in which I could understand their experiences of menopause and hysterectomy. These experiences are part of the female mystery, which at that moment remained inaccessible, far ahead of me. . . .

Now, on this sunny Wednesday in July sixteen years later, sitting with Julia in the shaded patio area, I listen carefully to what she tells me. I am no longer an outsider to such female mysteries. I try to thank Julia for her support, and my gratitude is genuine. But I conceal my acute sense of our differences. Her surgery is over while mine lies ahead. She has never invested as much emotional energy in her capacity to bear children; the hysterectomy was a relief to her because it ended bouts of sudden hemorrhaging. For me the surgery will bring to a close the state of fertility that I continue to value and cherish. I conceal my feelings not because I am afraid to tell Julia about them, or because I have defenses against them.

I conceal them because I do not know how to express them in words. I cannot shape them into forms of meaning. Yet the feelings rise up in me with great force as I sit in the sunlight with Julia. How odd that they are so invisible, so incommunicable to my friend.

Later I try to talk to my friends Esther and Margaret. They are both women who are my age and who have chosen to have tubal-ligation surgery. Esther, nine years ago, carried out a plan she had predetermined for herself. This plan was to wait until her youngest son, Jeffrey, was two years old. Then, with her family complete and secured, she would make a conscious and deliberate commitment to adult life. I recall how she went to New York City in order to have the operation done in a major hospital. Characteristically overestimating her own powers, she had expected to drive back to her home that same day with her husband, Bruce. Instead, debilitated and uncomfortable hours after she was released from the hospital, she ended up unexpectedly in bed at my house, while Bruce returned alone to their home in order to work and take care of their children. Esther had allowed me to provide only very little for her—one small toasted English muffin—despite her obvious physical discomfort. I recall now how unable I was to understand why she made her choice to have the tubal ligation, how certain I was that I would never choose that option for myself. As I watched her cope with the immediate aftermath of pain and discomfort, I felt compassion for her, along with a greater relief for myself, relief that this was an experience I would never need to have. Now, nine years later, I feel frightened for myself as I face what she chose to undergo on her own; I feel like a person sentenced to death by execution.

"I've had a difficult time adjusting to it," Esther tells me, with her characteristically direct honesty, when we meet for coffee. "Even now, I sometimes feel terribly mutilated, and wish I could undo the surgery. Funny how these feelings persist, even though I've already gone through menopause. I thought that women who had tubal ligations would experience an easier time at menopause because they would have already dealt with the loss of fertility. But I find that the two experiences are completely different."

"I can't believe that we've never talked about this," I respond. "I had no idea that you had these feelings. I've always assumed that you were pleased with the choice you made and that you never had a moment's regret."

"Maybe a lot of women who choose tubal ligation do feel that way," Esther answers. "I'm just not one of them."

"Well," I say with a sigh, "I'm not sure it would have affected my decision, even if I'd known about the problems you had afterward. I have to make absolutely sure that I won't become pregnant again; I could never go through another abortion. I don't even know yet how I'm going to live with myself after the abortion I've already had—even though I'm so grateful I had the freedom to choose it and even though I made the best choice I could. At this point I feel so terrible about choosing to end the pregnancy, I'm mostly staying on earth because I couldn't devastate my children and Michael by abandoning them. A second unplanned pregnancy—there's no way I could survive it psychologically."

A few days after my lunch with Esther, I take a walk with Margaret and tell her all my fears about the anesthesia. "I don't like the idea of not knowing what's happening to my body. And the idea that I could be put to sleep and never wake up again just terrifies me."

Margaret, who is at such an opposite pole from me in so many ways that we are constantly mystifying and baffling each other, differs from me here, too. "I loved the anesthetic when I had my surgery!" she exclaims ecstatically. "It was the best part—just to relax, to float off. . . ." she continues, with evident visceral enjoyment of the opportunity to reminisce.

"Oh, Margaret!" I sigh. "I can't even begin to imagine having that degree of trust in the world. I wish I could borrow your attitude just for twenty-four hours!"

"I'm not so sure it's trust," Margaret muses. "Maybe you should call it denial!"

Although this difference in our outlook, whether it be named trust or denial, should have served as a warning to me,

I cannot suppress my need to ask her for reassurance about the actual surgery. "Look, Margaret," I say, "I'm terrified about having this tubal ligation. I know you survived it in good shape, and I need you to reassure me that I'm going to be all right. Tell me that I can go through with it!"

Unconscious of her impact as she speaks her mind freely, Margaret instead proceeds to tell me the disastrous story of her friend May, a woman I do not know. "May had terrible complications following her tubal-ligation surgery! Everything that could go wrong did, and it took her a long time to recover." She adds blithely, "You'll probably have complications too. Like May, giving birth has meant so much to you; it's been so important in your life."

The panic balloons inside me career wildly—but I do not share my distress with Margaret until later that evening when we both attend a large social gathering, a fund-raiser for a professional organization we both support. I test out my ability to express my hurt in words by sharing my feelings first with Margaret's husband, Martin, who always lends a sympathetic ear. "That's awful!" he exclaims, to my satisfaction. "How could Margaret do that to you! You didn't need to hear about May now!" Armed with the support that his empathy provides, I search Margaret out among the crowd to confront her with my feelings. It's not hard to locate her, with her bright red hair and emerald-green dress.

"Margaret!" I say to her, "I have to talk to you!" I gulp. "You really upset me today when you told me that I'd have complications after the tubal-ligation surgery. I needed you to make me less anxious, not more!" These are daring words for me. I have had little practice in letting those I care about know they have disappointed me. It takes an event as catastrophic as the abortion or the impending surgery to push me to assert my needs when these needs might inconvenience others.

"Oh, Sue!" Margaret responds to me with an immediate and heartfelt apology when she understands the degree of alarm she has triggered in me. "If you pay me my hourly therapist's fee, I listen with full attention. Other than that,

I'm liable to say awful things without realizing it!" But her genuine concern and reassurance do little to calm the motion of the panic balloons inside me, because even now I can appreciate the uncanny accuracy of her intuition.

Unexpected support comes to me on Friday, the day before the operation, when I go to the hospital to have the required presurgical blood tests and to register at the hospital office. I am in the outpatient surgery department handing my forms to the nurse in charge. "Have you ever had surgery before?" she asks me. I tell her, "No, I haven't," and find myself adding simply, "I'm terrified." Although I have channeled my panic into the same words many times before, to many people, including close friends, this nurse hears them and responds to me in a different way. I watch her look up from the mass of paper forms in front of her and regard me intently, as if recognizing for the first time that an ordinary, vulnerable human being is standing, alone and afraid, behind the dehumanizing packet of mimeographed consent statements.

Immediately she takes charge. She locates the nurse who will be on duty the next day, which is no easy feat to accomplish since that nurse is on another part of the floor. She then introduces us so that I will know who will be caring for me the next day. Next she shows me the bed I will have and describes exactly what the anesthesia will feel like. "In just a blink of an eye you will be asleep and then awake again, as if no time at all has passed," she says. Her arm rests on my shoulder, and I fight back tears at the simple but profound comfort that its warmth and pressure brings. I feel a momentary relief from the panic, but when I leave the hospital and am alone again in my car as I drove home, the balloons resume their activity. Why won't they leave me alone?

Finally it is the Friday night before the operation. I am supposed to go to the ballet with Michael and our friends Katherine and Chris, an event we planned months ago when that universally comforting illusion of continuity carried me blithely through my days. They announced their plan to marry in the fall only a few weeks ago, and the unexpected opening up of the possibilities of marriage and motherhood that had seemed forever lost for Katherine had filled me with delight. I had been looking forward to the excursion to the ballet, not only as an evening of entertainment but also as an opportunity to spend time with them. But now I realize that I cannot go out for an evening of fun. All through the two months intervening between the abortion and this surgery, I have managed to keep all my commitments in the outer world; my crisis has been an invisible, internal one. This has always been my pattern; it rests upon the assumption that as long as I can function in the ordinary world, I am safe. I used to think of my capacity to function effectively in this way as a reflection of my highly developed sense of responsibility, a consistently superior level of "ego-functioning," a measure of my unshakable capacity to cope—no matter what. But tonight this familiar pattern gives way. For two months I have walked through my life carrying the enormous panic balloons inside, and now, my responsibilities to others essentially complete, I am exhausted. Michael, Katherine, and Chris encourage me to do whatever is best for me, and I stay home alone while Michael goes off to dinner and the ballet without me. Much later, when we both reflect back upon this time in our lives, Michael will tell me that he is appalled at himself for leaving me at such a critical time: "How could I have just gone off and left you like that!" But I will be able to reassure him honestly that I did not feel abandoned, that I needed to be alone with my thoughts and feelings.

Because Michael is away, I carry out the bedtime rituals with the children by myself. I anoint Jill's silky-soft brown hair with the motherly kiss that guarantees her sweet dreams and a safe night.

I call out "Good-night!" to Becky through her closed bedroom door. On nights when fortune shines upon me, her door opens and she emerges for a hug. Other nights, enclosed by those singular burdens that nine-year-old young ladies carry, she simply calls out, with an audible sigh of resignation. "Good-*night!*" I understand on these nights that any intrusion into her private world is intolerable, and I leave her alone. Tonight is such a night, apparently, and I accept her irritable reply with more than my customary disappointment. Tonight I would have liked the physical comfort of her hug, but I am unwilling to accept one that is offered on demand.

Slowly I climb the stairs to Ben's room. I feel as if I am a hundred years old, so depleted of energy and vitality am I; my spirit flame now burns low. I arrive at Ben's door after what seems like a journey of many miles, and I knock, careful not to dislodge his store-bought Beware of Dog sign and the homemade one that says, Off Limits—Entering These Premises Is Hazardous to Your Health! I look in and see that he is reading a *Garfield* cartoon book in bed, chortling away to himself. For several minutes his vibrant sense of fun transports me out of myself, and I am able to laugh at the jokes he shares with me. But once I leave his room, I am outside the sphere of his buoyant energy and must reenter my own inner world, one that is dense with sorrow. Tomorrow the fertility that generated the lives of these three children, that embodied their spirits in separate and unique physical forms—spirits that miraculously continue to expand beneath my eyes—tomorrow this fertility will cease, terminated by my own choice.

My children are eventually all asleep, leaving me, finally, alone. I sit in the small armchair in the corner of my bedroom, just as I had the night before my abortion. Now, in the quiet of late evening, I savor my last moments of fertility. Oddly I find I am calm now. The panic balloons, although present, are at rest, hovering silently inside me. I look out the darkened window at the stars and tell myself that I will see them again in just twenty-four hours. I will be alive tomorrow, even if unalterably changed. Yet the stars will look the same, at least to my inadequate senses. The thought of stars evokes a memory of how my mother tried to help me cope with my fear of being homesick when I was child, about to leave home to attend a one-week sleep-away camp. She had told me, "When you're in bed at night, look up in the sky and find the very brightest star. Then think to yourself that this very same bright star is looking down on me, too." Once settled at the camp, I had followed her directions to the last detail, propelled by the urgent necessity of that sick feeling in the stomach that homesickness brings. The chosen star had in fact bridged what would otherwise have been an unfathomable distance between my mother and myself on that first night away from home. Last year, when Jill went away to camp for a week, I passed on the same instruction to her the night before she left. When I kissed her good-night at bedtime on her first night back home, she volunteered that she had located the brightest star in the sky and had even tracked its movement across the night sky during her week away by measuring its distance from the tallest pine tree near her sleeping bag. Now, even though I am an adult in years, my needs are similar to ones I had as a child and to Jill's. I recognize that I want to create an equally essential bridge for myself, powerful enough to carry me across the most frightening separation I have yet experienced. It will need to be strong and solid enough to carry me from my familiar self, through the blackness of no-consciousness, to a new, altered self. The image of a star, one small eternal light in an infinitely vast darkness, seems a fitting symbol. Holding this image in my mind, I go to bed and sleep.

FIVE

Tubal Ligation: Event

Just as, in the case of the moon, an order or rule underlies her [woman's] conduct, so with woman also a rule or law underlies her apparent fickleness. Yet this law ruling woman is no more obvious or simple than the law ruling the moon, which to the average layman is by and large incomprehensible. So also the feminine principle, which underlies so great a part of woman's conduct, is not to be easily understood. . . .

This is very difficult for a man to understand because his inner principle is the Logos; and by this principle if a thing is right today, it will still be right tomorrow. . . .

Men, who experience life primarily through their rational Logos nature, are unable to appreciate the quality of the woman's perception as being equally valid with their own. It is a truism that we have no exact knowledge of things as they are; while we all have the prejudice that they are as we see them. . . . So that, naturally, we have no way of knowing whether men may not be as much deceived by their masculine nature as women are, obviously, by their feminine nature.

—ESTHER HARDING
Women's Mysteries: Ancient and Modern[1]

(The first incision is made straight, not curved, from one indenta-
tion to the next, regardless of previous scars on the abdomen, in the
skin.) . . . (The next incision is made in the subcutaneous tissue
down through the fasciae in the midline to one and one half inches
only.) . . . (Fascia is cut open by going under the subcutaneous
tissue. The scissors are placed in the space between the two rectus
muscles and opened in the line of the incision. This gives a space
into which the forefinger of each hand is now placed.)[2]

Because we know ourselves to be made from this earth. Temporary
as this grass. Wet as this mud. Our cells filled with water. Like
the mud on this swamp. Heather growing here because of the
damp. Sphagnum moss floating on the surface, on the water
standing in these pools. Places where the river washes out. Where
the earth was shaped by the flow of lava. Or by the slow
movements of glaciers. Because we know ourselves to be made from
this earth, and shaped like the earth, by what has gone before. The
lives of our mothers. . . .[3]

—From Susan Griffin, *Woman and Nature, The Roaring Inside Her*,
in which she juxtaposes two different voices. The author labels
the first voice as patriarchal—objective, detached, and bodiless—
and the second voice as matriarchal—embodied and impassioned.

In the morning before my tubal-ligation surgery, the ever present panic balloons remain quiet, but now they have a different quality, a kind of rigid stillness. I am taut with anxiety and tightly controlled. I feel like a coiled spring, in danger of bursting apart at the slightest touch. My coping, competent self takes over for the vulnerable, frightened child-self within. It wakes me up and provides enough energy for me to exercise at dawn, knowing that the increased circulation, the lively, compelling music, and the warm shower will make me feel alive.

Michael and I ride silently to the hospital at 6:00 A.M., just as the sun begins to cast its early-morning rosy glow over the deserted city streets. I think back to our ride to the same hospital when Ben was born. He happened to arrive on a Saturday, too; the streets were just as deserted then, and the sun was also beginning to rise. Jill and Becky were asleep, unaware that Kristin, their favorite babysitter, had come to take care of them in our absence. Today they, along with Ben, are looking foward to the pancake breakfast that Lynn, their current babysitter, has promised to make. Our mood when Ben was born was one of happy anticipation and excitement. Now I feel as if I am heading toward certain death, and Michael's grim expression indicates a similar fear.

The outpatient surgery department seems like a dark cave, far removed from the dawn-fresh outdoors from which I have come. An efficient nurse instructs me to remove all my clothing, even my wedding ring, and gives me a plastic bag labeled with the hospital's name in which to collect all my personal belongings. I am surprised at how frightening it is to be stripped naked. Without my wedding ring, my concrete tie to Michael is gone. I did not appreciate its importance as a symbol of relatedness, of human connection, until I was asked to give it up. Now without it, I feel like a lost, anonymous body. How will anyone identify me without my ring when I am unconscious from the anesthetic?

In minutes I am lying naked on a narrow metal gurney, covered with a thin white sheet. My hair is completely concealed under a paper cap. I am wheeled quickly to the elevator by an unseen male attendant, who remains behind me, outside the range of my vision. I feel totally disoriented: stripped naked, flat on my back on this narrow cart, unable to locate myself in space since the blank walls of the hall and ceiling—all that is visible to me from my horizontal vantage point—offer no landmark upon which I can focus. I derive some comfort from Michael's presence as he strides rapidly next to the gurney, working hard to keep up with the rapid pace of the attendant. But all too soon we arrive at a crossroad: the elevator door. Michael is not allowed to come further. I am convinced that my eyes have a wild, pleading look as I try to say good-bye. I hope he will find some way to come down to the hospital basement with me. He must know that I do not want him to leave me. But this moment quickly passes, and we merely wave good-bye with forced smiles on our faces while our eyes meet for a brief moment of true contact. The elevator door closes, and I begin my descent to the hospital basement, where the operating rooms are located.

The basement is a cold, bleak place, barren of windows. I am wheeled by my invisible, silent attendant down a wide corridor devoid of human activity, lined only with closed doors. We come to an abrupt stop at a room that appears to be some kind of temporary parking area, a large room without any lights on, filled with unused equipment. My attendant deftly wheels me around and literally parks me, like a used car, next to another body on an identical gurney. This body is wearing a green cap like mine and is also covered from chin to toe with a white sheet. But the patient is so still that I realize she or he must be sedated, unlike me. A tubal ligation must be categorized as such a minor medical procedure that pre-operative sedation is unnecessary. And as with the abortion, no medication exists to calm one's soul.

I am left alone. I have no idea what time it is or how long I will be left to wait here. A wave of anxiety ripples through me, and I begin to shiver with cold and fright.

Finally a green-gowned male figure appears and tells me, "Sorry, there's been a delay. The doctors are still occupying the surgery room. I don't know exactly how long you'll have to wait."

I battle briefly with embarrassment and shame and then ask him, "Is it all right if I use the bathroom?" A red wave of humiliation swirls around me as I struggle to comprehend the meaning of his reply: "Don't worry—they'll take care of that in your surgery." Without waiting for a response from me, he turns quickly and leaves.

There is a clamor of discordant voices in my head: Can I wait? What will they do to my body when I am unconscious? Do they drain urine from my bladder as if I am a piece of meat? I try to breathe deeply, to focus on my breathing, to allow the clamor of these voices to subside. My limbs seem no longer to belong to me; I notice that I am not moving my arm to scratch an itch. When I direct my arm to scratch, it does so sluggishly, feeling heavy and clumsy to me.

Only my eyes and ears seem to function automatically. But there is nothing in this large room to see and no sound to hear. I try to turn inward, to imagine myself lying on my back at a beach in the warm sun. Unable to conjure up this picture, I try to visualize myself at home in my own bed. But I cannot create a visual image strong enough to compete with the cold emptiness of the room I am now in.

A new concern suddenly wells up inside me: I cannot tolerate not knowing the time. The absence of a clock seems unendurable to me. It signifies the absence of a connection to the world I know. If it is 8:00 A.M., then Ben is waking up. Michael will be out for a run. What *time* is it? I need to know, desperately. But there is no one I can ask.

The presence of the person next to me suddenly looms large and absorbs my attention. I cannot tell if it is a man or a woman. I look for some visible sign of gender and finally notice the shadow of a reddish beard. I am lying next to a man. I wonder how he can lie there so quietly; is he asleep? I wonder why he is there; how will they assault his body? Craving a human connection, I wish we could talk. But we are both silent.

Eventually a male attendant comes to the man and with total disregard for my proximity—our gurneys are about eight inches apart—announces, "I've come to prep you for your surgery." With a mixture of horror at what is happening and relief at having some human activity to focus on, I watch with fascination as the attendant pulls up the sheet covering the man and begins to shave his right leg from groin to ankle. I overhear that the man is to have vascular surgery. The anesthesiologist comes and informs him about the mixture of gases he will be given. By now I understand viscerally that I have no personal meaning here. This man, myself, we are both nondescript physical bodies being prepared for mechanical procedures.

This comprehension brings with it an agony of soul in full force. Is this the way the gift of my twenty-five years of fertility will end? I had welcomed it as sacred and vowed to guard it at all costs; the fertility that has always been precious to me now must be surrendered without ceremony, impersonally, to strangers, while I am not even consciously present to bid it farewell. I fight back gulping sobs. There are no tissues, no room for tears, no room for emotions, no place for my selfhood. The lump in my throat is enormous; I am choking with pain, suffocating.

The anesthesiologist finally arrives, a bulky man in surgical robes. He is speaking to me in an unfamiliar foreign language; I cannot understand a word he says as he explains the mixture of medicines that he will use and forewarns me that I will have an I.V. inserted in my arm. I know that my inability to comprehend what he is saying has something to do with the stripping away of my identity, with the loss of will that has resulted. There is no "person" in my body to respond to him; my selfhood has been demolished. What remains is the anguish in my soul, the grief in my heart, at choosing this violent, inhuman ending to a vital, joyously alive, and beloved essence of me.

Finally the surgical team is ready for me. Now everything must move quickly, in stark contrast to the long, stagnant wait, to conform to the busy schedules of the surgery room, physicians, nurses, attendants. Not a second is to be lost. I am wheeled swiftly into the operating room, an experience that elicits a powerful memory. . . .

I am being wheeled with equal haste into a waiting delivery room, fueled by an urgency created not by the schedules of men but by the pressure of nature. A new life is emerging— hurry, hurry, hurry—a new life is emerging and will not wait! Jill, my first child, is about to be born; I am twenty-seven years old. Pain beyond any experience of pain I have ever endured, pain that so exceeds the threshold of pain that it can no longer be named by this word clouds my vision, blinds me. In the center of my darkened vision the double doors of the delivery room come swiftly into focus, looming larger than life, golden gateway to an unknown world. The doors burst open in front of me, and I am quickly transferred by green-gowned figures from the gurney to the delivery table. I am now the respected carrier of new life, surrounded by the anonymously gowned forms of my husband, the nurses, my doctor. I feel special, the only unique and identifiable human being present, in center stage and surrounded by attentive and helpful assistants as we participate in the ceremony, the mystery, of birth.

Memory fades abruptly into the dark reality of the present. I am now surrounded by four men, each intent on a different activity with a different part of my body. The anesthesiologist is inserting an I.V. into my left arm, someone else is attaching a blood pressure monitor on my right arm. An attendant has both my legs in tow and is slipping a white tube onto each of them. I am literally being pulled apart into fragments, with no regard for the dignity and integrity of my being. This rough treatment of my body is shocking, producing a kind of stimulus overload, and in the end I find myself welcoming the dread blackness of the anesthetic. It comes suddenly, without warning.

"Wake up, Sue! Wake up, Sue! Your operation is over!"

These words are harsh and loud, startling me out of a peaceful reverie. Dream images had begun to form in the midst of utter blackness. I do not want to wake up and I resist opening my eyes, but the insistent voice calls to me sharply again. I force my eyes open, and a nurse immediately thrusts an oxygen mask over my nose and mouth, instructs me to breathe deeply, and then leaves me alone before I can react at all. To my horror, I discover that I am unable to swallow. My throat will not close. I try to call the nurse back, but my open throat is a rigid channel through which it is impossible to shape sounds. The necessary muscles simply will not respond to my mental command to move. When I realize I am unable to signal for help, my competent coping-self takes over for me as it has before and instructs the frightened child-self to stay calm and to breathe deeply. The child-self obeys her, and after several deep breaths, I find I am able to swallow again. Like a child who has fallen down, whose mother comes and checks to see what the injuries are, the competent coping-self assesses the state of my body, limb by limb, and begins the process of reclaiming it. I am surprised to find myself awake and alert, having expected that the anesthetic would leave me sleepy and groggy. I locate a clock on the wall and orient myself in ordinary time again. It is only one and one-half hours since I left the outpatient surgery department. I imagine that Michael will have been waiting. Nothing else seems to be causing me pain. I am eager to be taken upstairs, to see Michael, to show him that I am alive, I have survived.

I am wheeled back upstairs to outpatient surgery, but Michael is not yet there. His absence feels dreadful to me, so hungry am I for human connection, so in need of experiencing a living bond to someone who knows and loves me. I have no idea where he is or why he is not waiting for me. Fortunately he arrives in a matter of minutes, a smile of relief softening the contours of his face. I feel a brief moment of elation—the operation is over. I am glad to be alive, to be conscious, to be home in my body again, to be with Michael.

Michael and I hold hands, and this fundamental human

connection restores me to myself. I ask him, "Where were you? Why weren't you here!"

"I was too agitated to sit in the waiting room, and they told me it would be at least an hour before I could see you. So I decided to leave the hospital and go for a walk to calm myself down. I was so nervous I forgot to duck down when I went out through the back of the hospital where they're doing that renovating. I hit my head on the makeshift door. For a second, I thought I'd knocked myself out!" Michael explains in a rush, and I comprehend that he needs to be restored to himself as much as I do.

I look closely at him and see a lump on his forehead. "Oh, Michael! Just like at our wedding, when you went into the men's room and walked straight into a full-length mirror!" I start to laugh, but discover that it hurts. I am experiencing the odd, "referred" pain in my shoulder that Dr. Hodge warned me about. Still it feels so good to laugh, to be free of the anxiety about surviving the anesthetic and the surgery.

I have to stay in the hospital for several hours because the remaining gas in my system makes me feel nauseated and dizzy whenever I try to sit up or stand. Michael leaves me for a short time to get something to eat in the hospital cafeteria. While I wait lying flat in my bed for him to return, I listen to a young girl crying in the bed next to me. Overhearing fragments of her interchanges with the pleasant nurse, I learn that she is sixteen and that she is suffering considerable pain following a surgical procedure on her bladder. Her urologist apparently has neglected to prescribe pain medication for her, and the compassionate nurse is helpless, unable to give her a pill or injection without a written order from the physician. I listen as the nurse calls different departments in the hospital and finally reaches the doctor on the phone. She asks the doctor to order pain medication, and I can tell from her responses that the doctor is refusing her request. The nurse finally asks that he at least stop by and check on his patient in person. I am touched by her efforts on behalf of her young patient. I listen as she tells the young girl not to worry, that her doctor will be there shortly. The girl continues to cry softly; meanwhile, her parents arrive and sit quietly with her.

After a time the doctor arrives, and I listen in silent rage as he berates his young patient: "Young lady, you have to expect some discomfort. Now, I am going to send you home, and you take a warm bath. Life has its aches and pains; you can't expect to feel fine all of the time." I wonder if I would allow him to speak to me like this, whether I have learned to be assertive at this stage in my life. I feel a powerful impulse to intervene on behalf of this young woman. The compassion of the nurse for this young patient, her affirmation of her patient's pain, seems to me to contain the seeds of what I will come to think of as a feminine form of healing, a form that is by no means limited to women and that is accessible to men as well. The attitude of the doctor is familiar to me because it is the dominant cultural attitude, expressed by both men and women. It reflects our devotion to the admired and highly valued ideal of carrying on heroically in spite of obstacles, in spite of pain. Though I will myself to speak out, instead I remain silent; beyond the inappropriateness of intruding, my role of patient has deadened me into a submissive state, and my own experience of passivity in a dehumanizing situation is too close.

Finally I am able to sit up fairly well, and Michael goes to get the car from the parking lot. I am wheeled to the emergency room door by another anonymous attendant and then helped into the backseat for the ride home. By four o'clock in the afternoon, only ten hours after leaving home with Michael, I am lying in my bed as if it were a completely ordinary Saturday, as if nothing unusual had occurred.

The activities of the other members of my family are going on in a normal way. My children acknowledge my return as casually as if I had been out grocery shopping, which is a great relief to me. Michael and I had told Jill, Becky, and Ben that I would be going to the hospital to have a minor medical procedure done and that I would be tired and need to rest when I came home in the afternoon. Later I had explained to them as truthfully and simply as I could that their father and

I had decided not to have any more children, that our family is complete as is. I told them that the doctor could close off the tubes through which the egg travels from the ovary to the uterus and that this would keep me from becoming pregnant. They were not particularly interested or concerned and didn't ask me any questions, which seemed to me to be a normal response on their part. I couldn't even be certain they were taking in what I was saying. But I felt that their fantasies might be more frightening than the truth, and I was not sorry to have given them an honest explanation. Lying in bed, I can hear the reassuring and soothing sound of their voices rising and falling in other parts of the house as they call out to one another and to their neighborhood friends. Yet I feel detached and separate from them, as if I exist in another dimension of reality and simultaneously in ordinary time with them. They are in the world of the living, and I am there with them only in physical form.

Lost in a separate dimension as if in a science fiction time warp, unable to stand outside of it in order to describe it, I simply repeat to myself over and over the same refrain, varying the words in rhythm: "My fertility is gone, I am sterile, I am infertile, I will never again be pregnant, I can never bear another child." Such thoughts recur automatically. Only later will I realize that in this way, I am working to absorb and integrate the irrevocable physical alteration that has occurred, that I am trying to adjust to the new and permanent path I have chosen for myself. In the moment, however, I simply feel as if I am chewing on an intractable, indigestible, solid lump of matter that I am being forced to ingest. I cannot spit it out, and I cannot make it dissolve.

I remember the violence of my reaction after my abortion. It seems at this point to have occurred in another lifetime and not a mere eight weeks ago. In contrast, I lie here now feeling empty, lethargic, uncaring. I have no sensations, no reactions, only a sense of deadness, a vacuum in which the same statement repeats itself automatically, over and over—I am sterile, this is final, this is forever. So accustomed am I to judging my inner emotional states as pathological, rather than adopting

the neutral psychological attitude toward them that would
enable me to recognize their adaptive value, that I feel a
thinly veiled terror at the depth of my lethargy. Only later
will I come to understand that such profound inertia can be
understood as a natural state for a woman whose biological
fertility, itself a powerful form of energy, has been abruptly
terminated. Before the energy can be redirected into a new
channel, it needs time to accumulate, to gather itself into a
deep pool so that a new river can form.

I do not know how long I remain alone in my room.
Eventually I hear the faint ring of the doorbell and the sounds
of adult voices. It is Katherine and Chris. I overhear from a
distance that they have come to visit me and have brought
spaghetti sauce for dinner so that neither Michael nor I will
have to cook for our family.

Michael comes up to the bedroom and announces cheerfully, "Katherine and Chris are here to see you!" He is so
ebullient with understandable relief that I have survived physically that he is oblivious to my psychological state, my utter
lassitude and detachment.

"I don't want to see anyone," I answer. "Just tell them I
don't feel well and leave me by myself," and I turn my head
toward the wall. But only a moment later Katherine comes
bursting into my bedroom, radiating a soft, loving energy.
Without uttering a word, she sits down close to me on the
bed; her physical proximity alone brings me immediately into
relationship with her. I cannot recall any significant occasion
in my adult life that has not included her presence. So,
despite my overriding impulse to retreat and withdraw, I am
happy she has come, glad she has ignored my efforts to push
her away. Prompted by her interest and her questions, I tell
her every detail of the surgery, mastering a trauma in the
process. We acknowledge together the ironic crossing of our
life paths at this particular moment in time. Katherine, who
longs for the fertility and unborn child I have just renounced,
is heading toward marriage and the hope of pregnancy and
childbirth; having sacrificed my pregnancy and fertility, I am
moving away from these precious experiences toward an un-

defined future. My contact with her carries me for a brief time into what feels like the dimension of the living.

When Katherine leaves and I am alone again, I find myself slipping back into that other dimension. I try to describe it to myself, to give it a name. Surely, I imagine, it is a realm that others must also have entered. Perhaps if such solitary states could be shared openly, rather than hidden because they may be alarming and difficult to describe in words, or because they put at risk our ordinary competent selves, the unthinkable isolation and aloneness that accompany them might be lessened.

My sense of living apart from others in this strange and empty world persists, even after I have healed physically from the operation, even after I have picked up the many threads of my ordinary life. Later I will ponder this extraordinary dimension and will name it the "Dead Zone." In an effort to preserve for myself the subjective experience of being lost in this empty, lifeless, Dead Zone, I write an entry in my journal, in which I address Michael, my friends, and Dr. Ross collectively as "You" and attempt to explain to them what it is like to dwell within this orb of utter desolation:

The Dead Zone is a private, empty realm in which I am completely, utterly alone. I have left behind my husband, my children, my friends, and even and especially, my former vital and alive self. No one can choose to join me here. This is not a place for the living, not a place for the people I know who are busily engaged in activities, social interactions, relationships, careers. This is not a place for the people I know who have desires, fears, appetites, dislikes. This is not a place where the person I used to be belongs. Where I am is nothing, no-thing. No energy, no life, no spirit, no-thing that matters, no way to make anything matter.

You cannot choose to join me here. This is a Wasteland that You cannot enter. Nor can You retrieve me from it and bring me back into Your world of life and spirit. You delude Yourself if You believe that Your curiosity about this place, Your interest in me, Your concern for me, even Your love for me, will enable You to join me. You delude Yourself if You believe that Your wish to help me, Your compassion, Your commitment to be with me, will enable You to be here too or to bring me back to Your world. Do not mistake me. I have not chosen to come here, nor do I want to stay. Oh how I, like You, wish that all these things would be enough to take You here. I want You to know where I am, to understand. But all these qualities, even taken together, are not enough to bring You here. They belong to the world of the living, the world in which it is human nature to care, to invest life with meaning. They will keep You from me, will keep You away, and You cannot even see this.

To come join me here, You must do as I have done. You must choose as I have chosen: to annihilate the source of life and energy, the source of meaning, deep within Yourself. There is no quantity of attachment to me that is powerful enough to compel You to make this choice. You cannot of Your own volition choose to come to the Dead Zone. Your attachment to Your Self, to Your life, is too great. What would compel you to join me here?

In the beginning, I, too, thought Your love, Your compassion, Your commitment, Your empathy, would bring You here. I thought You would rescue me, carry me cradled in Your arms back to life. I was so certain You would come. I could even feel myself being drawn back to life. I did not expect to dwell in the Dead Zone for so long. I, too, did not understand that the very energy of Your attachment to me kept You away. And so I accused You of not caring, of having no feelings, no capacity for empathy. I believed that You would not, could not, leave me alone here for so long in this place of Deadness if You cared. I thought You would find a way somehow, if You cared. And so I kept waiting, kept hoping, for You to come.

When You did not come to take me back, when no one came for me, I tried to find my own way back to You, to Your world, to my former world of light. I thought that if I stepped back into the tracks of my own life, walked in my own footprints, I could rejoin You in Your world. But the contents of my life alone do not give it meaning, joy, and vitality. The forms alone are not enough. The energy source is gone, and I cannot find a way to rekindle the essential flame. And because I appear to You, to everyone, to fit,

*to belong in this world of the living, You cannot see, no one can
see, that a flame no longer burns inside me.*

Putting words to the strange internal territory in which I
find myself somehow encircles it for me and renders it manageable rather than overwhelming and alarming. Liberated for
the time being from its deadening effect, I begin, without
consciously planning or knowing it, the long and difficult
work of mourning the loss of my fertility. I start by recalling
its birth. . . .

It is fall, and I am fourteen years old, still waiting for the
onset of menstruation. Most of my girlfriends have already
started having their periods. I feel excluded from the mysterious female world into which they have been initiated, as well
as vaguely worried that there is something physically wrong
with me, that I will never have a period and never be able to
bear children. Ever since the fifth grade, I have watched the
very same movie, available only to girls, which was shown in
special school assemblies. I have read carefully the pamphlets
peppered with Walt Disney cartoon characters that we were
given and pondered the diagrams of my female insides with
awe. I have shared in the incongruous mixture of superiority
and embarrassment that the girls felt in relation to the boys in
our class, who were not permitted to see the movie with us.

Lying in bed now, my reflections are bittersweet. Picturing
the movie, recollecting the sanctimonious male voice that
described the ways my body would soon be changing, I find
myself amused by the comical, even humorous aspect of it. I
might as well have been watching a documentary on the
technical aspects of how bees produce honey. But my midlife
consciousness adds to this humor a deep sorrow that the
information was not imparted to me in the context of a
personal relationship with a mature woman passing on the
wisdom of her life experience; that the masculine voice of the
narrator did not communicate the sacred and mysterious aspects of the physical changes that would occur in my body;
that there was no ceremony planned to mark this powerful

feminine rite of passage, to celebrate my initiation into the profound feminine mystery of fertility and birth.

My fourteen-year-old self knows about the two sanitary pads and new sanitary belt in a box on the shelf in my bedroom closet. My mother has given them to me to keep so that I will be prepared when my period comes. As they sit conspicuously gathering dust, I try not to think about them. I try to keep myself from worrying about how I will ask her for more when I need them. Embarrassment and shame predominate; at this stage of my life, I have no way of making a distinction between an experience that is essentially private and interior because it partakes of the sacred and one that must be shamefully concealed.

My experience with boys has been limited to contact in school, in class and on the schoolground, and at parties attended by groups of boys and girls rather than by couples. At parties we vote self-consciously, in our awkward and idealistic democratic manner, whether to play kissing games. The girls always vote no and the boys always vote yes, as we faithfully enact the sanctions we have internalized from our parents and our culture. Somehow the girls always manage to win. Collectively we uphold the image of chastity that we have learned must be protected at all cost by women who wish to be worthy of respect.

In the summer after eighth grade, I attend my first coeducational overnight camp. A boy walks me home after a camp dance. We stop by a tree, and he pulls me toward him for a kiss. For a moment I imagine myself to be a participant in one of the romantic scenes from the movies I have seen where the handsome young man and beautiful young woman kiss. But my illusion is rapidly shattered; my prevailing response is revulsion, and I push him away. Though he seemed friendly enough at the dance, now he seems alien and strange; I do not want this unfamiliar male person to have such intimate access to my body.

Soon it is fall, and I am at a party. I am wearing a matching turquoise sweater and skirt, in keeping with the fashions of the time, and my private secret underneath the sweater, a padded bra. At fourteen, I am ashamed of my flat chest and worried that boys will not be attracted to me. Shielded by my secret underwear, I display my exaggerated feminine shape proudly and deliberately, testing my skill in attracting boys. The atmosphere is thick with sexual tension at this gathering of swiftly ripening adolescents. Though summer heat has yielded to the crisp cool of autumn, the room feels steaming hot, warmed by the youthful blood circulating in our veins. There is tantalizing talk about the physical act of sex. The girls feign ignorance and ask the boys to explain what "pumping" means. Now it is the boys who carry the aura of sexual mystery. A boy I've never met before does ask me to dance, to my great satisfaction, but just as I had in camp, when he holds me close to his body I push him away. I am puzzled and confused by my ambivalent behavior.

In the middle of the night after this party, I awaken and move sleepily to the bathroom. I sit on the toilet, my flannel pajama bottoms—a remnant from childhood that I have carried into adolescence and that will metamorphose into a love of flannel nightgowns by the time I reach adulthood—pulled down around my feet. I regard the massive wet, dark red stain on my pajamas with a rapidly shifting sequence of emotions: first puzzlement, then fright, and afterward a slowly dawning comprehension. I am having my first menstrual period. Confusion follows until my coping functions gradually take over and organize my actions. I clean myself off and wash out my pajama bottoms in the sink, careful not to leave any telltale sign of pink in the bowl. I clumsily put on one of my two sanitary napkins, struggling to read and comprehend the written directions that come in the box with the belt. I walk awkwardly to bed, unaccustomed to the soft bulk between my legs and the uncomfortable pressure of the wide elastic belt around my waist. My body feels strange and unfamiliar, as if it has been completely transformed into something new. I gingerly arrange myself in bed and lie rigidly under my covers. In spite of the warm blankets, I am unable to stop shivering. I feel as if I am in a bitterly cold climate and cannot get warm.

Even now I feel intensely aware of the responsibility I carry. With every ounce of my fourteen-year-old wisdom, I believe that a priceless gift has been bestowed upon me. I have been given the capacity to produce life, a precious and sacred responsibility that I must protect. I have a firm sense of conviction, centered in the totality of my wisdom, that God has chosen this moment to give me my period because I have passed a significant test. I have not yielded indiscriminately to my budding sexual stirring, nor have I given way under pressure from the boys who have approached me. I have shown that I can be trusted with the privilege and responsibility of fertility. It is a sacred gift, mine to cherish, to protect, to defend. I have not needed to be taught such conviction; I carry it within my physical being, within what I will later come to know as the feminine archetypal layer of my consciousness. I vow to myself, as I shiver in my bed, always to be worthy of this gift.

Two years later I have a similar feeling of responsibility for protecting and respecting the sanctity of human life when I arrive at that universal adolescent rite that transcends gender: I pass the test for my driver's license. My mother gives me the keys to the family car for the first time, and I drive off on my own to the market. Unexpectedly, I do not feel joyful exuberance, a sense of carefree liberation, or even the inflation of pride. Instead I pull over to the side of the road and cry, overcome with awe at the enormity of the new status I have just earned. I have been deemed worthy of operating a vehicle that has enough power to endanger my own life and the lives of others if I should be careless or irresponsible.

But unlike my response to the genderless rite of the driver's license, a powerful feeling of shame attaches to my initiation into the feminine mystery of menstruation, to the priceless gift of fertility. I quickly discover that I wish to conceal the pivotal female experience of my first period from my father, not only because I am embarrassed or wish to keep it private. The following morning, the first day of my first period, I tell my mother what has happened to me. I come to her with a complex mélange of anxiety, embarrassment, and shy pride.

She is taken completely unaware, and I see the shocked expression on her face before it quickly transforms into a huge and, to my adolescent vision, inauthentic smile. "Oh, Sue, now you are a woman!" she exclaims, as she engulfs me with a hug. Her voice gushes with a baroque pride that must have masked other complicated feelings that were then beyond my capacity to comprehend.

With desperate intensity, I ask her not to tell my father. This worry captures all my attention. I also tell her I need more sanitary pads, assuming that she will get them for me. But somehow I find myself alone in the car with my father going to the store. How could I not have told her that this errand was too hard for me? Even to purchase such an intimate item by myself feels completely beyond my capacity. To make the purchase in front of my father? It is unimaginable.

In the market I manage to escape from my father, who goes off to shop for the items on the list he has been given by my mother. I quickly grab a box of pads and, carrying it buried between my arm and my body, rush to the single checkout counter that has a woman checker. I am in a panic that my father will finish his shopping and see me before I can go through the line and pay. I count out my own money and pay for my purchase as fast as I can and then run to our car with my paper bag, which I hide on the floor of the backseat of the car. With equal haste, I run back into the store and find my father, trying to pretend that nothing special has occurred, that I have just been browsing through the store, while inside my heart pounds wildly, still reacting to the challenge of going through the checkout counter and feeling the eyes of the checker and nearby customers upon me, penetrating my new, secret, private physical state.

My father and I drive home silently, while I wonder whether he has seen me hide my secret purchase, whether my mother has told him what happened to me, whether he *knows*. I wait to retrieve my package from its hiding place in the car until all the other groceries have been brought in and put away. After this, I never ask my mother to buy sanitary napkins for me, nor do I ever discuss any subsequent periods with her, even to complain about cramps. I hoard boxes of pads, which I purchase when the circumstances are right, which means that no other customers are present and the checker is female. When I suffer from cramps, I buy myself Midol, which I have learned about from reading magazine advertisements.

My adult mind, free to roam at will while my body rests in bed, now moves across the years, until it comes to rest upon a conversation I had with Jill when she was ten years old. She is blossoming into young womanhood in the loveliest way, a flower unfolding its petals so very slowly, fragile and new. She approaches me after school one day in a rare state of openness. I recognize immediately in her the same mélange of emotion I had felt with my own mother so many years ago—embarrassment, anxiety, pride. She waits until we are alone in the kitchen and then tells me that the older sister of one of her classmates got her period for the first time that very day in school. Jill's friend told her that her sister had stained her pants and felt horribly humiliated and embarrassed. Having said this, Jill waits with baited breath for my response.

I pray silently, this time with that capacity for humor that sometimes comes with age, to the same God who had gifted me with the power of fertility such a long time ago: "Don't let me say the wrong thing now, God." My batting average in responding to Jill in just the right way (in her critical eyes that are so similar to the way my own eyes once were at her age) is running pretty low. Taking a deep breath and plunging into an answer, I groan empathically (I think) over this terrible embarrassment and tell Jill, "You'll probably be getting your period soon, too. I already have a box of sanitary napkins for you in my bathroom. Do you want to keep it in your room?"

Jill shakes her head no. "Nope! You can keep it for me!" She then goes off to her room, her long ponytail bouncing in time with her energetic strides.

"Thanks, God!" I murmur silently.

Chuckling to myself as I savor this memory, I recall another facet of this conversation with her. Jill, so like me when

I was fourteen and trying to keep my shameful secret from my father, does not want Michael to know about our talk. "Don't tell this to Daddy," she orders me. Unknown to both of us, however, he has been sitting in the next room simply by chance. When Jill leaves, he comes into the kitchen and tells me that he happened to hear parts of our conversation.

"It sounded pretty important," Michael says, "I was wondering what you and Jill were talking about."

A bright red bubble of rage, perhaps twenty-five years old, explodes within me: "It's none of your business!" I answer, with more anger than the current situation warrants. Raising his eyebrows into his "Oh, what I have to put up with" expression, he shrugs and returns to his study. We have not discussed that conversation since.

With great difficulty, the day after my tubal-ligation surgery, Jill tells us a dream at the family dinner table, the first dream she has ever shared with us. I understand immediately that she is impelled to tell it to us because it continues to frighten her. She wants to get rid of it, to forget it, and hopes that by saying it aloud and depositing it with us, she will be cleansed of its lingering effect. As she tells it, she cries openly, another unusual response for her. Normally Jill is introverted and keeps any pain she feels locked far inside, well hidden from view.

While Jill speaks, Becky and Ben remain silent, somehow sensing on their own that it is important for them not to interrupt their sister:

"Our family has moved to a new house. It's blue, with white crisscross trim. Ben isn't at home, and Becky's at school. I come home, and Mommy isn't there to greet me like she always is. So I think the worst to make sure the worst will not be true, just like I always guess the answer on a test that isn't what I first think it should be when I'm not sure. So I think about Mommy, maybe she's dead. Daddy and I rush up to Mommy's room. Mommy is lying on her bed, completely flat, like a balloon without any air in it. I push her because she doesn't move. Mommy groans, a terrible sound." Jill begins to cry and covers her ears, as if the memory of this inhuman sound still reverberates in her head. As if unaware that her hands are still covering her ears, Jill continues to tell her dream. "Daddy gets mad at me for punching Mommy. He doesn't understand that I'm just trying to wake her up. Then Mommy groans and tells me to go away. She asks me to let her die in peace."

Jill then tells us what happened after she awoke from her dream:

"When I woke up from my dream, I was so scared that I turned all the lights on in my room. That didn't help, so I went upstairs really quietly and tiptoed into your room to check and see if Mommy was alive, just asleep. I didn't wake you up, I just checked to see if Mommy was breathing. Then I went back to my room and looked in my closet to make sure it was empty. Then I got back into bed, but I couldn't sleep, so I just stayed there awake."

Jill remains afraid of going to sleep for some days after this and tells Michael and me that she is afraid of the dark. I talk with Jill about her dream and tell her, "I've been thinking about that dream you told us last week during dinner, and I've been wondering if you had it because you know I'm sad about not having any more babies. I'm not sorry that I chose this for myself—Daddy and I are so grateful that we have the three of you—but it's a big change for a woman. Just as big a change as it'll be when you get your first period. When I'm going through a change, I always feel sad about what I'm leaving behind. I don't mind feeling sad—it's a way of honoring the importance of my life. And afterward I'm ready to welcome whatever will come next." Although Jill only looks at me with an expression embodying her own unique blend of suspicion and disbelief, I am certain she has understood me. Within a few days her fears subside.

My distress at having alarmed my daughter prods me to think more about the nature of my emotional response to the tubal ligation. I ponder again the beginning of my own fertility and the oddly pervasive sense of shame that accompanied it. For the first time in my life it occurs to me that shame is not an inherent part of the menstrual cycle itself, nor is it a pathological feeling response. This shame may instead mark an unfulfilled need for feminine wisdom, a wisdom that could not be passed on to me because a connection to it has been lost. I was not made aware that certain female experiences are private and that these experiences cannot be directly known by men, just as certain sacred male experiences can never be known directly by women. If I pay attention to my experiences as a woman, instead of glossing over them as I am accustomed to doing, perhaps I can retrieve the feminine wisdom for which I yearn.

I begin to imagine that I may also feel a similar shame about going through menopause, that phase of life during which women are embarrassed by hot flashes and apologize for their uncontrollable changes in mood. How can menopause be welcomed as the beginning of a valuable new stage of life in a culture that perceives aging as a terrifying prospect, in which older women are rendered invisible because attention goes automatically to young and beautiful women, are feared as if they are witches with evil powers, or trivialized as silly and witless (as in the expression "little old ladies in tennis shoes")? The transition from a fertile to an infertile state, whether achieved by nature or medical intervention, is certainly not one that all women can look forward to eagerly, in spite of the efforts some of us make to rationalize it in such positive terms as "freedom from the demands of parenting."

Even though as a psychologist and therapist I might have recognized the basis for a profound response to the loss of fertility in a client, I am unable to stand far enough outside my own experience while going through it to comprehend the underpinnings of my reaction. For now, I am left to ponder the recent demise of my fertility and to bear my private sorrow alone, acutely aware that no ceremony marked its birth and that certainly none has marked its end.

SIX

First Anniversary

To men these cyclic changes [inherent in women's nature] are most incomprehensible, and in their endeavor to escape from the dominance of the male, inherent in our patriarchal civilization, women themselves disregarded the effects of their own rhythm and tried to resemble men as closely as possible. Thus they fell once more under the dominance of the male. This time it was not under the male without, that is under men, but under the rule of the male within.

—ESTHER HARDING
Women's Mysteries: Ancient and Modern[1]

It's possible I am pushing through solid rock
in flintlike layers, as the ore lies, alone;
I am such a long way in I see no way through,
and no space: everything is close to my face,
and everything close to my face is stone.

I don't have much knowledge yet in grief—
so this massive darkness makes me small.
You *be the master:* make yourself fierce, break in:
then your great transforming will happen to me,
and my great grief cry will happen to you.

—*Rainer Maria Rilke*[2]

During the first six months following the abortion and tubal ligation, I continue to lead my ordinary life, working and taking care of my family. I hope that the mere passage of time will help me put these traumatic experiences behind me. Much of the time I am indeed distracted by my involvements in work and relationships. Participating in Katherine and Chris's wedding in the fall, helping to ease the beginning of the new school year for my children, and focusing on the ongoing challenges of Michael's and my work lives certainly engage my interest and energies. I find that the abrupt and irreversible severing of my fertility gradually becomes a manageable loss, though I have some sense that there is more to understand.

But sharp blades of grief and despair about the abortion continue to pierce through the smooth surface of my life, especially when I am alone and undistracted by my work or the lively interactions and demands of my family. I find myself unable to accept having made the choice to have an abortion, even though I am glad I had the right to choose it, even though I believe wholeheartedly that I made the best possible decision in the circumstances, and even though I do not believe the decision was either wrong or a mistake. Immobilized by the conflicting pulls of these paradoxical realities, I cannot free myself. When terrible feelings about having chosen the abortion break through each of the psychological walls I work hard to build, I feel overwhelmed with hopelessness: I will never find a way to live with the reality of having terminated the life of my unborn child. In this hopeless state I feel as if I completely lack the inner fortitude necessary to continue on with my existence. I can only conclude that in preventing my fourth child from having a life, I have unwittingly fractured my own; like Humpty Dumpty, my life, my self, is beyond repair. I have made a decision that I am utterly

unable to integrate into my sense of who I am. The strength
of my belief in the "rightness" of the choice of an abortion
given the context of my life and in the necessity for women to
have the legal right to make the choice that I exercised enabled me to carry out my decision; but these convictions do
not protect me from suffering the consequences of my choice.
My convictions, strong as they are, do not enable me to
construct a scaffolding that can keep me safely above the flood
of feelings pounding beneath.

I think back to the lively debates that took place in social
gatherings about the right of women to have abortions, particularly when the *Roe v. Wade* decision of the Supreme Court
seemed to be in jeopardy yet again. I remember vividly how I
always asserted so emphatically, "I think women should have
the right to choose an abortion, but *I* would never choose it
for myself. It wouldn't be right for me." I wasn't being
simplistic or naive in those discussions. I spoke the truth in
those debates: Abortion *isn't* right for me. But which me? The
me that exists in my family, that exists in relationship to
Michael, that has reached middle age? Or the me that used to
be: younger, without children, with still very young children, facing a seemingly limitless, expansive future?

I find that my consciousness about the issue of abortion has
been permanently and drastically altered. References to it no
longer glide past me without registering; I am often appalled
at what now catches my eye. In assorted news articles I find
that abortion is most often considered from the perspective of
the unborn fetus and its right to have a life, or from the
perspective of the pregnant woman completely separated from
the fabric of her existence. Although there must certainly be a
father in the picture, he is invisible as a person in his own
right, with his own complicated psychological makeup. Like a
two-dimensional cartoon figure, he either abandons the woman
to make her own choice, is left on the sidelines to mourn the
loss of the child he would have loved, or else is a shadowy,
supportive figure who provides money and/or hand holding,
behaviors that absolve him of additional responsibility. The
spotlight remains focused upon the woman—but upon her as

seen from the perspective of the audience who watches her and never from the vantage point of her own subjective experience. In the harsh glare of this spotlight, she is judged rather than understood, either for the choice she makes or for her reaction to the experience. Pro-choice advocates perceive the woman who communicates her sense of guilt and despair to be out of touch with her own needs, either deficient in feminist consciousness or victimized by Right-to-Life propaganda. Right-to-Life advocates perceive the woman who displays no feelings as either inhuman and insensitive or as a victim of a culture that permits her to be indifferent to the value of life and provides her with no other options. Where, in this culture, can I possibly find a mirror of my subjective experience? How can I remove myself from the cultural spotlight that shines so relentlessly upon women long enough to reach a sense of myself that is not influenced by the standards and assumptions of our culture?

Most distressing to me are the professional articles I read that include case studies of patients who have had abortions. Hidden and unquestioned judgments about these women used to remain in the background, but now they leap forth and are starkly apparent. I see clearly now that the woman is always an object of judgment, whether the judgment is positive or negative: She has made the "right" choice, or a "good" or "bad" decision. Not only is the woman judged for her choice, but she is also then judged for the emotional reaction she has had to it. A woman who suffers in silence and is stoic is seen as strong, whereas a woman like myself, who mourns long and deeply, tends to be regarded as pathologically grief-stricken. Even the way a woman shows her feelings is judged on a continuum of health and pathology: Crying an "appropriate" amount is healthy; staying in bed immobilized is not. I begin to wonder why no attention is paid in these professional articles to the therapists who are working with the women: How adequate are they to grapple with the issue of abortion? Who will stand outside and judge the judges?

I am upset not only by the judgments in the articles, which are now impossible for me to ignore, but also by something elusive in the manner in which they are written. There is a quality in the attitude of the authors, who are both male and female—that disturbs me. For example, one article on the general topic of terminating psychoanalysis written by two highly regarded psychoanalysts and published in a respected journal provides four case examples. My altered awareness helps me notice that by coincidence, two of the four cases are women who have had an abortion. In the first of these two cases, the woman's abortion is part of her reason for seeking help: "The patient, a twenty-five-year-old violinist, came into analysis as a low-fee case because of anxiety and depression over an automobile accident and an abortion, both precipitated by her own denial of danger."[3] Not only is a pathological defense—denial of danger—successfully located in the patient outside the context of her relationships, and not only is the complex event of an abortion reduced to a single cause, but the tone of the language used to make this assertion as it comes across to me is devoid of compassion and empathy.

In the second case example, abortion occupies a more central role. The patient enters low-fee analysis following "a panic attack precipitated by an illegal abortion."[4] The meaning of the panic attack, according to the authors, resides in the patient's abandonment when she was three by the Mexican maid who cared for her from her birth, compensating for the inability of the patient's mother to nurture her child adequately. The maid coincidentally came from the same town in Mexico in which the patient's abortion took place. The awareness of the connection between the maid and the abortion led to the patient's realization that "she had felt abandoned by her maid-mother, and that, by aborting her own child, she had turned passive into active [i.e., actively doing to her unborn child what she had passively experienced being done to her]."[5] This case example, like the first, considers the abortion solely in terms of the woman's early experience, and conceives of the choice in relation to a defense mechanism that operates in a pathological way.

As I ponder the references to abortion in this particular article as well as others, I eventually realize that I am both-ered by the consistently dry, rational, medical-model, analytical stance of these articles, a stance that now feels limited. Prior to my own lived experience of the abortion, I might well have joined the authors in having the same attitude. I now realize that a larger perspective is needed, one that includes the rational principles that are necessary for ordering our complicated world but also balances them with an equally important attitude of compassion and empathy, of respect for individual differences and needs.

My quest for a perspective on the rational attitude embedded in these articles takes me back to notes I preserved from a college philosophy course. Shuffling through pages of notes that my nineteen-year-old self recorded diligently more than twenty years ago, I discover that the foundation of the rational, analytical approach in the professional articles is *logos*, the Greek word for "word, reason, plan." *Logos* was used in Greek theology and philosophy to express the divine reason implicit in ordering the cosmos and giving it meaning. Heracleitus, a philosopher in the sixth century B.C., discerned a *logos* in the cosmic process that he conceived of as analogous to the reasoning ability of human beings. Our culture is patriarchal in form; men hold positions of power, and descent and succession are traced through the male line. The capacity for rationality and reason, the *logos* principle, has been both dominant and highly valued in our culture, and it has been associated with men. Consequently the *logos* principle can be referred to as the masculine principle, although it exists equally as a capacity within women. Men in this culture have traditionally held positions of power and are deemed to possess the *logos* principle. Women have had to fight for the right to be viewed as equally capable of reason; they have had to cope with the opinion that they are too emotional to make rational decisions. Given the centrality of the masculine *logos* principle in our culture, it makes sense that most professional articles, like the one with the two case examples, would be written from this perspective.

But, the Greeks also have another noun—*agape*, which means "love." But, I find in my notes, the *Agape* refers to the love of

God for humankind; it is mirrored in the love of human beings for God and for other human beings, the spontaneous and self-giving love that goes beyond reward to the giver, beyond the worthiness of the receiver. Saint Augustine of Hippo, a great thinker of Christian antiquity (A.D. 396–430) who lived in Roman Africa, conceived of *agape* as founded upon *amor*, the ethical appraisal that influences action, and as the supreme good in the expression of which human beings reach perfection. *Agape* thus refers to a love that includes empathy and compassion. My forty-year-old self does not want to take for granted words I thought I understood half a lifetime ago, and I turn to a dictionary. *Empathy* means an understanding so immediate and intimate that the feelings, thoughts, and motives of one person are comprehended by another. *Compassion* refers to a deep feeling of sharing the suffering of another, in an inclination to give aid or support.[6] In college when I first took notes on these words, I had not yet had a life experience that embodied their abstract meaning. Now, from the vantage point of wife and mother, I can understand intuitively (with my heart and my intellect) the experience of love that is symbolized by the Greek word *agape*. It seems to me that the experience of motherhood in its highest form must be grounded in the *agape* principle. The *agape* principle can also be named the feminine principle; though, like the masculine principle of *logos*, it exists in potential form equally within the male gender.

I realize that I have missed a tone of empathy and compassion, the presence of the *agape* principle, in the professional articles and that it is understandably absent. The feminine *agape* principle has been subordinate to the *logos* principle in our patriarchal culture because women, those most likely to embody it, have been perceived as inferior and have come to accept this position (that is, until the feminist movements of the last several decades). Yet the feminine *agape* principle contains an ethical and moral foundation upon which both men and women can stand, one as essential to the well-being of humanity as that provided by *logos*. If the attitude toward women in our culture could be broadened to include recognition of the importance of the *agape* principle, and the empathy and compassion it includes, both men and women would benefit. While the male and female genders may embody separate connections to *logos* and *agape*, these complementary capacities exist within each of us, regardless of our gender, and both are fundamental in shaping and supporting our individual modes of being in the world. What I miss in the professional articles so full of hidden judgments is the presence of both these essential capacities.

I ponder the nature of my relationship with Dr. Ross in this context. I see that he, despite his good intentions and in common with most of us, has been firmly rooted in the masculine *logos* principle so highly valued in our patriarchal culture. I have stood alongside him on this familiar ground. Now, despite my positive regard for him, I am being pulled steadily and reluctantly away from him by the sheer emotional energy generated by my experiences. I do not leave the comfortable masculine territory of our relationship by choice; the new and feminine ground that awaits me feels both unfamiliar and unstable. I am beginning to fear that we will be unable to reach each other across the chasm that is widening between us. Yet the loneliness I feel, isolated with my experience of and response to the abortion, impels me toward a relationship grounded not only in masculine *logos* but also in feminine *agape*—a relationship in which I can experience fully the depth of my despair. Dr. Ross remains for now the person to whom I hope to bring my broken self. I feel like a bird who has unwittingly flown into a glass window and broken its wing, and I yearn for him to be the compassionate healer as well as the reasonable wise man who picks me up and cares for me until I can restore myself. Michael and my women friends have their separate lives as well as their own needs; these are relationships of mutuality, and the pain of my wounds from the abortion has propelled me onto a one-way street. I do not want to strain these relationships with the weight of my heavy feelings, and I know that I am in no condition to shoulder even the lightest of their concerns.

From my perspective, therefore, Dr. Ross's office is the one place where I can legitimately claim time and attention solely for myself. But I feel stuck in my work with him, as if powerful forces are restricting me to the rigid and narrow path of being a "good" patient, which means always being rational, in control of my feelings, and not making distressing emotional demands upon him. No matter how hard I try, I cannot seem to break free of this pattern; I cannot find the gateway to a relationship of a different order, a relationship that includes both masculine and feminine principles.

"Why don't you see a different therapist?" Michael and my friends ask me. "Maybe you ought to see a woman," they suggest, recognizing my need for compassion. I ask myself the same question, but the prospect of trying to find a new therapist is too discouraging. Even if I could come up with the name of someone new, starting from the very beginning feels impossible to me. I feel that it would take me years to convey a sense of myself to a total stranger, that years would have to pass before I could even get to the immediate and pressing crisis of the abortion. Moreover, I feel both a personal and professional pressure to have a happy ending with Dr. Ross. I long to feel a sense of completion to my years of analysis with him; I want to end our relationship in a satisfying way. I want us to feel good about our work together even as we acknowledge its inevitable limitations. The prospect of leaving my therapy feeling disappointed, angry, and dissatisfied is dreadful. As a therapist, I do not want to face the possibility of having an unsuccessful therapy. If Dr. Ross can fail me, despite his good intentions, then I might fail my own clients just as profoundly, no matter how hard I struggle through difficult issues with them. I am coping with all the despair I can handle for now, despair about my chosen profession will simply have to wait.

As a temporary compromise, I do the best I can on my own, mustering all the resources I have and resolving to try to help Dr. Ross help me. Toward this end, I read as much material as I can find that is written for and about women, searching for renderings of issues pertaining to female experiences that will help me recover from the traumatic aspects of the abortion. I find that I am not looking for ideas that will appeal to my intellect, to the masculine *logos* side of my being. I am searching instead in a realm that I have left unexplored until now; I am searching not with my mind but with my heart for images that will appeal to my intuition, to the feminine *agape* side of my psyche.

My imagination is kindled by the image of a waxing new moon cradled in my right hand, and a waning, dying crescent moon cradled in my left hand, which I come upon in Nor Hall's book, *The Moon and the Virgin*.[7] I share this image with Dr. Ross, hoping to teach him about the realm of the feminine as I learn about it myself. I tell him, "The waning crescent moon in my left hand is me, leaving motherhood forever behind. The task of bearing children belongs to women who are reflected in the light of the waxing crescent moons." Dr. Ross is interested in my image, but I quickly intuit—as patients in intensive therapy come to know their therapists—that he has not yet had a life experience of suffering that has included the healing potential of symbolic images, the healing potential of the feminine *agape* principle. His lack of affinity for symbol creates a gulf between us that I keep trying to bridge. But I discover that without a lived experience of the healing power of symbols, Dr. Ross's genuine curiosity and intellectual interest in the symbol of the moon, the moon that changes cyclically yet remains essentially itself, are not enough.

On my quest for symbolic images that will reflect and contain my anguish, I discover the Japanese musician Kitaro. I come upon an exquisitely accurate reflection of my emotional state in the haunting melodic line of his song "Silver Moon." The melody embodies in liquid, flutelike sounds the visual images of the waxing, full, then waning, and finally dark moon. I carry it inside me and listen to it at will, each time feeling the wistfulness that its melancholic sounds evoke, each time experiencing anew the cycle of the moon and my pervasive sense of loss, the loss of my child, the loss of my fertility. I am discovering that images can be auditory as well as visual and am discovering, as well, how healing they can be. I bring a tape recorder to my session so that I can play the music for Dr. Ross in an effort to communicate my inner state. "How loud is it?" he asks me. "The walls are thin, and I don't want it to disturb the other occupants of the building." Irritated, I tell him, "I'm much too considerate to bring in loud music—it's not rock 'n' roll!" Finally he agrees to listen to it with me. But I sense that he is still worrying about how loud the music is, or whether he should have agreed to listen at all. I know that he is not listening on the wholehearted, empathic level that I need from him; he has no comprehension of the symbolic meaning the music has for me. The hour ends with both of us feeling dissatisfied and disappointed.

I am enormously comforted to find the profundity of my loss affirmed in Nor Hall's chapter entitled "Spiritual Pregnancy": "When the mother is separated unwillingly from the child or when the fruit is *taken* from her rather than *given*, a certain understanding is lost, an organic bond severed that severs the mother from her own life's meaning."[8] I can see with ever-increasing clarity that my unwilling separation has left me with a sense of loss and of inner emptiness that is so huge, so overwhelming, that I cannot integrate it by myself. I need help in transforming the feeling of loss into a sense of new potential. I need help in shifting my generative and nurturing energy from caring for biological children to nurturing other "children," metaphorically speaking. Help in making this transformation cannot come from Dr. Ross, but I do not know where else to turn. In this culture, so far as I am able to see, psychotherapy is the appropriate *form* of help, but many psychotherapists, like women in our culture, lack an understanding of the dilemma of abortion that will enable them to provide it.

Most of the experienced therapists I have admired, and from whom I have learned, freely acknowledge that their patients were their best teachers. I, too, share this debt of gratitude to my clients. But women have not yet been able to teach anyone, let alone psychotherapists, about the experience of abortion. Women like myself, preoccupied with obtaining abortions and saddled with intense feelings that have little place in our culture, have hardly been able to allow the experience of abortion fully into consciousness. And as long as abortion continues to carry the dark cloud of taboo that weights it down in our culture, women will be prohibited from fully exploring their subjective experience of it.

Until psychotherapists can be taught by women clients, healing modalities adapted to this complex issue cannot evolve and women will continue to lack the empathy, compassion, nurturing, and comforting that are essential to coping with the dilemma of an untenable pregnancy. But I reach this awareness only by going through my pain; my insights evolve too late to comfort me on the way. For now, inertia and the hope that Dr. Ross might still be able to learn enough to help me, the hope that I might yet be able to carry us into uncharted seas, keeps me treading water.

By the time spring is in full bloom, bringing with it the first anniversary of my abortion, my body, as if it has a life of its own, begins to behave strangely. My period, which still arrives with great regularity every twenty-six to twenty-eight days, suddenly does not appear on schedule. Instead, I begin to reexperience symptoms of early pregnancy—sore breasts, fullness in the lower abdomen. Encouraged by these unusual symptoms, I start to have the fantasy that my fallopian tubes have healed themselves (as the doctor had warned me they do in rare cases). The fantasy quickly becomes an intense wish. Perhaps my body has healed itself, is no longer damaged as I envision it to be—the healthy tubes now burned in the middle beyond repair, my abdomen scarred by tiny scalpel cuts. Perhaps I am whole again; perhaps I have been blessed with a second chance, another opportunity to create life. If so, I vow I will not make the same choice this time. This time I will choose life for myself, for my baby, life for both of our souls. But my period finally arrives one week late, and my hope for a second chance, a rebirth, is dashed to pieces.

"Anniversary reactions are quite common," Dr. Ross announces upon hearing my story, pride in his accumulated knowledge showing in his face. "Research studies by Mardi Horowitz in San Francisco have shown this to be true." I shake my head in disappointment, recognizing yet again that

Dr. Ross can stand only on this familiar masculine ground of rational, logical principles. Much as I might wish it otherwise, angry and disappointed as I feel, he cannot leap with abandon to the feminine companion ground of feeling and compassion. Where is his recognition of the powerful yearning conveyed by my physical response? Where is his recognition of my shattered hopes? I wonder whether other women and men find themselves standing alone on such separate ground yearning for a bridge to connect them to others. If such a bridge is needed, perhaps it cannot be constructed without time and effort and risk on the part of both women and men to develop the complementary capacities for both *logos* and *agape* that are within each of us. Meanwhile, I tell Dr. Ross indignantly, "I am not a statistic; this is not a matter for scientific research!" He is puzzled by my indignation but lets it fade away without comment.

Springtime, season of blossoming green fullness, season of ripeness in which I extinguished the life of my fourth child one year ago, passes inexorably into the blazing yellow light of summer, the season in which I annihilated my fertility in the cold basement hospital operating room. It is July, one year after the tubal ligation. I face a five-week separation from Dr. Ross, which will include a four-week vacation of my own. During this time, I will leave behind the supports and structures of my life. I am having a difficult time.

My fortieth birthday will take place during my summer vacation. This birthday would have been difficult under any circumstances, bringing with it the inescapable tasks associated with midlife—facing limitations, the narrowing of options, and coming to terms with mortality. Most of the men and women I know have had similar reactions to reaching forty. For me, this particular birthday now represents not a developmental milestone, not a new beginning, but rather an ending, a death, a time to mourn. In the context of such loss, this birthday cannot possibly be a celebration of a new beginning, the birth of the second half of my life.

My vacation will also include a visit to my grandmother, who has just celebrated her ninetieth birthday in the nursing home in which she lives. Though I rarely speak with her on the telephone these days because she is not always able to respond, I have called to let her know I am coming and that I am bringing Michael and the children. "If you live to celebrate ninety years of life, you are entitled to have your great-grandchildren brought to you!" I tell her. Since her home is located three thousand miles away from me in a place to which I have no other reason to travel, it seems likely that this will be our last meeting. I love her: I love this once-warm, once-round, white-haired woman who cared for me as a baby and who spent every spring of my childhood in my home, enjoying being able to spoil me ("That's what grand-mothers are for," she would say), loving being able to love me in her selfless, undemanding way, loving me simply for who I was, for existing, not for anything I had ever done. It will not be easy for me to say good-bye to her.

My vacation this summer will also include a visit to my husband's parents, where I will confront my formerly vigor-ous, energetic father-in-law in his gravely deteriorated, stroke-induced disabled condition. I will see my mother-in-law, always stoic and uncomplaining but clearly weighted down with the enormous physical effort of caring for him. Her physical exhaustion is the only visible sign of the hidden burden of her loss. Already feeling fragile, stretched taut from containing my own guilt and loss, I feel overwhelmed by the prospect of these visits.

To make matters worse, I have a dreadful session with Dr. Ross two days before we are to leave. I know that I have been wanting to count on him, on his understanding of how diffi-cult a time I am having, to be my anchor during the weeks of separation that lie ahead. Because I am so accustomed to serving this function for my own clients, carrying a sense of continuity for them and an empathic recognition of their pain at impending separations, I assume that Dr. Ross will provide it for me. Unfortunately he instead appears to be eager and happy to be going away on his own vacation and seems remote and withdrawn rather than emotionally present in my hour. In the last minutes of the hour, as if to cheer me up, he tells me the old joke about the rabbi and the minister who debate whether life begins at the moment of conception or the moment of birth—not a very sensitive choice of topic for me. He laughs as he tells me the punch line: Life begins when the dog dies and the children leave home. This misguided albeit well-intentioned attempt to lighten my mood and perhaps connect with me as one therapist to another only leaves me feeling misunderstood, as though I am a burdensome client he will be happy to see go.

Fortunately I am helped by my friend Katherine. We meet by chance the next day, good fortune for me, at a local swimming pool where we both swim laps for exercise. In the bright summer sun we sit together on one of the redwood chaise lounges at the far side of the pool, and I pour out my feelings. I tell her how I dread saying good-bye to my grandmother, how hard it will be to sit with Michael's father, how my therapy with Dr. Ross seems to be at a complete and utter impasse. The tears I have been storing up in anticipation of the vacation stream from my eyes in Katherine's company.

She lends a perspective to where I am and murmurs words of support. "It *will* be hard to say good-bye to your grandmother, but it's also important to go, to let her know how much she means to you and to bring her great-grandchildren to see her. That's a way of completing her life, of giving it meaning. Your visit to your father-in-law is the same. Part of what's so hard for you about your work with Dr. Ross is the way he pulls back from you when you're most upset. People who are upset need to have others stay with them, even move toward them. Your father-in-law doesn't want you to stay away from him because he's disabled. That's probably his worst fear. I think you're upset now because Dr. Ross couldn't let you have these feelings with him. He needs to stay afloat, above his feelings. I think he must be afraid to let himself feel upset. So he made a bad joke instead, and you were left abandoned and alone with your pain."

As I listen to Katherine, I know that everything she says is completely accurate. But it is not her words, or even her understanding, that help me the most, although both are important and offer a temporary way to bear my pain. The most helpful part of my time with her comes at the end, when she simply puts her arms around me and gives me a long, firm hug and I find myself crying in her arms, a rare and precious experience for me. I am held by her, both literally in her arms and symbolically by her feelings and words.

As I drive home, feeling soothed and calm for the time being, I find myself comparing how satisfied I feel now with how empty and alone I so often feel after my hours with Dr. Ross. He is so accustomed to expecting rational thinking and competence from me, responses that I have always provided, that he, like me, has lost touch with the capacities for feeling, for human relatedness. But if I am to recover from my abortion and tubal ligation, I will certainly need to rely upon these capacities in addition to my intellect and competence. Katherine's compassion, her understanding, her instinctive hug— qualities that leave me feeling securely enfolded within her being—have helped me more than any therapeutic insight I might have had.

In the evening I attend a birthday dinner to celebrate my fortieth birthday. It is the night before we are scheduled to leave for our vacation. The dinner is an annual event with a ten-year history and includes Julia and Stephan, Katherine and Chris (our newest member), myself and Michael. I am happy to be spending our last night in the company of close friends. As a special birthday gift to me, they have chosen two beautiful art books. I appreciate the thought and effort that went into choosing them. I enjoy their quality, their permanence, the awareness my friends have of me and of my interests. I do not know now that two months later, when my long-suppressed agony over the abortion erupts in full force, I will give these books to Michael to hide from me, because I am afraid I will not be able to stop myself from destroying them, from ripping them apart page by page, an effigy of myself. But tonight I take them home with me carefully, treasuring even the wrapping paper.

Only thirty-six hours after my birthday dinner, I have been transported three thousand miles through the air to the home of my grandmother. I find myself in a quiet, stately brick home for the elderly, surrounded by peaceful lawns on which Jill, Becky, and Ben play under Michael's watchful eye. I sit and hold the hand of my grandmother, who, though ninety years old, looks like an angel. The cloud of soft white hair that I have always loved—though I've been told by my mother that it was once a rich, vibrant auburn—still frames her face in an ethereal aura. I reach out with my free hand and gently pass my palm over its surface, as unable to resist the urge to feel its softness against my palm now as I was when a child. I look intently at her face, trying to drink it in so that I can carry it away with me to have forever; I am so afraid I will not see her again. Though her once-round cheeks are hollow now, and their smooth surface etched with the finest of wrinkles, the serenity I have always sought and found in her face remains. She is still beautifully groomed and dressed, though she needs the help of her loyal and loving nurse, Myra. Despite the ignominy of being helpless in a wheel-chair, unable to use a bathroom or walk on her own, reduced to eating pureed and finely chopped foods, she still exudes a familiar calm and dignity.

I am content simply to hold her hand. I do not need or wish to talk to her. I do not attempt a conversation, because she lives now entirely in the present, often drifting softly to sleep in the middle of conversation. I watch her struggle to relate to my children, her great-grandchildren. When I was their age, she always seemed to find exactly the right words to say to me; now, a generation later, she is hovering close to the edge of losing physical and mental control of herself. She repeats over and over, unable to stop herself, as she grips Ben's head so tightly that Myra must pry her fingers loose, "Are you a nice boy? Come give me a kiss!" But Ben does not complain; he senses that this is not an ordinary encounter. He seems to understand that she cannot help being how she is. (Later he will behave quite differently with another older woman resident who reaches out to kiss him without his permission. He will back quickly away from her and an-nounce, "Just a handshake'll do!")

The next day I have my last visit with my grandmother. This time I sit with her in her own room instead of downstairs in the lounge. Unlike the cheerfully cluttered apartment she moved to after my grandfather died, and in which I spent many happy vacations during my college years, the room is completely devoid of personal belongings, not because they are prohibited but because they could be stolen. Even the perfume I bring her is quickly put away in Myra's purse. Myra must take it home with her because anything left in the room would quickly be taken. Now, in the last years of her life, my grandmother does not even have a room to herself. Costly as the home is, there are no private rooms. Her roommate is a woman even older than my grandmother. This woman occupies the bed nearest the window and is curled on her side in a fetal position, facing away from us. Another older woman, who, Myra tells me, is her sister, is sitting near her, lovingly caressing her forehead. "She comes here every day to be with her sister," Myra confides in a whisper.

My impulse to find ways to convey verbally to my grandmother how important she is and always will be to me wither inside my mind, unspoken. I realize my words would not be meaningful to her, for in fact we now inhabit separate worlds. The invisible structures of memory and meaning within her that preserved our relationship, that contained the multitude of our experiences with each other over the course of my lifetime, have been eroded by the passage of time and the diminution of her physical capacities. No longer am I the beloved first grandchild, for whom she cared during large segments of my life. No longer am I the special grandchild with whom she spent each winter. No longer can she recall my visits to her during my college vacations, the fun we had together. I exist for her now only when I am concretely in her presence and, even in these precious times, I exist only for brief instants before I blend in her mind into her sisters, her daughters, or her other grandchildren. But I can sit and hold her hand, and this simple physical connection is enough. I sit in her room, joined by visible touch and by invisible feelings to the mother of my mother even as the elderly sisters sit together next to us. I am acutely conscious of knowing, as women and men who have access to their feminine capacities for empathy and compassion know, how to reach another human being: not only through rational, conscious thought and language but also from the deep intuitive center of the heart. How tentative, how uncertain, such knowing seems to be for those who do not have access to these capacities. Why is this, I wonder; must it be so?

Though my grandmother has drifted quietly, over time, into another dimension and is now far removed from me, I still have within me those memory traces that preserve and keep safe her meaning to me, though after this last visit I will not be able to acquire new ones. I will have my memories for as long as they survive in me, until time erodes them for me just as it has for her. So, in this final visit, I only hold her hand, and we touch across the boundary of our separate worlds. And though I am not yet ninety, may never be ninety, I now know what it is like when the structures of meaning that have always supported us dissolve. My abortion shattered the frame that gave my life meaning and, isolated by the profundity of this experience, I too have moved into the center of a world whose outer boundaries seem impermeable to others as they are to me. Trapped inside. I long once again to have someone who can understand the magnitude of my loss sit with me and, with this knowing, with this understanding, simply hold my hand.

Our subsequent visit to Michael's parents echoes this message. My father-in-law, now damaged from his stroke, is a mere physical shell, a vacant image of his former self. My heart is heavy as I witness my mother-in-law's fatigue and sorrow and Michael's quiet agony at the impossibility of relating in familiar ways to his father. I bear silent witness to my father-in-law's extraordinary effort to rouse himself to be with his beloved grandchildren, and silent witness to the loss for Jill, Becky, and Ben of all that he could have offered them, of all that might have been. I frighten myself by projecting myself into a terrible future, into the loneliness of my mother-in-law's situation. I cannot bear to have such thoughts, yet they keep coming unbidden. How would I cope? I cannot envision having the same resilience and courage that she displays without ever stumbling.

And yet, even the magnitude of my pain at saying goodbye to my grandmother and at the untold sorrow of the situation with Michael's parents, the quality of that pain, is different from the agony I have tried to share with Dr. Ross. The rapid descent toward death of my grandmother, of Michael's father, is part of the natural human course, part of the destiny that awaits each of us sooner or later. They are struggling to bear a fate that has been visited upon them, whereas my pain has been brought on by my own choice. I have been the cause of my own suffering; a terrible event has not simply happened to me. The element of choice makes all the difference in the world to me and has left me feeling at odds with nature, in disharmony with myself.

For the first time, I begin to wonder if my sense of disjunction with the natural course of life, of being out of step with nature, is a necessary burden that I must carry for the rest of my life. After all, I think to myself, human beings intervene actively with medical technology to alter individual fates by curing disease and prolonging life. Such interventions are not perceived as unnatural, because they are directed toward alleviating pain and suffering, a goal that is universally valued and accepted. Yet to many of us, suicide, like abortion, is considered an unnatural and unacceptable choice, as is euthanasia, or intervening actively to allow death to occur when it is inevitable. I can see that decisions in these painful domains of human existence arouse nearly unmanageable anxiety because they border on darkness, they move us to the edge of death. I wonder whether such anxiety makes the choice to bring about death seem unnatural or wrong. Isn't death as natural as birth, even though it frightens us, and aren't there circumstances in which death is as acceptable or necessary as a choice as birth or the continuing of life is in other contexts? I know that death, after all, is the normal counterpart of life. But I do not know whether death by choice, in every circumstance, is necessarily outside the realm of that which is in harmony with nature. Perhaps the conscious renunciation of life is as much a uniquely human option as the conscious effort to affirm it.

SEVEN

Maelstrom

I felt a cleavage in my mind
As if my brain had split;
I tried to match it, seam by seam,
But could not make them fit.

The thought behind I strove to join
Unto the thought before,
But sequence ravelled out of reach
Like balls upon a floor.

—Emily Dickinson

A death-blow is a life-blow to some
Who, till they died, did not alive become;
Who, had they lived, had died, but when
They died, vitality begun.

—Emily Dickinson

Over the remaining weeks of my summer vacation, I struggle to stay afloat above a mounting despair, which I am less and less able to ignore; the struggle leaves me increasingly depleted and exhausted. As my physical and psychological energies diminish, I hold on to the hope that a return to the structures of my ordinary worklife will help organize and focus me, as well as replenish my energy for life. But after I return home, settle my children in school for the new year, and return to work myself, I am not rejuvenated. Instead, I continue to feel a loss of life energy; my former vitality seems to have been permanently extinguished. I simply cannot come to terms with the chaotic mix of feelings and thoughts that surged forth after my abortion. Almost as soon as I create a way of thinking that binds my sorrow over the renunciation of my unborn child, the thought seems to dissolve, and sadness returns, as immediate and intense as if the event had just occurred. Much as I wish to feel relief at having made the best choice, I cannot will this feeling to arise.

Michael and I have endless debates as I prod him to bear at least some of my pain. Sometimes we end up storming angrily away from each other, certain that our marriage cannot survive. At other times our commitment to work through this crisis prevails, and we cling to each other in mutual anguish. But no matter what the outcome of our debates, the loss of our fourth child simply does not have the same meaning to him as it does to me.

"It isn't fair that I'm the one who has to suffer! You helped make our baby, too!" I moan.

"I can't help it!" Michael retorts. "I just don't have the same level of feeling that you do. I don't even want to have your feelings. There are times when the child seems real to me, or times when I look at Jill, Becky, and Ben and wish that they had a brother or sister and wonder how they'd be with that child. But those times pass by, and I go on to other things."

"I wish I could be like you! But I can't seem to recover from having chosen not to let that baby live. Maybe I feel different from you because I made the choice; I'm the one who took responsibility for it," I say.

"I don't know why we're different," Michael replies, as perplexed as I am at how disparate our reactions are.

"But what about your fertility?" I ask him, shifting ground in an effort to find some way to reach Michael, to make him understand not only the intensity of my feeling but also the important new awareness that grew from exploring the meaning of my subjective experiences and from the seeds planted by reading Nor Hall's book. Although my biological fertility was sacrificed without honoring it as having psychological and symbolic meaning, generative energy, of which biological fertility is but one example, remains alive in me. My task is to find a new direction for the fertility that until now has been channeled into bearing biological children. I struggle to give Michael an analogy that will communicate this awareness. "Try to imagine having a vasectomy if being able to have children mattered to you, if your manhood, your virility were bound up in it. How would you feel if you went to a doctor's office, had a routine medical procedure done very matter of factly, without any appreciation of emotional and psychological significance to you, and you came out one hour later emasculated?"

"My fertility just doesn't have the same meaning to me as yours does to you! I don't think I'd like going through with the surgery, but I doubt that I'd have the same feeling about it as you. We're just not the same!" Michael insists.

"But it's this difference that's making me feel all alone, that something is the matter with me!" I protest. "I can't understand how you can be so disconnected from your body, from the phases of your life, not to have any sorrow now that you've passed through the stage of having children! I know how much you love our children, how devoted you are to them. It doesn't make sense to me that you don't have an

emotional response to losing your fourth child or that you
wouldn't have an emotional response to losing your fertility! I
can't understand why making the choice to end a life, exercising that kind of power, doesn't feel awesome, monumental,
absolutely huge to you!" Slowly I begin to see that our
different attitudes toward fertility are related to the separate
grounds upon which we each stand during the time we have
our discussions. In our discussion I am rooted in feminine
ground, which is linked to the earth, to the physical cycles of
the body; Michael stands upon different, masculine ground,
which is linked to spirit and consciousness, to rational principle.

As I acquire a better understanding of our different foundations, I see that at other times, on other issues, we can reverse
our positions. Masculine and feminine principles, *logos* and
agape, exist within both of us. Often when Michael tells me
about clients he will be representing in court and asks me
what I might decide if I were on the jury, I can be completely
objective, operating strictly on the basis of rules. Michael can
become exasperated with me, with what he calls my utter lack
of compassion. Feminine ground is clearly not reserved exclusively for women. But during the moments when I am having
debates about the abortion with Michael, I feel isolated and
alone in the struggle to ward off a sense of something being
terribly wrong with me.

"What I *do* feel bad about," Michael says thoughtfully, "is
how unavailable emotionally I was to you when we made the
decision. I know I abandoned you, that I didn't want to have
any feelings about the abortion and tubal ligation. I needed
you to make a decision about them—the decision that I wanted
you to make—and to go on with things. For me, that's enough
to warrant my continuing to be in psychotherapy, to learn
more about how I could have let you down that way." Michael's recognition that the emotional response I needed from
him was absent helps me, but it takes time for my hurt and
anger to diminish.

"Well, I'm glad you're doing that, but I can't help feeling
angry, that it's too late, that I'm still left with my suffering,
that it matters more to me than to you," I tell him. "You get

to be the good guy who stays in therapy because his wife is so difficult, and I'm still left holding the bag! It isn't fair!" I am working myself up into a rage, and I try to stop, knowing it won't help. But Michael and Dr. Ross blur together in my mind, becoming a single giant, unempathic Man. Neither one of them, it feels to me, really wants to hear my pain nor does either one of them want to feel any himself. Where can I possibly go to find an affirmation, an understanding that something huge has happened in my life, something so monumental it cannot simply disappear? I have to integrate this monumental event so that it doesn't overwhelm me, and I don't know how.

Finally my inner stalemate comes to an end: The dam breaks, the storm arrives. Although it is terrible in its intensity, it is a relief after the long, sluggish, humid period that has preceded it. The immediate trigger is the pregnancy of my friend Katherine, whose path had so dramatically crossed mine at the moment of my tubal ligation. As I feel her happiness at the new life beginning inside her and feel my own pleasure for her, for the opportunity she will have to experience motherhood, all my long-suppressed feelings about the choice to terminate my own pregnancy and to destroy my fertility erupt with white-hot immediacy and intensity. This time I cannot, will not, seal them over or attempt to climb above them on a scaffolding of rational concepts. This time I cannot, will not, protect those I care deeply about—husband, children, friends, therapist—from the tumultuous onslaught of my despair, rage, and grief. This time I cannot, will not, protect myself from experiencing these emotions. The storm is a hurricane, and I will fight my way through it to the center.

Over the next six weeks my hours in the office and responsibilities with my children will provide the only respite from this internal storm, the only times when my attention is focused outside of myself and when the pressure of feelings is temporarily held at bay. In the free spaces of unstructured time, my feelings erupt in mounting waves, unrestrained by duties. Indescribable guilt over having taken the life of my child, rage at myself for allowing this child to be stripped from my body, and a barely tolerable self-loathing for my mutilated and sterile body overtake me in a great tidal wave.

I finally hit rock bottom with Dr. Ross. I will never forget the depth of my misery, or his, when I try to describe my dreadful inner state to him. Everything he says feels more and more off-center to me, either completely irrelevant or woefully inadequate. The pale reflection of the intensity of my feelings in such comments as, "It must be terrible to feel that way," or a timid silence, seem to be all he can muster by way of response. I keep telling him that he is not helping me. I persist in refusing to pretend to feel better for his sake. He keeps trying to say something empathic, until I feel battered with the barrage of his useless interventions and guilty for rejecting his pathetic offerings, for refusing to appreciate him when I do not feel comforted. He is a nice man, and he is trying hard, but I can no longer betray myself for his sake. Finally I sit and sob quietly. I hear him chant in a background litany, "This is awful. This is awful." Ironically his direct acknowledgment of my state brings us together for a moment; Dr. Ross joins with me in feeling isolated and alone. He finally tells me, "You've stopped my thinking!" and I answer, "Good! I'm glad! Your thinking isn't helping!" I am so immersed in my anger and disappointment, and he is so caught up in his unsuccessful effort to supply the response I need, that neither of us can appreciate that what matters most now is not the content of my complaints but the fact that I am finally directly expressing my feelings and needs. Lost among the trees, neither one of us can see the forest.

We remain immobilized and helpless in this state of impasse for several weeks. I am no longer able to wait for him to learn how to help me; my needs have become too urgent, too pressing. Only a matter of life or death, such as the abortion, could possibly have propelled me to this state. I can see that the intensity of my feeling is frightening him and that he cannot grasp that I need him to relate to me, I need him to resist his impulse to withdraw out of fear. I need him to know that my feelings, no matter how intense, cannot hurt him. In one last effort to impress upon him how much I need him to stay in contact with me, despite his fear of my feelings, I bring in some paragraphs I have written in my journal. The words, like the earlier image of the waxing and waning moon and like the melancholy music of Kitaro, are my attempt to articulate what I need: someone to accompany me while I descend into the depths of my feeling. In this way and for this reason, what will later become the manuscript describing my experiences has its origins:

Please move with me into unfamiliar territory—region of high anxiety, fright, terror—dark space with no guiding light, no exit in view, and the entrance lost behind somewhere. I am not used to being here, either. I did not ask to come, nor did I try to find my way to this place. Suddenly I find myself alone in a dark space, though still a small piece of me exists in the more familiar (to You) realm of light, with the structure of time, plans, appointments, commitments physically to do or be somewhere. But this realm of light, which used to be the only one for me and which once felt so substantial, so secure, sane, real, has now lost that substance and mass and is the in-sane, un-real, in-secure place to be (although I know You may not yet see this). Now the formless darkness is all-encompassing, is engulfing me, and I do not know how to exist in here. There are no familiar rules—I cannot see, I cannot hear, I cannot think, I cannot feel, I cannot smell. There is no external or internal boundary, nor any object upon which my senses can focus. There is no resting place.

Will You come and be here with me?

I do not want to tell You who I am and how I live in the world of light, the world You know, the world we share, the only world You know. I do not want You to help me alter this world, to expand it for me, to help me to be different inside it. I do not want to adjust to it, or to make it adjust to me. I do not want to know who You are or how you live in the world of light. I need to return to the dark space with no form, where I lose my form, inner and outer. I want to learn to be here without terror or alarm. I want You to come here too.

In this dark space I no longer understand our collective need to create a myth of normality, to create labels of "neurotic," "psychotic," "disturbed." I do not understand our collective need to help, even to force people to live only in the world of light. Is it so those who are labeled "normal" can remain omnipotently secure and superior, able to maneuver successfully in this world, able with boundless compassion and mercy to help others to be the same, to be "normal" too?

The more successful I became in the world of light, the more unfamiliar and frightening the dark space seemed, and yet the more insistently it pressured me from all around. This world of light is only a small sphere surrounded by black, by the dark space, a sphere that shrinks under the pressure of the black the brighter and better articulated it becomes. The brighter and more differentiated the small sphere of the world of light became, the more I sensed its lack of importance, reality, solidity. Does it exist for You?

Will You come and be here with me?

Please move here with me, despite Your fear, despite Your assumptions and judgments, despite Your labels for this space. I can no longer live in the world of light alone, denying the existence of the dark. I choose to know both worlds, for they each exist, inside and outside of me. They each exist inside and outside of You.

After reading these words, Dr. Ross tells me, "This description is very powerful; it draws you right in." In this moment I sense that he understands now what response I am seeking from him—that I am asking him to leave the cognitive realm of thought and face my darkest feelings with me. I understand that he simply does not know how to do this and that I cannot teach him. Much as I had hoped our termination would be different, I realize that I must let go of hope for a different outcome and end my analysis.

The illusion that help from him is just around the corner is not easy to give up, but I am resolved to do it. I tell Dr. Ross in the next session, which takes place on a Friday, that I have decided not to come back anymore. He makes what feels like a halfhearted effort to encourage me to stay: "Are you sure you want to stop today?" So great is my disappointment in this ending that if he had taken even a slightly stronger stand, asked me to come for at least one more week, asked that we allow some time together to end, my resolve would have crumbled in an instant. Sitting in my comfortable, familiar patient's chair for the last time, looking clearly and directly at the mixture of sorrow and relief on his face, I feel completely alone. When I leave his building for the last time, after the years of regular visits, I feel as if I am shutting a door on my past, on my former self, a door that will remain forever closed.

My internal storm reaches its peak during the weekend that follows this final therapy session with Dr. Ross and continues through the next weekend, punctuated only by the normality of the work week. The loss of Dr. Ross, added to the weight of the feelings I am already carrying, pushes me relentlessly to the bottom of my whirlpool. I am fearful I will never be able to ascend. Pain spills from within the confines of my psyche unchecked. I see no way of living with the guilt, loss, and anguish I feel, and now there is no one left to help me find a way. I know that Michael has been trying hard, but he needs and wants me to be restored to my former self. But I know that such a restoration is simply not possible. I need someone who can hold the fragments of my shattered self until I can put them back together in an order that will endure. I am in a box with no visible exit. In it, I flounder, helpless, alone, and desperate. I have fallen into a black hole, leaving all my capacities to cope aboveground. Ordinarily able to explore my inner experience, to make sense of it, to observe states that are painful either until they are comprehensible or until they pass by, I find even these capacities have deserted me to such an extent that I cannot imagine they will ever return. The inner torment is so unbearable to me that the only peaceful state I can imagine is death.

It is Saturday morning, the day after my last meeting with Dr. Ross, and I am running on the Anderson Memorial hiking trail. My foot is sore from minor surgery; I have not been running distances of more than three to four miles. But I cannot feel any pain in my foot or any fatigue in my muscles. I am lost in an inner world of grief, of which the only externally visible sign is the gulping, gasping sobs that come from deep in my chest. I notice the distance markers as if in a dream: .5 miles, 1.0 miles, 1.5 miles; they seem to appear only instants apart, as if I have not run from one to the next. When I arrive at the end of the trail, at the five-mile marker, I feel as if I could continue forever. I am outside of ordinary time. But however fragile it may sometimes seem, a thread links me to life, pulls me around, and I return home after an eleven-mile run. I never experience a sense of fatigue, my foot does not hurt, the entire eleven miles (the farthest distance I have ever gone) seems not to have happened at all. I am disappointed, because I had hoped, prayed even, that I might exhaust myself enough that the racking waves of anguish might cease, at least for a few hours. I have chosen to annihilate a life I cherished, and now I want to annihilate myself. I have lost my sense of worth, my value as a person.

When night arrives, I cannot sleep. When I do fall asleep eventually, exhausted, I awaken after only an hour to find that I am back in the nightmare. In my other life I would awaken gratefully from a nightmare, relieved that I had only been dreaming. Now my life is the nightmare to which I am forced to awaken. I yearn for the darkness of sleep; I want to sleep on and on. It is my only hope of comfort. My other life ended at the abortion; the abortion was the "singularity," the term physicists use to describe the boundary or edge in time at which space ceases to exist, the moment of the big bang.

I can find no resting place. I have no inner center of peace and calm to which I can retreat from the pressure and stress of the external world. There is only the anguish, the torment, the shredded remains of my annihilated child, my Self the murderer, confronting me like the garish, alarmingly bright figures that pop up unexpectedly in the horror rides at amusement parks. But rides last only a few minutes, and people choose them for the moments of thrill and excitement they provide. My ride is endless, a hell I can't escape. No one is in control. I cannot make it stop . . . STOP . . . STOP . . . HELP ME . . . PLEASE . . . PLEASE . . . ENOUGH . . . NO MORE, NO MORE. . . .

On Sunday I try again to exhaust myself through physical activity, but this day it doesn't work. I run with Michael on the hiking trail in the heat of midday. On the way back I am overcome by the heat; my head is pounding, my legs barely move in response to the command from my brain. I go through brambles, unable to direct myself to move around them. A small hope surfaces: Perhaps I can die if I keep going in this heat. I force myself to keep going, faster, faster. Unseeing, I miss a shortcut, and Michael, who was with me, cannot find me. I hear him calling me through a gelatinous fog, telling me to stop and wait for him. I will my feet to halt and stand still until Michael arrives. I see through the fog that he is worried about me, hear him tell me that I look the way his father did after the stroke. But the blackness of unconsciousness that I yearn for does not come; instead I feel nauseated and chilled. I cannot drive my physical body to death. I am a Frankenstein who has transformed myself into a monster that will not die.

Death! Always feared, always viewed with dread, always put off to the future, as far away as possible. Now Death becomes my beloved friend, my only source of comfort, the only focus that can organize the scattered fragments of my torment. I evolve a suicide plan that feels just right and I find relief in picturing each step of it over and over again. I no longer believe that losing me will cause my family any harm; in this state I believe that any harm I might cause them would come not from my dying but from my continuing to live. But I do not tell anyone the details of my plan, not now, not ever. I keep it to myself, in reserve, a resource that offers the only comfort I can find.

I share my thoughts with Michael, because he is there and Dr. Ross is not. Without my knowledge, Michael had phoned Julia, Katherine, and Margaret on Friday evening and again on Saturday to find out if they thought my life was in danger.

If I had known then about these calls, I would have laughed sardonically, because from my point of view the only life that mattered to me and that was once worth saving already ended at the singularity, that point at which everything changed unalterably. My physical remains are unimportant. The question is not how to preserve these physical remains but how to cross back over the space/time boundary to re-create my soul. But Julia, Katherine, and Margaret told Michael that he must listen to my feelings and bear them, too, that I will not harm myself, that if I had a place for these feelings, I could come through this crisis. Later Michael will tell me, "Without Dr. Ross, I felt like I was on an airplane with you that had suddenly lost its pilot and copilot. We were heading toward the ground, and I was the only one there who could save us." Without Dr. Ross, Michael is left to assume the task of holding on to me until I can come through the storm of my feelings.

I telephone Michael from a public telephone booth in front of the grocery store on Sunday afternoon one week after my hot afternoon run with Michael because I feel compelled to tell him my thoughts. Later Michael will give me a small piece of paper with notes on it. He will tell me that he took the notes while he listened to me on the phone call. Terrified by what I was communicating, he wanted to be able to ask for help from our friends and was afraid he wouldn't be able to remember everything I had said. Later I will be able to appreciate the full extent of my frightening impact upon him. But not now; in this moment, I am lost in anguish.

I call Michael because I do not want to wait until I arrive home. I believe that I am seeing clearly now; the kaleidoscopic fragments have organized themselves into a pattern, and I am impelled to describe it to him. I am so happy there is a pattern; as long as this pattern endures, I am not lost in the maelstrom. It gives me a place to stand until the next wave comes to sweep me away. If I can share this pattern with Michael, perhaps it will survive in him, protected from the shattering impact of my thoughts and feelings.

I tell Michael the pattern I see: My period is coming. I will

not be able to endure it. It is symbolic not only of the loss of
my pregnancy, of my baby, but is also a reminder that I have
sacrificed my fertility as well. I cannot imagine surviving
beyond this menstrual period and the vast emptiness it represents. For four or five days, unlike a thought or feeling that
lasts only moments, my period will be a constant physical
reminder. My body will become an enemy, attacking me,
tormenting me, reminding me ceaselessly, "See, your baby is
gone, your pregnancy is over, you ended it, you killed your
baby, your body is sterile, your period is a mockery of
fertility, a mockery, a mockery, a mockery, as you are a
mockery of the human being you once believed you were.
You are a travesty of the human being you wanted to be,
committed to valuing every human life, to mothering, to
nonviolence, to compassion for others. . . ." I am terrified that
these thoughts will go on and on, like the horror ride, and I
won't be able to stop them. I know as I hold the telephone
receiver that I will not be able to make Michael understand
me, but I have no one else to tell, and I must communicate
the pattern.

I can feel him listening intently to me, even over the phone,
so I keep going, giving him everything, giving him my pain,
no holds barred, the pain I had wanted to bring to Dr. Ross. I
tell Michael, "I feel so terrible, I only want to die. My true
life on this earth is already over; I have died a spiritual death.
Only physical death remains for me. This physical death will
be a gift to my children. I want them to see that life is worth
living only if you are true to your Self. If you violate any part
of your essential inner core, you cannot continue to live in a
meaningful way. I want them to have known me, to remember me before the singularity; what has continued on after
that is only a travesty of the mother they know. I have known
for too many years what it is like to live life primarily accom-
modating myself to the needs of others instead of freely,
spontaneously choreographing my own part in the universal
dance of creation. To live life in this way is empty, unsatisfy-
ing, and always carries with it a sense of unrealized potential.
Unfulfilling as it is, it is at least tolerable because there is

always the hope of shifting into a different mode of being. But living life as a travesty of one's true self is intolerable, unbearable, full of endless pain and anguish. My capacity to endure this pain in the hope of finding an endpoint is diminishing, my hope is diminishing, I am so tired, my reserves are so low. . . ."

I pause, and hear only a sigh from Michael, so I continue. "Michael, please let me have the calm of death. Please, I want to die in the midst of my family, surrounded by your loving arms. Please, won't you release me from this intolerable imprisonment in the physical remains of the former self that I once could love. Don't make me stay alive only to protect you and our children from your imagined loss of me. My physical life is worthless, it allows you only to maintain the illusion that I am alive; but I know I am no longer alive. Spiritually I am already dead. If you love me, if my children love me, you will all let me leave you, let me go in peace. Instead you're all clinging to me, grasping at me, out of your own selfish needs. You are all selfish, wanting your own lives to continue without disruption. You are unable to see the price you are making me pay to let you have this illusion of continuity. Please, do not ask me to pay this price. I am trying so hard, I am trying so hard for you and for the children, but I don't think I can go on much longer.

"Understand that I feel good about the life I have lived. I am grateful for everything that life has offered me. I am grateful for my relationship with you and all we have shared. I am grateful for having had my children, for having lived to see them develop each in their own special way. I have had so much. I have had enough. Let all this be, let it stand as is. Do not tell me that my death will erase it. Do not tell me that I will harm you, harm the children, if I leave you. Can't you see that I am trying to preserve the good that has been, that I don't want to diminish the good by my continued existence? There is no way I can live with the knowledge that I killed my child, I have tried everything I know. My period is coming, the clock is running out, my emotional reserves are so low—I cannot withstand this new onslaught, I am exhausted. . . ."

My despair is a nuclear fuel that has shot me like a rocket into another zone, and I am light-years away from Michael, receding from him like a galaxy into outer space. But Michael refuses to release me. I hear him tell me that he will not let me go, he loves me, the children love me, he cannot imagine his life, their lives, without me. He orders me to come home, and later when we talk again, I see him cry. He will not stop fighting for my life. He becomes a bulwark against my despair. Other times during the rest of that Sunday and during the week that follows, he rages at me and tells me he cannot listen to me anymore now. He has had enough for now, he must get away. Many nights over the coming week we sleep in separate rooms. On one of these evenings, I hand him the art books my friends gave me for my fortieth birthday; my pain and self-hatred is so intense, I am afraid I will destroy the books because I cannot abandon Michael and my children by destroying myself. Repeatedly Michael tries to shoulder his share of the blame, telling me he does not like how he pushed me to make the decision to have an abortion, that the baby did not seem real to him, that he did not grasp how very real it was to me. But feeling rage at him is no better than feeling rage at myself. It is myself that I must accept; it is rage against myself that I must withstand.

But because of Michael, even for him, I try my best to hold on to meaning, I try to survive. Only later will I be able to marvel at how the strength of Michael's love and commitment anchored me to life. Only later will I come to understand that with the will and capacity to look squarely into the depth of my misery, he gave me the secure sanctuary I had longed for. Only later will I be able to recognize, and then to respect, how he managed to set aside his own needs in order to understand and to meet mine. Only later will I realize that my descent into despair sent him on a corresponding and equally difficult journey. When that time comes, I will truly know that "life's most difficult burden is the incommunicability of love."[2]

But for now it is still a perilous time. I am just managing to survive, barely continuing to live. I am clinging with my fingers to the edge of a cliff; I am treading water in the midst of an ocean with the last of my energy; I am locked in an airless coffin, with only a little oxygen left; I am crushed beneath rocks and boulders, using all the strength I have to hold them off so that I can breathe. I am praying for rescue, hoping against hope to be rescued, but I have no idea who will come, or whether help will arrive in time.

EIGHT

Crossing a Boundary

A religion that valued the feminine contribution would accept the collective assumption of this sacrifice [abortion] and associate with it a ritual to express its terrible and necessary dimensions. At the present time, the fetus is sent down the sewer, without any form of farewell, and the operation obeys the rituals of medicine. In many places, abortions are serial operations, and it may happen that not one word is addressed to the woman, except to verify that she has fasted and has filled out four copies of the bureaucratic forms. . . . This ritual may vary in its details, but its principle quality is to be as bureaucratic as possible, clinical, and asceptic of all emotion. What happens to all the fear, the guilt, the pain, the solitude and the suffering? The guilt, and sometimes revolt, may be crushing and unjust, insofar as the woman bears alone a burden that belongs to all of us.

—GINETTE PARIS
Pagan Meditations[1]

Responding to the urgency of my need, Michael, out of his own growing desperation and alarm, comes upon the idea of calling Planned Parenthood for help. "We have to do something!" he says to me on Saturday morning of what will be the final day of the worst of my inner storm. "You don't have Dr. Ross anymore, and we have to find someone else." We are sitting and drinking coffee together. The children are still asleep, and we have a precious hour to ourselves.

"What else can I do? I don't know who to call. The therapists I know probably wouldn't be any more effective than Dr. Ross," I answer, weeping silently inside.

"What about Planned Parenthood? I've seen articles in the newspaper about them. They must have a list of professionals who know something about abortion," Michael asks me after a pause. "They have a branch not far from here."

"I can't bear to call. It's too humiliating. Here I am, a therapist myself, surrounded by friends who are therapists, a patient who has had years of analysis. . . . I try to picture myself on the telephone making an appointment, and I cannot imagine speaking coherently about my situation to a stranger on the telephone.

"I'll call for you," says Michael. "It's not hard for me to call. I'd do anything to get you help."

I leave the table and go back to bed. I feel an unfamiliar sense of calm for the first time in many days, both because Michael is actively taking care of me and because a new possibility of help has opened up from an unexpected direction. Solidly middle-class, we have always sought and paid for private medical care; the idea of seeking help in a public clinic represents to us the crossing of a boundary into territory that is completely new.

We are fortunate. Michael reaches Robert Weston, a supervisor in charge at Planned Parenthood, without any delay.

The clinic has Saturday hours, and the receptionist puts Michael's call through immediately. When he attempts to explain our situation, he is amazed at Robert's immediate empathy for and comprehension of our needs. Robert does not even seem surprised or appalled at my extreme state of despair. In fact, he tells Michael that my reaction is not at all uncommon. Robert refers us both to Karen Ortman, a relatively new counselor on the staff, who, he believes, is just the right person to help us. Michael puts in a call to her right away and is even able to make contact with her on the weekend. She returns his call on Sunday and, responding to the urgency in Michael's voice, she schedules an evening appointment for us both the next day, Monday.

We drive together to the clinic to see Karen. Now I cross another boundary. I have always sought therapy from the older and more senior members of the psychotherapeutic establishment, known for their experience, training, and the wisdom of their more advanced age. Karen, in contrast, is a thirty-year-old woman who has been a counselor at Planned Parenthood for less than a year. Yet I am now in the position of relying upon her for my life. She represents my only hope for finding a way to live with myself and with the choices I have made, to differentiate myself from individuals who use their power and authority to harm other human beings. In my worst moments, the atrocities committed by a multitude of nations, from the beginning of written history in the service of a political cause, feel no worse than the one I committed in destroying the life of my child.

Michael and I park in the relatively empty lot in front of two small and somewhat run-down buildings; this agency is not the beneficiary of extensive public funding. We climb the short staircase to the larger of the buildings and go through the door. Inside is a rather shabbily furnished waiting room, with only a single narrow window to one side of the reception area. A gray-haired woman is sitting at a worn oak desk; she has a pin that has "Volunteer" printed on it.

"We're here to see Karen Ortman," Michael tells her, holding my hand tightly. He knows how hard this is for me.

"Oh, yes," she says, checking the appointment book. "Oh, yes. Karen left word for you to meet her in the other building. It'll be quieter in there, as we have a class going on here Monday nights. Just walk across the parking lot and she'll be there."

Still holding hands, Michael and I walk slowly over to the smaller building, open the door, and cross the threshold. Inside the narrow corridor, dimly lit, with gray walls and gray industrial carpeting, we hesitate, uncertain of the next step. Suddenly a young, dark-haired woman dressed in wrinkled green pants and a bulky sweater emerges from a room off the hall.

She greets us with a warm and open smile. "Hi! I'm Karen! I wanted to meet with you here because it's much more private. Let's go on back to the rear office. Follow me."

Michael and I follow her into a tiny, cluttered office, where the three of us sit on a mismatched assortment of hard-backed chairs that we help carry into the room together. I think of the luxurious private offices in which I have sat, all nicely carpeted, furnished with deliberately chosen, comfortable chairs, the walls decorated with specially selected paintings. I have always felt that creating a nice office environment is important and that the office reflects the personality of the therapist. But now, focused on the soul-agony I am in, issues of environment have become inconsequential to me; they do not matter at all. It is the person, the presence, of Karen that now counts for everything.

I sit facing Karen, who is looking directly at me with genuine warmth and interest, without a set "professional" manner. Michael, Karen, and I have arranged ourselves in a tight circle, our knees almost touching; here is another contrast to the more distant arrangement of chairs in the therapy offices I have been in. We are a tiny human group, joined together to confront human pain.

Despite her acknowledged inexperience (she tells us immediately that she has been with the clinic for only four months), despite her limited professional training, despite the absence of a traditional professional demeanor, and despite her casual appearance, Karen is quite firm in taking charge of the session. She informs us right away that she understands something of our anguish.

"I want you to know that two years ago I had an abortion. Over these past two years, I've had to work very hard to grapple with the multitude of issues this experience raised for me. But it's this personal experience that will help me to help you." Without dwelling further upon her own experiences (though to be told that she has spent as long as two years struggling with her experience is already helpful to me), Karen proceeds to ask pointed and specific questions. She clearly has an agenda in mind. First, she directs us to tell her our stories and moves without hesitation into the most difficult areas— our anger at each other, our disappointment in each other and in ourselves. We are both relieved that we are finally in the hands of someone who will take charge and, more importantly, someone who seems unafraid of the worst of our feelings. Momentarily spared the enormous weight we have each carried floundering separately, we are able to see, reflected in Karen's eyes, how solid our relationship is. In fact it has been elastic enough to withstand great stress, and we leave the session with a sense of pride that sustains us in the midst of our trial. We make another appointment to see her on Thursday evening, and the simple awareness of having this time ahead of us is comforting.

The days until Thursday pass by with a whisper of the wonderful ordinary quality that has been missing in our household for a long time. This return to routine is for me precarious at best, because I know that I am at the beginning of whatever I will have to do to come to terms with my feelings. I manage to get through the three days with a mixture of dread and hopefulness that the hint of normality has kindled. I am not looking forward to the work of facing my rage and grief head-on, but I now have the possibility that relief awaits me.

At the second session it quickly becomes apparent that the

task of integrating the experience of both the abortion and the tubal ligation is primarily mine. Had I been the partner who wanted the abortion, and Michael the one who wished for our child to be born, the task of renouncing the child and of enduring the grief would have belonged primarily to Michael; I would have suffered, as he is, the pain arising from having my more urgent needs outweigh his. I feel a powerful sense of kinship in this moment with men who have had to bear the loss of progeny, and I wonder how we have managed to prevent our anger and grief from destroying our relationship. Somehow Michael and I have survived as a couple; our relationship is strong enough to bear any remorse we still feel at our manner of reaching the decision to have the abortion. At the end of the second joint session, Karen says to me, "I'd like to meet with you alone, Sue. Even though Michael is suffering, too, you're the one who's sitting with the most grief, guilt, and anger about the abortion." I know she is right. The pockets of intense pain are mine alone to explore, much as I wish that they were equally within Michael. I must venture alone on the next step of my journey in search of healing.

As I drive by myself to the clinic for the first of the three sessions I will have without Michael, I miss him for another reason. He will not be present as a safety net in case I fall, nor will he be there holding on to me with an invisible but unbreakable lifeline, preventing me from being lost forever in the dark territory of grief and anger. Without him, I will have to rely upon Karen to perform these functions, and I have no confidence in her ability to stand firm or in my own capacity to lean.

I harbor a secret hope that we will sit and talk; this is the mode of communication I am most familiar with as both therapist and patient. But Karen suggests that we jump right in, using Gestalt techniques. "I think that this method will help you bypass your rational mind and help us reach your feelings more directly. I've worked this way myself for many years, and it's my intuitive sense that it's right for you." I know immediately that Karen is correct in her assessment. I am skilled at talking about myself, but a newcomer to being myself with another person. So in response to her instruction, I close my eyes and let her voice take over for me.

She begins by asking me to scan my body and to report on whatever sensations stand out for me.

"I feel a huge lump in my throat," I tell her, shocked at its presence and by the choking sensation it is causing.

"Now, become the lump, and tell Sue what you are doing there," Karen's voice intones.

With a surprisingly easy and fluid shift of the center of consciousness, I, as the lump, reply. "I am there to keep Sue's feelings under control so she can continue to function in her life—do her work, care for husband and children, be available to her friends, attend to chores, run the household. Most of the time Sue isn't even conscious of my presence. I am noticeable only if attention is specifically focused upon me."

Karen's voice says, "Now shift back to being Sue," and, after shifting, again with surprising ease, I experience an overwhelming sense of respect for an adaptive mechanism I had not even been aware existed. In fact, had I become aware of the lump in any other context, I would undoubtedly have wished it away without any idea of its value to me.

But Karen does not permit me to rest here for long. "Let's start out with the hardest part first: anger! List the people you feel anger toward."

My voice grows louder with her permission to feel my anger, without worrying about whether it is fair or appropriate. "I'm angry at my doctors for not appreciating the emotional aspects of this choice, I'm angry at my friends for just assuming I ought to go ahead and have an abortion, at Michael for not wanting this child and for making me have the tubal ligation, and I'm angry at my former analyst, Dr. Ross, for being afraid of my feelings, and I'm angry at myself."

Karen says, "Let's start with the hardest one first: your anger at yourself. Visualize 'Sue' in an empty chair directly in front of you, and tell Sue about your anger at her."

Hesitantly I begin to address "Sue," but Karen interrupts. "Repeat your words in an *angry* voice, and talk to 'her' in the present tense." This simple technique, one I had read about in studying Gestalt therapy but have never tried or experienced, has an extremely powerful effect. The intensity of my angry feelings increases exponentially. This is the very first time in my crisis, and perhaps in my entire life, that anyone has not only been willing to listen to my angry feelings but has actually chosen to move toward them by telling me not only to have them but to amplify and express them in a safe situation.

I talk to Sue loudly, accusingly, my loathing of her oozing out of every pore. My hatred—unleashed only with Karen's explicit command—is vicious and intense:

> *I HATE you for depriving me of the experience of being pregnant, of delivering and mothering my precious fourth child. I HATE you for killing my fourth child. I wish you had chosen to kill yourself instead. Your child's life is worth more than yours is now and ever will be. You are a MURDERER and you will NEVER be forgiven. I will never forgive you for what you have done. I can NEVER live with you. I hate you for depriving my child of life, of the opportunity to be in this world, to know its family, to find its way in the midst of this family.*

Karen's voice is calm as ever when my tirade eases off. "Okay," she says. "Now, I want you to switch seats, and to be the 'Sue,' at whom you have this rage. As this 'Sue,' I want you to speak to the 'Angry Sue' and tell her how you feel."

As I switch chairs without opening my eyes, I cannot imagine that the "Hated Sue" will have anything to say. Surely in the face of such hatred she will be speechless; there cannot possibly be any defense she can make. There is nothing she can say, no reply to make, no reply that even should be made, to the Sue who is so filled with justifiable rage.

My emotional experience as I take this chair is overwhelming, completely beyond anything I had expected. As soon as I sit in the new chair, I feel enormous compassion for the "Angry Sue," for her pain and anguish. How can I begin to find the words to tell her how I feel, and even if I can, will she be able to hear me through the wall of her fury, and through the wall of her agony lying so close behind the hatred? Slowly and through tears, the "Hated Sue" begins to speak to her agony counterpart:

> *I was in an impossible situation, with so many factors to weigh. Your wishes, and the baby's, were only a part of what I had to balance internally. Michael was struggling with his high blood pressure and was feeling he had to work less or he would literally die. I wasn't certain he could manage to be responsible for another child, a lifetime commitment, beginning at the age of forty-six. And even though you so strongly wanted this child, I was not at all sure that you could manage the responsibility for another life. You already have three children who are healthy and lusty in their needs for attention and family supplies. What would the presence of another little person competing for the same supplies mean for them?*

And then unexpected words emerge from the "Hated Sue":

> *How could I have known the future? There was no way I could have known that Michael would stay in the psychotherapy he began after his father had his stroke. I didn't have any way of knowing he would get control over his blood pressure and would shift his role in the office so that he would be under less stress. There was no way I could have foreseen that Jill, Becky, and Ben would continue to be healthy and energetic. I could choose based only on the situation I knew at the time. And for all you know, if I hadn't made the choice I did, it's possible that you wouldn't be in a situation right now where you could even wish that I'd chosen differently. If things weren't going well for you now, you'd be feeling gratitude for my choice.*

Karen's voice intervenes again, a constant and steady guide. "Now I want you to shift chairs and to tell this 'Sue' how you're feeling."

I speak once again on the part of myself at whom I have been feeling such unspeakable rage. My attitude has been transformed:

I never thought I'd stop feeling angry at you! I can't believe it, but I'm beginning to feel some respect and compassion for you. I can see that you had such a terrible choice to make, and you balanced the priorities as best you could. You were courageous to bear the entire burden of this choice yourself, holding only yourself responsible for whatever consequences arose.

Thus ends the first piece of work that Karen and I accomplish together. Before bringing me back into the room from the soul-place deep inside me to which I have traveled, Karen again has me scan my body. I notice to my surprise that the lump that was so vividly present in the beginning has disappeared. I immediately realize that it is gone because I have not needed to contain my emotions while I have been in her presence. I need the lump only when it is necessary for me to be my own "container." Without any conscious effort, I have come to lean on Karen. I share this insight with her and then slowly open my eyes and return from my first real excursion into grief in the presence of another human being. For this precious hour in time, I have not felt like an outcast, an untouchable, a pariah.

After I leave this session, I feel a sense of wholeness that has been missing ever since I had the abortion more than one year ago. I also notice another change; I happen to park my car next to a station wagon that has an empty infant seat with a cozy-looking blanket in it, all ready for the return of its small occupant. Automatically I look away quickly, trying not to feel the grief and pain for the empty space inside me that will never hold my lost baby. But when I recall Karen's willingness to go with me into the pain and I remember my hour with her, I realize that I not only survived the experience but also ended in a better place. So I deliberately turn my head back and look intently at the empty infant seat with its waiting blanket. I do feel a tremendous sense of sadness, but I stay still, allowing myself to feel it, until it passes away, and then I continue on my journey home.

I experience the familiar anxiety and apprehension before my second visit to Karen but make myself go by holding on to the memory of how helpful my first session had been. There are so many pockets of pain I could fall into—which will we choose for today? I do not relish the thought of moving into any of them.

When I arrive at this session on a sunny fall afternoon, I tell Karen that I have resumed functioning effectively—at work, as a mother, as a wife—and that I am not sure if I need to be here with her or not. Her reply is thoughtful: "I'm glad to hear that you can function again. I know from my own experience and from that of women I've worked with that working through an abortion is a process that takes time and that it doesn't always follow a steady course. My own abortion took place over two years ago, and it was only last May, in a meditation retreat, that I was finally able to come to terms with my guilt. I went to Sari, the leader of the retreat, a woman in her fifties from Thailand, and asked her what the Buddhist attitude toward abortion is. She told me that there's a concept of 'water baby' in the Buddhist tradition, a baby not yet human, and that I should think about my aborted child in this way. But it was her forgiving presence, more than her words, that enabled me to feel forgiveness and compassion for myself. It was at this retreat that I made the decision to become an abortion counselor, and in June I began working at this clinic. And I'm only now beginning to work on retrieving my sexuality. So you may find that we're on a plateau; we did an intense piece of work last time. I don't know how long the plateau might last; it could be a week, a month, or even a year or more."

Karen's openness in sharing her own unresolved issues somehow frees me to say that sexuality is also a big problem for me. Instead of feeling free, sensuous, sexual, I feel like a "thing," a piece of meat, existing only for the pleasure of my husband and deadened to any possibility of pleasure for myself. The loss of fertility is another issue for me, one that feels related to my deadened sexuality. In this way Karen and I happen upon fertility as the appropriate pocket of pain for this session.

Karen again moves right into my feelings with her Gestalt

technique, catching me off guard, bypassing my cognitive shields. She has me close my eyes and scan my body just as she did in the first session. I tell her the first feeling that comes into focus: "I'm feeling just an intense appreciation for your not taking my capacity to function effectively and competently as an indication that I don't have any other needs. Most of the time, it's my 'competent, cognitive, therapist self' that people in my life see. I don't think I've ever had the experience of someone appreciating that I also have a vulnerable side. I recently ended my analysis with a very experienced psychoanalyst who couldn't keep that side of me in his view, even after I warned him in my first session not to be taken in by my competence. Here you, so new at your profession, have the intuition and sensitivity to sense this vulnerability and to comment upon it in such a respectful manner, without my even having had to tell you about it."

With my eyes closed, again guided by Karen's quiet voice, I begin to experience myself as the "Fertile Sue." I try to describe in words the joyous and full feeling, the sense of complete harmony with life, that fertility carries for me:

> *Having the option to create life yet open to me, even if I might choose to let the opportunity pass by, is a wonderful, even miraculous, sacred state of being. Fertility to me has always been a priceless gift and responsibility that I had so looked forward to as a child and had vowed to cherish; I can't believe that it's over, gone, finished forever. I had such a sense of pride in my body for functioning so perfectly, automatically empowered by forces transcending my limited conscious control. How could I ever have chosen to demolish that capacity, to mutilate myself? I have brought a precious gift, a harmonic state, to an abrupt, violent, and permanent end. How will I learn to live with the pain of this choice?*

Karen continues to guide me. "Now shift to the other chair, still keeping your eyes closed, and see the 'Sterile Sue' in the chair across from you. Tell me what you see."

I follow Karen's instructions, shift chairs and look at myself as the "Sterile Sue." I can hardly speak, the vision of what I see is so dreadful to my inner eye.

I see an empty, deformed, shriveled, grotesque, shapeless woman trying desperately to care for her useless body through endless exercise, repetitious and joyless. She is condemned now to age inexorably and die. Her purpose on earth, her connection to life, to the life cycle, is over. There is nothing left for her except to pass the time until the end comes.

Tears flow as they never have before in the presence of another person, as I sit with painful feelings of self-loathing, revulsion, disgust, and hatred. They swirl in waves around me in a state of being outside ordinary time. But very gradually a new feeling emerges as I watch the image of "Sterile Sue," so repugnant, so loathsome. The new feeling is compassion: "Sterile Sue" is alone to face this abrupt transition in her life without the compelling guidance of the physiological changes that accompany a natural menopause and without having voluntarily sought her condition. My heart aches with pain for "Sterile Sue," for the difficult task she faces completely alone. She has only whatever inner resources she can find to rely on. In the face of such hatred, I cannot envision how she will ever retrieve any resources from within.

I continue to speak to Karen. I tell her, "There is no 'rite of passage' for Sue, no community of women to surround her as she faces this transition."

Karen asks, "What ritual might help Sue? After my abortion my friends suggested a ritual for me to enact around the loss of my unborn child. It really helped me to carry it out."

Together Karen and I create the vision of Sue going to a place outdoors, in nature, where she will say aloud words of farewell to her fertility. Picturing the scene in my mind is enormously comforting; the image heals simply in the having of it. "Sterile Sue" must consciously claim her place in the ever-recurring cycle of fertility, with its waxing and waning for all women, even if she has propelled herself there in an abrupt, disjunctive way. I wish to help her with that difficult task, and I see clearly how my disgust and contempt for her have only made it worse, if not completely impossible.

The compassion and the healing images combine to provide a restful state of calm, which I savor in Karen's quiet presence. Her intuition is so accurate; it guides her to leave me a period of silence within which I can experience this long-absent state of being. Finally the session "feels" over (she has never held us to a specific amount of time, yet each session lasts about one hour; this is yet another crossing of a boundary for me, so different from traditional therapy frameworks). The separate "Sues" merge together and return to the small office, to the hard-backed chair close to Karen's.

Before I leave, Karen announces, "I have an 'appreciation' of you that I want to share. I was anxious before I met with you and Michael the first time. I wondered whether I would be able to help you. I have confidence in my skills, but I'm pretty new at this work, and I've been uncertain as to whether I chose the right path for myself. It was pretty intimidating for me to meet with an attorney and an experienced therapist! Your appreciation of me has really been validating and affirming. It's helped me feel that I've made the right choice of career. So you came to me at just the right moment in my life. I thank you for it."

With this acknowledgment of the mutual "rightness" of our intuitive responses to each other, we end the session with plans to meet a third time.

Before my third visit to Karen I again feel the familiar wish to cancel. It has been several weeks, I have been feeling more like myself, energetic and functioning well, and I seem to be "healing." Yet, I am afraid not to go to see her because I am fearful of leaving the abortion behind me. I don't want to seal off the experience as I did once before, only to have it burst upon me later; and I don't want it to fade away either. I feel I am the only living person who mourns the loss of the life of my unborn fourth child. If I stop mourning the loss, who else will know and care?

I feel torn by conflicting feelings for Karen, too. I don't want to disappoint her, to let her down by canceling, and yet

I don't want to go to the appointment to take care of needs I imagine her to have. This conflict is very familiar; it is part of that long-established inner battle over whose needs—my own or those of another person—will have priority. Another part of me looks forward to seeing Karen, to hearing about her experience in the meditation retreat she has attended between our sessions. I smile to myself as I remember how she told me about her one-week vacation, so unlike the traditional therapeutic mode of imparting such information to clients. She had started the second session by saying, "I would like to tell you about something nice that's happening in my life!" How refreshingly different from my accustomed way, learned from sessions with supervisors, teachers, and my own therapists. Therapists learn to inform the patient of the dates of the vacation in a neutral manner, nothing more, and then to prepare for the onslaught of feelings of abandonment, hurt, and anger that are likely to follow. My smile is not because I believe these difficult feelings are not present, or because I believe they are not important to experience, but because I can see so clearly how, through the filter of our guilt, we assume that those are the only feelings patients have and ignore the part of the patient that can feel pleased for the therapist-person who will be away.

With these conflicting feelings racing around inside me, I go to my appointment. I always feel a bit out of place when I arrive at the clinic, bustling as it always is with teenagers and volunteer help of all ages and demeanors. And yet, as always, I am greeted with an open friendliness and attention that are humanizing and heartening. This is not a waiting room where one could enter and be overlooked or forgotten.

A pleasant, receptionist, takes my name and tells me, "Oh, yes, Karen just called in." My heart sinks unexpectedly; perhaps it is Karen who will cancel. I am upset by my sudden awareness of her importance to me, which has been masked by my resistance to seeing her at all. My urge to cancel suddenly comes into clearer focus as a fear of being disappointed by someone who I hope will be reliably there for me. In only two sessions I have developed an intense and powerful attachment to and reliance upon this young woman. The receptionist's voice continues: "Karen is waiting for you in the other building and wanted me to tell you to go right over."

My anxiety instantly dissipates, and I hurry across to the other building, where I see no sign of Karen. I peer into a large meeting room. A group of people are seated around a table, but they are friendly and one of them asks me if she can help. I reply, "I'm looking for Karen," and someone else tells me that Karen is not there. But now I am confident she is present and, in fact, Karen appears just then with a warm smile. We go to our small room in the back, where Karen spontaneously offers a hug. I feel so glad to see her, this young woman with whom I have spent so little time. Karen and my time with her are both very precious indeed. A few minutes of connection around an issue of soul seems to have accomplished more than years of analysis.

Karen begins by telling me about her time at the meditation retreat, which was difficult for her in a number of ways. In turn, I share my gains in various areas—work, sexuality, relationships. I also tell her of my concerns about keeping this appointment with her: One part of me wants to keep moving ahead in my life, but another part of me fears leaving the abortion behind. With that opening, Karen leaps in with the confidence and assertiveness I associate with her youth, but that must actually have more to do with her own experience as a patient and her trust in her intuition. I feel an awareness of my lack of trust in my own intuitive capacities. Karen trusts herself to leap into darkness, whereas I walk cautiously, always seeking a well-lighted path. The capacities I have been developing to enable me to enter dark places with clients seem now to be well-lit choices, sanctioned by traditional therapeutic techniques. It is Karen's leap of faith that I have not yet learned to take.

We sit in a close-knit formation: Karen, myself, and an empty chair. I close my eyes and allow her soft voice to guide me, first taking me into my body, which today I sense to be relaxed and comfortable. She then suggests something differ-

ent, something I could never have imagined doing. "I want
you to visualize the unborn child in the other chair."

This is the moment the unexpected occurs: I look over at
the empty chair with my inner eye, anticipating with dread
the sight of a baby who will be so tiny, so vulnerable, so
helpless, that my heart will burst into flames, each flame a
cry of anguish that I chose to prevent its birth. But to my
utter astonishment, the child is not there! Nor is the chair
empty. I do see something there, but what is it? I try to focus
the image more clearly: It seems to be a kind of formless
mass, but it is shimmering, as if filled with life energy. I
comprehend that my unborn child has somehow dissolved
into this pure and unboundaried life energy. Words come
pouring out as I try to articulate this unexpected and extraordinary occurrence. I tell her, "Karen, my baby isn't there! I
see a whole mass of life energy that isn't in the form of a
baby! It isn't in the form of anything. I can hardly explain
this to you; I just hope you can understand. I didn't annihilate a life. I only prevented this life energy from being channeled into my fourth child's body, but that energy is still
there! IT IS STILL THERE! I didn't annihilate this life
energy!" The energy, a fluidly shifting force that I can only
sense rather than see, is now assuming a benevolent, formless
presence in the other chair.

Karen instructs me: "Now I want you to shift into the
other chair and 'be' this energy."

As I settle into the new chair, I am no longer my familiar
self. "Sue" is in the other chair, appearing rather like a lifeless
small doll. I somehow become a boundary-less life energy; I
feel ageless, wise, and benevolent. I feel as if I have tran-
scended the fragile beings that are known as Sue, Karen, and
even the unborn child. I explain to Karen, "Sue, like the
unborn child, is simply one manifestation of my plentiful life
energy. This energy reappears moment to moment in a multitude of forms. Sue does not have the power to kill the source
of this energy; she could only prevent one form of its
manifestation—her unborn child—from coming into being.
This form is only one among a multitude, like a particle of

sand on a beach. The terrible, painful separation and loss that occurred when Sue denied life to her unborn child is very real, but it is not the only way of understanding the abortion. The energy of life itself will continue on, though not specifically through the being of Sue's fourth child." I feel enormous compassion for the deflated, small figure of Sue, who, from the perspective of my embodiment of a bountiful life energy, has had to carry such a heavy burden.

There is no more to say. Karen has me return to the other chair. I am glad to be back in my body, back in my familiar self. I feel as if I have come home after a long trip, and I am glad to be in my own "house" again. I have a sense of peace and calm; some of the benevolence that was present in the other chair remains with me still. I feel lighter, unburdened for the moment of my concerns about sealing off the experience of the abortion and leaving my child forever behind.

The journey has surprised me. Even my worries about disappointing Karen now seem silly to me. I comprehend that Karen does not have a specific goal for me. She is interested in the journey itself, welcoming its surprises and comfortable traveling in the dark. She is a mountain goat in the realm of the spirit. I, in contrast, am a trail horse, relying on familiar landmarks, looking for guideposts, at a loss if they are not there or if my guide is gone. For Karen, there is only the journey, so there can be no disappointment if the landmark is missing; it was never needed or sought.

Karen brings me back to the room. When I open my eyes, I am disoriented, confused about the time, uncertain as to where I am and how long I have been away. Even if the dimension of reality I reached in that other state is impermanent, to have had even this brief contact with it has made an indelible impression. Life in its usual sphere, in my ordinary plane of existence, will not seem quite the same again, now that I know that another level exists.

Karen and I chat a bit and then walk out together into the darkness of night. During my late-afternoon journey, the sun has set.

This is the last session I have with Karen, although we are

to remain in contact by telephone and letter over the next few years. After this session I write and send the following letter to Robert, Karen's supervisor at the clinic:

Dear Mr. Weston:

I am writing to let you know how appreciative I am for your help in referring my husband, Michael, and myself to Karen Ortman. Although I am a therapist and surrounded by a circle of close friends who are therapists, it was Karen who was able to provide exactly what was needed to help me turn a crisis of despair into the beginning of a constructive experience.

I am sure that you may already be aware of the special qualities that Karen brings to her work, but I would like you to have my comments as someone who has directly benefited from them. Briefly put, these qualities include first and foremost, a keen intuitive awareness of what the other person's central needs are and of what the best way to provide for these needs would be. Beyond this, Karen has the ability to trust her own intuition. This trust enables her to act without hesitation upon her sense of what a situation requires. Karen also has and can put to use extensive experience with Gestalt techniques, which are particularly effective in short-term interventions, as may often be required at your clinic (although they are of course useful in other situations as well).

The Planned Parenthood clinic is indeed fortunate to have Karen on its staff.

Sincerely,
Sue Nathanson

But the stable place of healing and recovery that I achieve in my three sessions with Karen unexpectedly turns out to be only a plateau and not a final destination. I soon find that another pathway opens up before me, not only inviting me to embark upon its unfamiliar byways, but demanding that I do so.

NINE

Meditations in Solitude

How can the mother *release herself from this [internalized mother image] imago which has arisen to distort the human reality both of herself and of her child? . . .*

The mother's release from identification with the good-bad maternal instinct can take place only through a psychological differentiation of herself from her children, by which she grants them the right to live their own lives and die their own deaths—to suffer as well as to enjoy. These are native human rights and no one may with impunity shield another from them.

—ESTHER HARDING
The Way of All Women[1]

Oh mother,
after this lap of childhood
I will never go forth
into the big people's world
as an alien,
a fabrication,
or falter
when someone else
is as empty as a shoe.

—from "Mothers (for J.B.)"
by Anne Sexton[2]

Shortly after my three sessions with Karen, I am unexpect-edly catapulted again into the maelstrom of feelings sur-rounding my abortion by a sudden surge of media publicity on the issue. Settling down one evening after a hectic day and a typically chaotic family dinner to relax with a new issue of *Newsweek*, I quickly discover that this magazine will not per-mit me much relaxation. The entire issue is devoted to the subject of abortion and to the intensely polarized conflict between the Pro-Choice and Right-to-Life advocates. The magazine is peppered with photographs that are appalling. My recumbent position on the comfortable and well-worn chair that Michael usually occupies is completely at odds with my inner tension as I stare at the hate-filled faces of abortion protesters carrying Right to Life signs. Next, I absorb the impact of the picture reprinted from the movie *The Silent Scream*, in which a developing fetus suffers horribly while being destroyed. I reverberate with pain for the sobbing women who are being escorted across picket lines by volun-teers, for the doctors who are harassed and even blackmailed for performing abortions, for the alarming fanaticism that is behind the bombing of clinics, for the zealous protestors who identify only with the helplessness of the potential lives being destroyed.

The next day another disturbing encounter with the forces opposing abortion occurs closer to home as I drive along the familiar edge of the college campus on my way back to my house. Students are picketing the college infirmary, the very building where more than once I sought medical care and solace during my graduate-school days. Today, instead of representing a sanctuary for the sick, the building has become the setting for a choosing up of sides, laying the groundwork for an all-out war. The actors are student picketers, their so-young faces teetering on the narrow hinterland between childhood past and adulthood ahead, faces now either intent with idealistic passion or grim with anger. But they are not performers on a stage. They are human beings in the real world, seeking to prevent abortions from being performed in their university.

When I arrive home, I go immediately up to my bedroom and sit in the comfortable chair by the window to think about what I have seen. Why is such rage and hate being directed at me, I ask myself, as if I were not already struggling hard enough with these feelings? Is this violent hate aimed at me-as-Myself, or is it coming toward me-as-Mother?

In the safe solitude of my bedroom, I think about how each of us must live with the awareness that we will be faced with loss and suffering and with the loss and suffering of those we love. To the extent that we think about our fate, we live on the edge of an abyss, tiny and vulnerable individuals, virtually helpless in the face of an indifferent universe. Yet there once was a time when each of us existed as an infant, when each of us was cared for by a mothering person, however inadequate, who cushioned and protected us as much as she or he could from the injuries and insults of the external world. As infants, we were not yet able to experience our mothering persons as separate from us, with independent lives and needs and limits. What a betrayal, what an enormous disillusionment, awaits each of us. Each infant among us will discover not only that the mothering person is separate, with often conflicting needs, but worse yet, that this person upon whom we depend faces the same indifferent universe herself. And what guilt, what enormous despair, awaits each mother when she faces the reality that she has brought a child into an imperfect world, into arms that, no matter how loving, cannot afford perfect protection from the suffering of life. Had I faced this reality fully, instead of shielding myself from it as I did with the comforting belief that I could make the world better for my children than it was for me, I am not sure I could have borne Jill, Becky, and Ben into this world. From the plentiful accumulation of moments in which I have been compelled to witness helplessly the suffering of my children, my mind alights upon a recent experience with Ben. Somehow, the lack of a serious or life-threatening component renders it even more poignant, as if reminding me that even healthy children are not invulnerable.

> *My heart fills with grief as I remain a helpless witness in the face of my son's pain. In my two-hour absence one evening, giant hives have erupted mysteriously all over his face and torso. He is waiting expectantly by the door when I arrive home, hardly able to wait to tell me his story. He informs me in his most adultlike manner that he has attempted to relieve the itching near his eyes by finding, peeling, and eating a carrot (shreds are left all over the kitchen sink); he remembered that carrots are "good for eyesight." When this remedy, the only blossom upon which his beelike young intelligence could alight, fails to help him, his hope remains located in me, in my arrival. I see his beloved and hopeful face, his soft and normally unblemished skin blotched with red eruptions, and I know I could not have prevented his suffering, nor can I cure it. I can only use my limited human remedies to soften this discomfort, which, though trivial in itself, to me in this moment stands for all the pain that his life will inevitably include. I know that I can offer Ben comfort and some minimal medical balms now, but these offerings seem paltry in the face of this misery, symbolic of all the suffering to come.*

The inevitable disillusionment of children who face the limitations and helplessness of their mothers, when it collides with the guilt of the mothering person, surely provides one piece of the bedrock for the hatred directed by the picketers toward women who have abortions. The picketers are demanding that women bring unborn children forth into life no matter what capacities the women have available to buffer these children from an indifferent universe. As long as all our attention remains focused upon whether women should deflect or accept the demands of the picketers and take on responsibility for giving birth to every child they conceive, none remains available for a deeper understanding of the source of the picketers' rage. As long as the sum total of women's energy is spent deflecting the anger and condemnation directed toward them, the hatred can only increase.

Sighing to myself, I begin to think about how much pressure I am under in my role as mother to protect my family from harm and to take the responsibility for whatever goes wrong. An interesting conversation I had with Becky at breakfast floats into my mind. Becky is an avid reader of the comic section of the newspaper every morning. As it happens, we generally arrive in the kitchen at the same time most weekday mornings and we sit at opposite ends of the kitchen table without speaking. Morning is not Becky's most cheerful time of day—an understatement; she has always been something of a night owl, ever since she was born, with a rhythm different from mine. Our opposite body rhythms used to create terrible conflicts in the morning, when I'd be eager for cheery greetings and conversation, only to bump up against Becky's grudging and taciturn responses. I have finally learned, not without considerable effort and with more than a few defeats, to keep my distance and to enjoy her silent presence, all the time watching for those rare openings when she is in a happy mood and I can slip in a few hugs and kisses and occasionally, a word or two.

On this particular morning, Becky sits at her end of the table in front of the Rice Krispies box, the nonfat milk carton, and the glass of milk to which we carefully add two tablespoons of my morning cup of coffee. These invariant components of breakfast are neatly arranged on the pristine paper-towel placemat that Becky improvises for herself each day (our ordinary vinyl ones are not clean enough for her taste). Suddenly Becky dissolves into giggles. Startled by such unusual early-morning cheer, I look up with surprise and see that she is giggling at one of the comics. "Read this!" she commands through her chortles. She shoves the carefully folded newspaper over to me and waits for my reaction. Only too happy to share any experience at all with my elusive little daughter, I locate the comic that has captured her and, not wanting to ruin this special moment by an unforgivable misunderstanding, proceed to read it with care.

In the first of the three frames, a small boy sits staring unhappily at a plate of food in front of him while his mother instructs him firmly, "Stop worrying about your peas touching your mashed potatoes!" In the second illustration, he reels with shocked disbelief and bewilderment as she informs him bluntly, "Inside your belly, everything gets mixed together anyway!" In the denouement, the distressed mother holds her sobbing little boy in her arms, patting his back. She thinks silently, "Sometimes we're not ready to hear the truth!"[3]

I have no difficulty joining Becky in her laughter. But it is only later, when I am by myself, that I recognize the more serious message hidden beneath the humor in this comic strip. In the story told so simply through cartoon illustrations, the mother is a paradoxically ambivalent figure: the person who both shatters the illusions of her young child ("Everything gets mixed together in your stomach") and who then holds and comforts the child when the illusion is lost. The little boy in the cartoon has worked hard to establish even a rudimentary control over his world, to achieve the cognitive capacity to make discriminations and to form separate categories, and to insist upon an ordering of the universe in whatever way he can, his domain extending only to the food on his plate. He, like each of us, is destined to bump up against his pathetically limited ability to control his universe. Where else is he more likely to direct his rage and grief than toward his mother, the person who both confronts him with objective reality and then comforts him when, his illusions of omnipotence shattered, he is wounded by the limits of this reality.

Thinking about this precious interaction with Becky reminds me of Jill and of the time when I took—"dragged" would be a more accurate term—her to the doctor to have a persistent sore throat checked for a possible strep infection. Enraged at me for exposing her to the humiliation and inconvenience of being examined physically by a doctor, even a woman doctor, frustrated at being sick, helpless in the face of her illness and my power to insist on the trip to the doctor, Jill repeated with great intensity and fervor, her words piercing my heart with an impact that surprised me, "I *hate* you! I *hate* you!" She then exercised the only authority and control available to her in the situation: She ordered me to stay in the waiting room while she went alone with the doctor into the examining room. I thus became for Jill the target and receptacle of her frustration, helplessness, and rage. Banished from the examining room and sitting in the waiting room with these difficult and unpleasant feelings now swirling around inside me and no longer in her, I understood that she was now free to be cooperative and polite with the doctor. Being aware of my function as a psychological receptacle into which Jill's problematic feelings could be placed certainly helped me withstand her rejecting behavior. I suppose I can willingly accept this role as an essential part of mothering, but it is not at all easy to be experienced in this way. Even with my awareness of the need for me to play this role, and even though it only lasted a very short while (by the time Jill emerged from the doctor's office, she had moved from actively raging at me to coldly ignoring me), I was nonetheless wounded by her negativity. As we drove away from the parking lot behind the building, I said to Jill, "Why don't we stop for frozen yogurt on the way home?" feeling that we both needed a treat after the stress of the doctor's visit and that sharing something pleasant would modify her mood. Jokingly, but very serious underneath, I asked her as we savored our treat, "Can't I at least be a good mother for just one minute? How about appreciating me for one little minute? I'll even take thirty seconds!" Jill, invoking her wry sense of humor, thanked me nicely for the yogurt, paused for a second, and then asked, "Is the minute up now?"

I function as a receptacle for blame not only in my role of mother but also in my work as a psychotherapist. I do it with great difficulty and pain. I think of my client Sandra, a young woman whose parents abused her physically and sexually and then died of different and unrelated illnesses when she was in her teens. Orphaned, never able to rage at her parents for their damaging treatment of her or grieve their ultimate abandonment of her, she experiences these intense feelings with me. When I sit in silence in order to leave room for her emotions to surface, I feel despair, too. She berates me for not helping her, tells me she has lost all hope that therapy will be of any use, rages that no matter how compliant she is in coming to her sessions, nothing improves. Her words push me to doubt myself, to face my own human limits: If I have any "techniques," any psychotherapeutic skills to help her, she asks me, why aren't I using them? She cannot bear to keep coming to see me for yet another three years if nothing is going to change, if she is not going to feel better, if the past cannot be changed. I can hardly stand the feeling of having nothing to offer her but my full attention and understanding. I have no remedy that will remove her anguish, no magic that will alter her life experience, no wise words that will provide instantaneous comfort and solace, no recipe for a shortcut through her pain. I have only my human presence to offer and a heartfelt conviction, based upon my sense of her courage and resilience, that she will eventually be able to shoulder her fate and integrate her terrible past experiences into her present sense of selfhood.

I so understand every feeling she is expressing. I had every one of these feelings in relation to Dr. Ross after my abortion. I remember all too vividly how abandoned I felt when he offered me medication to make my feelings go away, when he accepted my cancellation of an hour when I called and said I was too upset to come in ("Call me when you feel better," he had suggested), and when he simply withdrew inside himself. I do not want to abandon Sandra if I can possibly help it. My unshakable conviction that she needs to have the experience of raging at and grieving with a person who will not back away, who will not retaliate and harm her, who will continue to love and value her not only despite but because of her terrible feelings, helps me to withstand her doubt. I have come to believe that each of us needs such an experience. We must help one another bear the suffering that necessarily accompanies our efforts to live our lives in an imperfect world. If we make room for our rage and grief, we also create space for our joy and pleasure. But it is not easy to bear the blame, even temporarily.

I ponder further the blame that is directed at women who choose abortion. It seems to me that the mere idea, let alone the actual possibility, that a mother could kill her child, even when it is as yet unborn, generates anxiety that is simply unthinkable. The label "unthinkable anxieties" was coined by one of my favorite teachers, the British psychoanalyst D. W. Winnicott. Because he died before I came across his work, our relationship has been limited to my reading of his books and articles, but his writing has a vitality and immediacy that always leaves me feeling as if he is talking directly to me.[4] Winnicott believed that all babies exist on the brink of such specific unthinkable anxieties as going to pieces, falling forever (perhaps being washed down the bathtub drain when the water goes out), having no relationship to one's body, and having no sense of orientation in one's world.

I have come to appreciate that we never completely outgrow the unthinkable anxieties of infancy. That vulnerable child-self within us, always in jeopardy of abandonment, neglect, or even murder by our all-powerful mothers, never totally leaves us; it remains telescoped inside our adult selves. When we try to live up to the restrictive and confining myth of "normal adult," which does not allow for the continuing existence of this child-self, we are without permission to acknowledge and face the anxiety elicited when this helpless, dependent child-self comes forth. Consequently whenever we (including those who are active in the Right-to-Life cause) identify with an unborn fetus that some mother refuses to bring to life, and we experience the alarming state of unthinkable anxiety generated by this identification, we instinctively attempt to rid ourselves of the unwanted feeling as soon as possible. One means we have of ridding ourselves of this anxiety is to blame the mother for causing us our discomfort and to strip her of her power to place our child-self in danger. I picture again the determination on the faces of the protesters and understand their zealous efforts to protect and give voice to the unborn children who cannot defend themselves. But it is not humanly possible for any mother to be a perfect buffer against such terror. It seems to me that our conception of what constitutes a normal, strong, psychologically healthy adult needs to include the possibility of having a vulnerable infant/baby/child-self within us. We need to understand that these terrifying states of unthinkable anxiety that Winnicott describes in relation to infants are also part of adult experience; they are an inevitable part of the human condition. Perhaps then we might be able to cope with them in ways other than making them the fault of someone else or stripping women of the power and right to make inevitably necessary and difficult choices. Perhaps then our attention and energy can be directed toward sharing the moral responsibility for such choices; it is not an easy task to bear the close connection between life and death and between attachment and separation.

My thoughts about the intolerable anxiety generated by the *fears* of that vulnerable infant/child in each of us prompt me to think about its powerful *needs* as well. I come to another underpinning of the intense, even murderous hatred of women who have the power to choose to take the lives of unborn children. Perhaps our need for a loving attachment to a mother who has the power to buffer and protect us from an awareness of the vast and indifferent universe in which we must survive is so profound that we unconsciously demand that mothers provide perfect care for their children. No matter that such perfection is impossible: In the context of my circumstances I could not care for a fourth child, just as my mother could not care for me when she miscarried at the very moment I had my tonsils out. Our yearning to be loved and cared for unconditionally, and the unbearable wound we experience when this yearning cannot be met (as it never can be), run so deep that our pain may sometimes be channeled into our own murderous rage and into dark projections onto women and mothers in general.

I consider the tendency in human beings to locate the enemy outside of us, in the other. Our very survival in these times seems so precarious as toxic chemicals pollute our environment, viruses as lethal as AIDS spread unabated, terrorist activity continues, and weapons development continues. Our efforts to control and combat a host of such threats, important as they are, seem woefully inadequate at times. I wonder, as the very real threats to our continuing existence proliferate in our immediate present, whether woman-as-mother provides a readily available receptacle for culpability. Just as she embodies the power to create life, she also bears the responsibility for bringing about death. I think about the front page of the local newspaper that I saved back in 1985 because of the striking juxtaposition of the two major headlines of the day. In large bold type, the first headline read, MX CLEARS CRITICAL HURDLE IN SENATE. Directly beneath this blaring headline, not separated by any printed text, was a photograph. The picture showed abortion protestors marching with signs in front of a Planned Parenthood Clinic. Two of the large signs they carried could be read easily. The first sign, carried by a woman, read, Thou Shalt Not *Kill*. The second, carried by a minister, read, Planned Parenthood Killed One of *My* Flock. I could not ignore, even then, the juxtaposition of the two issues: At the moment when an increase in weaponry is sanctioned, when the young sons of our nation may be called upon to risk their lives in war, women are being condemned for murdering their children.

In the face of our enormous and understandable anxiety and fear of death, we fix the blame upon woman, giver of life, as if it is possible for any woman singlehandedly to avoid and prevent any death, let alone the violent ones that necessarily accompany the wars we wage. I doubt whether the weight of this blame can be lifted from the shoulders of women until our culture modifies our existing collective perception, not only of women, but also of death as a final ending. A huge sigh escapes me as I realize the enormous distance that must be traversed before such modifications can occur. This road seems as long as the one women must travel in order to affirm as sacred their capacity for procreation. In contrast to the condemnation women now receive for renouncing the lives of unborn children, and to their negative connection with death that this condemnation brings about, I recall that the matriarchal traditions of the Celtic "fairy faith" considered death to be the Land of Everliving Women. Rather than identifying women as purveyors of death, this culture imaged death as a realm in which older women who passed on before their children did were there waiting to receive, guard, and help their offspring.[5] No such comforting image of death, or of women in relationship to death, exists for us as yet in this time and place; for now, it is up to individuals to find and hold high healing images—both images of women and images of women in relationship to death—for the rest of us to see.

In my reverie in the solitude of my room, I recall that human beings *do* form intense loving attachments to their mothers, no matter how imperfect their mothers may be. The bond begins in infancy, or perhaps before birth, and endures through adulthood. I recall the powerful glimpses into the raw vulnerability that results from the strong bonds children form to mothers, glimpses that I have found in the works of a number of contemporary women poets. The women differ in age, sexual orientation, and literary style, but to me they seem strikingly similar in their capacity to find language that articulates the pain that the deep attachment to and irrevocable, inevitable loss of one's mother brings. They are also alike in their capacity to face the reality of death squarely. Although these poets are daughters expressing feelings about the loss of their mothers, I imagine that men have similar feelings toward their mothers. Opening my heart to the vulnerability and pain of some of these women poets provides me with a direct pathway to my own. "The Blessing" by Carolyn Kizer[6] and "What Remains" by Marge Piercy[7] are examples of longer poems; two excerpts from poems by May Sarton and Anne Sexton follow:

> *I saw my mother die and now I know*
> *The spirit cannot be defended. It must go*
> *Naked even of love at the very end.*
> *"Take the flowers away" (Oh, she had been their*
>   *friend!),*
> *And we who ached could do nothing more—*
> *She was detached and distant as a star.*
> *—from "A Hard Death"*
> *by May Sarton*[8]

My mother died
unrocked, unrocked
Weeks at her deathbed
seeing her thrust herself against the metal bars,
thrashing like a fish on the hook
and me low at her high stage,
letting the priestess dance alone,
wanting to place my head in her lap
or even take her in my arms somehow
and fondle her twisted gray hair.
But her rocking horse was pain
with vomit steaming from her mouth.
Her belly was big with another child,
cancer's baby, big as a football.
I could not soothe.
With every hump and crack
there was less Madonna
until that strange labor took her.
Then the room was bankrupt.
That was the end of her paying.
                    —*"Madonna," from* Death Baby
                       by Anne Sexton[9]

The special vulnerability and deep anguish that arise from attachment and inevitable loss, expectation and certain disappointment, surely require the most powerful buffers we might imagine. What can provide a stronger protection against the pain of loving and being disappointed, the pain of yearning for and never receiving enough of that unending, unqualified love and care that we crave from a good mothering person, than murderous hate?

I realize that my meditations are helping me distinguish the different components of the anguish that followed on the heels of my abortion. No wonder I felt such powerful self-hatred. The hidden expectations toward mothers in this culture are certainly an inextricable part of my expectations toward myself as the mother of my unborn child.

Musing again about my grief over the loss of my unborn

child, I find that my understanding of it is now more refined and detailed. The first thought that comes to mind is how absolutely enmeshed I am with family, how embedded my sense of self is with Michael and with each one of my children. The anguish my abortion has caused me must be considered within the fabric of my relationship to my family. My next thought takes me to a paradox so obvious that once I name it, I cannot understand why I did not see it before. The paradox consists of the fact that my unborn child was simultaneously separate from and part of me, just as Michael and each of my living children is. I am grieving for the loss of my unborn child as a separate being with as solid a separate reality as my three living children. And I am grieving for the loss of that unborn child as a part of myself. In fact, it seems to me, this paradox must be implicitly true in all intimate relationships; we fluidly shift from experiencing one another as separate from us and as merged with us all the time, without even noticing.

I think of a recent experience on a weekend trip that Michael and I took with Jill, Becky, and Ben. As I recall it now, it exemplifies for me the fluidity of boundaries that is part of all intimate relationships. The subjective experience of being merged with my family was so powerful, I wrote about it in my journal. Michael and I took Jill, Becky and Ben to a beach town for a long weekend, hoping for sunshine and relaxing beach weather. Greeted instead with unending fog and rain, we were left enclosed together indoors all weekend. Michael and I left the children and made a foray to the small fishing town near the house we had rented, searching for a place to buy food for dinner, intending to cook at home. By chance, we wandered into a busy new restaurant on the wharf, directly overlooking the fishing boats and stacks of lobster traps; this was a working fishermen's community, not a dock for recreational yachting or sailboats. Michael and I quickly agreed that an outing to this restaurant would be fun for all of us, an opportunity to glimpse another way of life. The hostess, an unaffected young woman with a friendly smile, was happy to make room for our three children and even agreed, despite the large number of people waiting for tables, to hold an available table for us for the ten to fifteen minutes it would take to fetch the children from the house and return to the restaurant. Michael departed immediately to pick up the children while I waited at the restaurant, token of our intention to return as promised! I was actually very happy to be left behind as collateral at the restaurant because I did not relish the task of gathering up three housebound, stir-crazy children, who might well be expected to growl and refuse to budge or to grumble with complaints about the food. In any case, I was certain they would not come along with smiles and light hearts, not out into the gray gloom to an unknown restaurant specializing in fish—to them synonymous with the word *inedible*.

As soon as Michael departed in our big green van, I began to make the adjustment to being on my own, my first block of time alone and away from my family for two days. It is difficult to find language for my internal experience as I hovered psychologically on the border between being part of a larger whole and being a separate person. Once the van carrying my family disappeared from sight, I felt as if my center of gravity still remained with them. . . .

I float invisible and formless among the chattering people sharing drinks and lively conversation at the small tables and long wooden bar, oasis of golden light in the darkening rainy night. Unobserved, I hover among the different groups, taking in conversations, creating scenarios in my mind. I watch the young teenage couple, twins radiant with youth and vibrant health, both blond, blue-eyed, dressed alike in blue jeans and sailor's white T-shirts, sitting knee to knee at the bar, gazing earnestly into each other's eyes, linked not only by appearance but by the intensity of their romantic passion. I float soundlessly over to the window, by now so accustomed to my ghostlike state that I no longer expect the cocktail waitress to approach me with the offer of a drink. Drifting to a new location, I position myself directly behind the hostess, inches away, becoming her wraithlike alter ego as she deals with a new group of people who enter the restaurant, shaking the rain off their jackets and off the little girl that one of the adults carries. I listen to the hostess tell them there will be a table for them in thirty minutes, and keep silent counsel as they decide to leave and return rather than stand inside and wait with their small child. I feel a slight pang of guilt upon realizing that it would have been easier for my family to wait than for them to, but I also feel some relief in knowing that our table will in fact be held for us. Lost in these rather vague and conflicting feelings, shrouded by my cloak of invisibility, I jump with shock when the hostess turns around suddenly and, seeing me just inches away, says, in an equally startled tone, "Oh! Hello!" Blushing, I apologize for my human presence, for simply occupying space: "I'm just standing here to keep out of the way." After this brief moment of contact, this brief experience of having mass and substance, I return to my state of invisibility. But I now find myself drifting over to the front door, made completely of glass, where I can look out onto the parking area and to the road beyond. That brief descent from my floating, trancelike state evokes in me a distinct wish for the arrival of my family and for the return of my sense of a separate self that they hold for me. Vigilant, I hover at my new post, scanning the road for our familiar truck.

How can I describe the relief and joy of seeing that green truck wind its way down the steep, two-lane road, on its way to the restaurant, on its way to me? The vehicle seems alive, human, its headlights a sign of warmth, the right-turn blinker signaling its entrance into the parking area the most comforting of winks, cheerily greeting me, calling out directly to me, "Hello, Sue! I'm here now! I've arrived!" As it makes its turn, I catch glimpses of the familiar shapes of my children, occupying their separate territories inside the van, long since claimed by "squatter's rights." Becky, a blur of bright turquoise, is a small but stately presence taking up the entire rear seat, middle child claiming her separate space alone in the back. In the next row I can see the tall shape of Jill and the smaller round head of Ben, oldest and youngest always at odds, at opposite ends of their row. And sitting in the driver's seat, a large oval form of tan, is Michael, pillar of fatherly strength, transporting my three little cubs, my "aqua-bears" dressed in different shades of blue, safely into my arms, safely home to me.

*My barely sketched outline quickly fills in as I move to the door
and hold it open for them, greeting each of them in turn with a
swooping hug and big kiss, swooping hug that is more than a hug,
big kiss that is more than a kiss, in that hug and in that kiss
creating them into them-selves at the very moment they create me
into my-self, I defining them, they defining me, beloved mother,
special child, special husband, each of us part of one another,
brother, sister, child, parent, husband, wife, each of us oddly
separate, too, Michael, Sue, Jill, Becky, Ben, three small bundles
all a different shade of blue, biggest hulk in tan smiling, and me
now standing out the most vivid, the most brilliant, the brightest
of all of us in my fire-red, ember-red, ruby-red rain jacket.*

The consequences of the paradox of being both a separate
self and yet a self that incorporates each member of one's
family are rarely as dramatic, rarely a matter of literal life or
death, as they are in the case of abortion. When viewed from
the crux of this paradox—in ending the life of my child, I also
annihilated a part of myself—the degree of my anguish becomes understandable. Closing my eyes, I see my three children as facets of myself: Jill, the embodiment of my own soft
center of vulnerability; Becky, who carries my stubborn refusal to yield against my will; Ben, spearhead of my playful-
ness and creativity. Once I comprehend how fluid and
permeable are the boundaries of my sense of myself, I understand that I am grieving not for one, but for three deaths:
myself as the mother of this child, my fourth child as a
separate being, and for the fourth child who, like my others,
remains forever a part of me.

With my eyes still closed and visions of these children
waxing and waning in the clear vision of my inner eye, I
wonder how I will ever manage to shift the direction of my
nurturing and creative energies from raising children to something new. The powerful wave of instinctive forces so alive
within me seem to have joined with the cultural undertow
that pressures women to be content with husband, home, and
family and that encourages them not to venture too far beyond
these boundaries. Yet content as I am with these components

of my life, I have come to understand that there is within me a creative energy, a generative energy, that now demands a separate outlet. Do I have the courage and fortitude to break free psychologically and stand alone, giving birth to metaphorical, spiritual children, as well as to continue existing within my family? Is it possible to do both?

In the solitude of my bedroom, I gaze out the window and realize that the sun has finally set. My meditations in this solitude, rendering a bit more comprehensible the intensity of my emotional response to the abortion, have left me feeling at peace with myself. My hunger pangs signal that it is time to cook dinner, and I rouse myself to walk down the hall to the kitchen to prepare food for my family. It will take the work of some months before the most shocking awareness about my abortion crystallizes in my mind.

TEN

Woman as Murderer

Abortion and infanticide, so abhorrent to the Christian stand-
point, have not always been condemned. They are freely practiced
among primitive tribes and were by no means uncommon in
ancient civilizations, as, for instance, in China. Abortion was
extremely common also in Europe up to the Middle Ages and the
present world trend is toward legalization under prescribed cir-
cumstances. But there remains a deep-seated sense that such an
action is wrong. This sense of the wrongness of abortion is generally
explained in terms of the taking of life—as a sort of murder. . . .

When the choice is made with full consciousness of what it
involves the outcome will not be all evil. For it is through just
such moral conflicts courageously borne that psychological growth
is brought about.

—ESTHER HARDING[1]
[Written in 1970, prior to
Roe v Wade decision]

In almost all cases, one aborts an impossible love, not a hatred. The child is sacrificed to a value that one judges at the time to be more important: either the children one has already borne, those one will have one day, or one's own psychological, economic, or physical survival.

I believe it is time to sacrifice to Artemis [the virgin goddess of femininity] the fetus to which we are not prepared to give the best of ourselves and our collective resources.

The universal unconscious has always utilized different methods of reducing population when space and resources are deficient. The most obvious is war. . . . The "sacrifice" of lives then takes place through men rather than through women, but the victims die at random, and the power of death is unleashed in all its fury, and beyond reason. . . . [We need to develop] as quickly as possible a collective consciousness which would establish a new sharing of the powers of death between men and women.

—GINETTE PARIS
Pagan Meditations[2]

The deepening understanding of my response to the abortion does not assuage a special, sharp, emotional pain I feel when confronted by the arguments of the Right-to-Life faction. Much as I had hoped the pain would dissipate as I became increasingly able to accept my choice, it simply will not go away. Ultimately it impels me to face the darkest part of myself, a part that in my deepest moments of despair I am not certain I can live with: In my heart, I believe the accusations and condemnation of the Right-to-Life supporters have merit. I did choose to end a life, and I do feel like a murderer. I must bear responsibility for this act.

Yet I am unable to reconcile the contradiction that accompanies this subjective truth. What am I to do with another part of me, equally real, that knows I also acted to protect lives? Murder, I believe, is wrong. Abortion—the deliberate termination of an actual or potential life—*is* a kind of murder. But abortion is too complicated an act to be considered wrong in the ordinary meaning of this word. We in this culture have not yet evolved an understanding of the concept of "wrong" that is differentiated enough to address the issue of abortion.

Books and articles are being—and will continue to be—written that are moving us toward a differentiated understanding of the rightness and wrongness of abortion. Scholars from many disciplines are debating the ethical and legal issues on the subject of abortion, deliberating the question of whether it can be justified legally and morally and whether or not or in what way it belongs in the political arena. I follow their efforts, which are solidly centered in the masculine *logos* principle with interest, and I consider them important. But as a woman who has personally confronted the abortion dilemma, and as a psychologist concerned with the subjective experience of individuals, I find that I miss the balance that a complementary perspective grounded in the feminine *agape* principle would provide. For some women who choose it (and for some men who have fathered the unborn child), the rightness or wrongness of abortion on any grounds may be irrelevant to managing psychologically the reality of the taking of a life—the reality of a kind of murder. Like me, these women (and men) are now left alone to find an effective way of coping psychologically and emotionally with this reality.

I ask myself whether every woman who chooses abortion feels that in exercising the power and right to terminate a potential life she is rendering herself a murderer. I believe that even if, like me, she consciously believes in her moral and legal right to act, has confidence in all the reasons for her choice, and feels only relief at the termination of the pregnancy, she may nonetheless be vulnerable, now or at some time in the future, to feelings of guilt for having chosen to end the life of an unborn child rather than to give birth.

These thoughts bring to mind a recent session with my client Liz, who synchronistically told me a story nearly fifteen years old, a story she had never told anyone else during all that time. Our meeting began as a typical therapy session, with both of us sitting in my office in our usual places. Liz is an attractive woman in her mid-thirties who always makes herself at home by plumping up the pillow on my couch, taking off her shoes, and reclining, knees bent, with her feet on the low table between us. I always find myself unintentionally mirroring her posture by slumping low in my chair and putting my feet up on the table, too, rendering it a bridge across the short distance between us. For some months Liz had been trying unsuccessfully to become pregnant. Recently we had weathered together the disappointment of discovering that a hoped-for pregnancy was instead simply a late menstrual period.

On this particular day Liz began the hour by saying she wanted to share with me an excursion into the past she had taken by herself the night before last.

"I found myself feeling vaguely sad all day, without any obvious event having occurred that could account for this mysterious feeling. No matter what I did, it wouldn't go away. Finally, Tim and I went to bed for the night. He went right to sleep—he always does—but I found myself unable to sleep. After tossing and turning for a while, I got up and went into the den to sit by myself. Once I was alone with my thoughts, memories of an abortion I had fourteen years ago, when I was only twenty years old, came up out of nowhere."

Liz stopped talking and began to cry, her hands covering her face. Her tears were as fresh as if the abortion had just taken place; the fourteen-year gap seemed to disappear in an instant. I sat quietly with her for a moment and then said softly, "I'm so sorry, Liz. I didn't know about the abortion."

Liz sucked in a deep breath as if in response to my echo of sorrow and took up her story. "My memories of the abortion led me on a search for the private diary I kept at the time. I'd written about it in my journal, and I knew the journal was somewhere on a shelf in the den. Finally I found it in a pile of papers on a dusty bookshelf. I snuggled into my favorite chair and started to read what I had written about how I got through the abortion."

It was easy for me to picture her, as she talked, curled up alone with her diary in the middle of the night in her silent house. Liz told me how she had taken a trip to Europe with her best girlfriend after their junior year in college and how they had paired up with some male classmates they had met by chance in a second-class train compartment. Free from the constraints of home and the moral prohibitions of her parents, exhilarated by their adventures exploring a foreign country, Liz had indulged herself in the forbidden pleasure of a sexual relationship with Andy, the young man with whom she had paired off. Her pleasure and exhilaration ended abruptly with the discovery that she had become pregnant. Andy was a responsible young man and offered to help her in any way he could—financially and by accompanying her to doctors. There was no question at all about whether to have the abortion; no other choice made sense to them. They did not know each other well enough even to consider marriage and, even if they had wanted to stay together, neither of them had completed their education. Andy in fact was planning to go to medical

school after he finished college. Although she was comforted
by Andy's support, Liz somehow felt better about going
through the experience that lay ahead of her with her girlfriend
She went on to describe to me, as if we were discussin
events that had just happened, her appointments with diff
ent foreign doctors that she made and kept, accompanie
her best girlfriend, in the European country they were
ing in together. To obtain a legal abortion there, she needed
to locate a doctor who would be willing to assert that the
pregnancy would endanger her health. Finally she located
one, but it was not easy going. Liz had to fight hard for the
abortion that, even then, as sure as she was that it was the
best available option, caused her no small amount of heartache.

The doctor examined her carefully and then took her into
the office, where his desk and medical books were kept, to
discuss her situation. He sat behind a large and polished
mahogany desk while she sat in a small chair in front, next to
her silent friend.

"I prefer not to perform an abortion," he pronounced firmly.
He went on to explain his reasoning. Though he spoke in the
language of his native country, which Liz had only studied in
school, he managed to make his thinking all too clear to her.
He was clearly critical of Liz, not only for becoming pregnant
without being married and for seeking an abortion but also
because she was traveling in a foreign country rather than
living at home in her own country working at a job. He
regarded her with stern dark eyes, his harsh stare magnified
by the lenses of his horn-rimmed glasses, the image of which
is indelibly engraved upon Liz's memory. "I prefer to send
you home to your parents rather than give you an abortion,"
he pronounced again. "You should have a job, go home!
Enough travel!"

"It's incredible, looking back, that I was able to stand up
for myself at all—he had such a forbidding stare," Liz told
me. "I tried as best I could—it was tough trying to communicate in a foreign language—to explain to him that I absolutely
did not want my parents to know, that the pregnancy was the
result of a sexual blossoming that wasn't bad, even if it wasn't

part of a permanent and committed relationship to a man. I tried to explain that I wanted to be a mother, but not till later on in my life, when I was settled myself and married. Somehow I must have managed to stand up for myself successfully, because he finally changed his mind," Liz said, unaware that she was shaking her head in wonder as she relived the experience.

"I can still see him closing his file folder in that forceful way, in keeping with his assertion of his patriarchal power and authority, acting as both judge and jury!" Liz recalled, a tinge of cynicism in her voice. "He pronounced, very reluctantly, 'Well then, I will give you a second chance.' As if he had the right to decide what course my life would take! And in fact he did have that power over me. It was a terrible feeling to be at his mercy like that. I don't think I have ever felt that helpless in my entire life. If he had made a different decision, I really don't know what I'd have done. I know I couldn't have faced trying to convince yet another doctor, and I simply wouldn't have gone to my parents."

Liz lowered her voice in shame and slumped down even further on the couch. After a pause, she told me in barely audible words, "I know that I'm having difficulty getting pregnant now as punishment for having taken the life of that unborn child then." We sat in silence together, feeling on both our shoulders the weight of this shame and the terrible punishment borne of it.

Finally, breaking the silence and drawing upon my own recent meditations upon abortion, I said to Liz, "With so much focus on the legitimate right of each woman to choose whether or not to bear a child, there is no one to help those women who need to face the aspect of abortion that to them feels like—in fact *is*—murder. There's no place for women to bring such dark feelings of guilt."

I will never forget how Liz looked at me then; there was an expression of shock on her face that was indescribable. She looked me straight in the eye and said, "When you said that word—*murder*—I just got chills. One of my diary entries— I've never told it to anyone and thought I never could, I wasn't even going to tell you now—reads: 'Elizabeth, You are a MURDERER. You committed MURDER on June 29, 1971.' I have never shared that thought with anyone until now. My girlfriend and Andy kept telling me I was doing the right thing, and it would have been too hard to go through with the abortion if I had tried to deal with feeling like a murderer, too. I couldn't handle both."

I went on to say to Liz, "You know, I think your concern that you are infertile now as punishment for the abortion fourteen years ago, and your sense of shame about that experience, are your way of trying to come to terms with the aspect of abortion that feels exactly like murder to you. It simply was not possible for you to face this feeling of being a murderer *and* go through with the abortion. So the feelings of guilt about the choice had to go underground for a while— fourteen years, to be exact. Maybe they would've stayed underground if you hadn't had this difficulty becoming pregnant. Now that they've surfaced, you have an opportunity to deal with them consciously in a different way."

I spoke more than I usually do in that session, but Liz was listening avidly to me, and I could see that my words were hitting home, forming a stronger bond between us than the bridge created by our legs across the table we used as a footstool. "Sometimes the awareness of having taken a potential life can operate outside of consciousness in subtle ways. It can deaden sexual desire, facilitate another pregnancy to make reparation for the lost child, or cause the end of the relationship with the man who fathered the unwanted child. These are only a few examples among many of the aftermath of making that impossible choice.

"It may be that you'll be better off for having brought the feelings of being a murderer into consciousness," I told Liz. "It seems to me that the feeling of being a murderer, if it isn't faced consciously, can remain alive in the unconscious. There it may manifest itself in a disguised form in the life of the woman who carries it within her. It doesn't just evaporate or disappear; the body recovers physically, but the experience of having taken a life, of having chosen to murder, to use the starkest word I can think of, remains alive in the psyche. It may remain alive in a way that never interferes with how an individual woman chooses to live her life. I know women who rarely give any thought to their abortion and, if they do think about it, only feel good about having chosen to have it. But the abortion experience may also surface in ways that make it essential for the woman who carries this knowledge outside of conscious awareness to face it fully, to face it consciously. She then faces a crisis that seems so deep—I use the word *deep* because it requires a permanent alteration in her cherished sense of herself—that I call it a crisis of her soul. And this crisis can precipitate a frightening descent into unbearable feelings."

I went on. "Someday I hope our culture will evolve a new attitude, one that will enable women to bear the responsibility for choosing life or death for our offspring in a different way than is possible now. We have lived in a patriarchal culture, where the father is supreme, for so many years that we've lost our connection to a source-ground of feminine wisdom. I know I have to explain what I mean by those words. In this patriarchal culture we lack fully developed images of woman-hood—images that I'll call archetypal—that we can respect and that would serve as models for all of us. By archetypal images, I mean images that are universal, prototypical, that exist within our psyches simply because we are part of the human race. Both men and women are deprived because our culture is devoid of these images of womanhood, to the detriment of everyone. Here's an example of what I mean. Imagine what it would be like if, as a culture, we had rites of passage for young girls entering puberty, rites that would welcome them with pride into their roles as women, into their awesome power to nurture a potential human life inside their body, instead of keeping this tremendous passage hidden, as if it were shameful! Imagine what it would be like if, as a culture, we could value wise old women, if the title of crone, instead of conjuring up the fearsome image of a witch, could be a title bestowed with pride and respect. If only we had an image in this culture of a Goddess as well as our lonely, powerful, masculine God. Archaeological finds from ancient cultures include representations of female goddess figures. I like to imagine that women and men in these ancient cultures were able to draw strength and pride from this feminine, yet nonetheless divine, image. I believe that women and men in contemporary times could also derive strength and wisdom from such archetypal feminine images. Maybe in a culture in which all of us were surrounded by these images, instead of the stereotypical images we see in magazines, women would be able to cherish as sacred our capacity to give birth rather than see ourselves reflected in a cultural mirror as wantonly sexual at worst or irresponsible at best, with pregnancy an unfortunate by-product!" I stopped myself abruptly, worrying that I had gone too far in sharing my deeply held personal convictions.

But Liz had visibly relaxed, and it seemed to me she was drinking in my words. "I totally agree with you in principle— but I don't see how that kind of major cultural shift ever can take place. I haven't come across any divine feminine images, except for the Virgin Mary, who was saintlike, and Eve, who was a sinner!"

Liz and I share a rueful laugh, and then I comment, "Well, I don't think we have to wait to recognize that women who unexpectedly become pregnant, as you did, will have to choose whether to bring forth that new life. I'm still in the process of developing my ideas about this," I told Liz, "but I'm coming to believe that the terrible and dark feelings of guilt over renouncing that life—murdering it—need not be experienced in a self-destructive way. These dark feelings can provide valuable access, a trap-door, into what I'll call the realm of the feminine, a realm that now remains outside of our patriarchal culture. This feminine realm contains all the subjective experiences related to being a woman that are ignored from the perspective of a patriarchal culture. In fact, without these painful feelings, there's often no access to this realm, because women have had to adapt to our existing society and disregard their own experience, often with great unconscious cost to themselves."

Then I heard myself say to Liz, though I was talking to both of us at the same time, "I have a parable about Mother Nature that you might be interested in hearing; it's in a journal I write in from time to time. I know I'm focusing only on the nature of being female and leaving out the masculine for the time being, but I think that this omission is necessary for now, at least until we explore feminine issues more fully."

"I'd like to hear your journal entry," Liz said. "I just told you about my diary, and now you're sharing your journal with me. That feels human and related, a sort of womanly exchange."

I got up from my chair at that point and picked up my journal from the desk across the room. After returning to my chair and settling myself in, I read my parable aloud to Liz. I had written it shortly after coming upon the quote from Linda Fierz-David that I had read aloud to Dr. Ross during the Saturday session we had after my abortion. Until now, I had not had an occasion to read the parable to anyone. But in this moment it seemed a fitting response to Liz:

In the time before the spark of consciousness was ignited in the first human being, the responsibility for the continuation of all living creatures resided with Mother Nature, who was as yet without consciousness Herself. Unseeing, unfeeling, unconcerned, Mother Nature simply obeyed the instincts that ruled supreme in Her deepest center. She just continued to issue forth life with unceasing persistence, enlisting the help of Man, who also obeyed His instincts without thought. Babies poured forth from Her womb, all without her personal regard. Some were runts, underdeveloped, undernourished, not yet ready to come forth into the light of day. Others were strong, healthy, feisty. Regardless of their state, Mother Nature just pushed them all forth into the world relentlessly, neither speeding up nor slowing down the pace at which she kept giving birth. The babies, once born, either lived or died, all in her unseeing and impassive presence, all equally unseeing and impassive themselves.

After eons had passed, a change occurred! The spark of consciousness ignited, and Mother Nature became aware. No longer did She continue to bring forth babies in a perpetual stream, without regard for their individual conditions. Now each offspring became a central focus of Mother Nature's attention and thought. Mother Nature began to notice that She could affect their safety and health. As more time passed, She became aware of her own feelings, desires, and needs, as well as those of her offspring. She discovered that She was no longer content to pour forth babies in an unceasing stream. She noticed Her fatigue at being a constant caretaker; She noticed Her own curiosity and eagerness to explore the world around Her. Man, too, responded to the spark of consciousness and began to regard His own personal wishes for the first time.

In the end, with Her more developed consciousness, Mother Nature began to exercise Her power of choice. She stopped producing offspring in Her formerly unconscious, instinctually based way. She learned to avoid the conception of babies. If, for any reason, She became pregnant and did not choose to nurture the new life, She would end that potential being's life. She began to listen to the needs and opinions of Man, but because the child lay within Her body, because She alone would give birth whether or not Man stood by Her, the decision remained Hers alone to make. In this way, with the igniting of the spark of consciousness, Mother Nature claimed the lonely power, shouldered the heavy fate, of a Murderer.

The new consciousness that brought Mother Nature an awareness both of Herself and Others and that empowered her with the choice that could make her a Murderer would not have been problematic at all were it not for the enormous range of that consciousness. If Mother Nature could have been conscious only of Her Self, Her own needs and desires, being a murderer would not have mattered; if one discards a rock, a piece of wood, spills some water, there is no cause for concern. But Mother Nature knew that the unborn baby She destroyed would have had its own conscious awareness, its own life trajectory, its own value and meaning. She could feel the powerful bond between the unborn baby and Herself, between the unborn baby and Man, between the unborn baby and its brothers and sisters, even at the very beginning. She understood *her responsibility for the life of the baby. There was nothing left for Mother Nature to do but to find a way to live with an expanded consciousness of Her own power and responsibility and to bear this consciousness with courage, with grace, and with dignity. . . .*

My voice trailed off, and Liz and I were silent. After a time, Liz gave voice to the question that I was thinking.

"I wonder how women in *this* culture will ever accomplish the task that faced Mother Nature in that parable?" she asked. "In reality, Mother Nature never has to confront the task, because She doesn't have that spark of consciousness you're describing. The real Mother Nature—remember those old advertisements for butter instead of margarine?—the *real* Mother Nature destroys individual lives, children and adults alike, through disease, accident, violent crime, war, old age, without cause, without reason, at least without reasons we can see."

I sighed and said sadly, "I don't know how we'll accomplish this task. Women in our time and place who choose abortion are alone, without any existing structures to rely on while they work to integrate this profound experience. Women have to develop themselves psychologically so that they can accept the consciousness of having the power and capacity to choose to end a life that is also part of their very own being. In this time and place, women who choose abortion are unprotected from the assaults of those who call them murderer; they can't shield themselves from these assaults at the same moment they attempt to confront their own inner judges. There are few therapists in general, and even fewer to whom they might have access, who can help them if they choose not to seal over the experience of abortion, not to deny its importance, not to deny its meaning, and to connect it with its deep roots in elemental feminine experience. Most important of all, there are no existing structures to help them weave it into the ongoing creation of their soul. Women in our culture who can't suppress or repress their experience of abortion must bear the burden of their consciousness alone."

I suppose in retrospect that I could not bear such pessimistic thoughts, because I found myself reframing them to Liz in a more hopeful way. I told her my thoughts: "This burden of consciousness, while a difficult one, also offers hope for a world where human beings relate to one another with compassion. When we begin to have compassion for women, for the lonely responsibility they bear, we'll carry part of their burden too. Just as when we begin to have compassion for the dilemma of the doctor who facilitates the death of a terminally ill patient instead of blaming him for shortening a life, we too will begin to shoulder the heavy fate of being human. The spark of consciousness that makes us human also enables us to become aware of the soul-wounds we have the power to cause in others who are grappling with the most profound of human issues. It's this very consciousness, so hard to bear, that may ultimately enable us to *contain* our power to injure and destroy, rather than to enact our impulses in violent acts."

We looked at each other, then, drained from the heaviness of these thoughts. Finally I smiled at Liz and said, "Whew!" She returned my smile and said, "I feel so grateful that I can come here. Your empathy and understanding are providing me with such a special place for my feelings."

"I'm grateful, too," I replied, and with that we ended the session.

Later, recalling this session with Liz, I give more thought to my sense of myself as a murderer. Clearly, whether an unborn child is viewed as an actual or as a potential life, for a woman to choose to end this life means breaking a sacred taboo. Just as incest is a sacred taboo, so too is infanticide. To choose abortion truly means daring to cross a moral boundary. I think of the agony of Abraham when God required that he sacrifice his son, Isaac. I think about the agony of Agamemnon, king of Mycenae, leader of the Greek expedition against Troy, as he faced the necessity of sacrificing his daughter, Iphigenia. I remember the scene in the movie *Iphigenia* in which Agamemnon's warriors were stranded on the beach, unable to sail for Troy because there was no wind stirring the sultry, stagnant air, no wind that could propel the boats. I remember how Agamemnon believed the oracle who foretold that the sacrifice of his favorite daughter would bring the wind so that his restive soldiers could move out to war. Ultimately Agamemnon made the choice to sacrifice his beloved daughter, despite the anguished pleas of Iphigenia as she begged for her life. I try to think about the symbolic meaning of Agamemnon's dreadful choice because its literal meaning is too painful. Symbolically the message I derive from this Greek myth is that the Feminine, represented in the form of the young woman Iphigenia, has to die, has to be sacrificed—killed—in order for the Masculine, in the form of Agamemnon and his warriors, to yield to the irresistible pull toward war and triumph.

It strikes me that both these examples, Abraham from the Bible and Agamemnon from Greek myth, are stories derived from a patriarchal culture. In both stories there is empathy for the fathers who, tested by male gods, must choose to sacrifice their children. Yet there is a striking absence of empathy in patriarchal culture, either in ancient or in modern times, for women who choose abortion or, more specifically, choose to murder their children. The myth of Medea comes to my mind as one example from the past. Medea is the woman who commits the unthinkable act of murdering her children in a state of unimaginable rage at their father, who has left her for another woman. She seeks vengeance and, rendered utterly helpless, is unable to channel her anguish in any other direction. There is no compassion for Medea; her act is viewed with abhorrence.

My thoughts of Medea lead me to the contemporary example provided by William Styron's novel, *Sophie's Choice*. How interesting, I think, that this book was a best-seller and was later made into a successful movie. Something about its theme must have resonated with a large number of people. The book affected me deeply; I found it both difficult to read and also impossible to forget. While not specifically concerned with the abortion of an unborn child, the novel is concerned with a situation in which a mother must choose whether an existing child will live or die at the hands of the Nazis. Sophie, confronted by a sadistic Nazi guard, is told that only one of her two children will be allowed to live: "You must choose!" the guard cruelly orders. In response to this command, Sophie chooses one of her children to live and allows the other to be sent to death. Ironically, the child she permits to live ultimately perishes in the concentration camp, thereby rendering her choice meaningless in the end. In the novel, as in ordinary reality, Sophie, like any mother, cannot completely control the destiny of either of her children. Crazed with grief, unable to live with having made her choice, she ultimately chooses suicide for herself and perishes.

I am struck by the thought that even in this modern tale it is a woman who must endure alone the unimaginable, unthinkable, and ultimately unbearable responsibility for choosing life or death for a living child. Sophie does not receive a hero's reward, like Abraham, for successfully meeting a difficult challenge, nor does she have Agamemnon's justification of carrying the responsibilities of a king. Like Medea's husband, the Nazi guard and the cruel order he issued fade into the background, and the spotlight shines on Sophie, who ultimately did not have the power to protect the life of either child or herself. Her belief that she had the power to choose life or death for either of her children was only an illusion, yet she took on a blame so enormous, so unbearable, that it ultimately caused her to lose her life.

The stories of Abraham, Agamemnon, Medea, and Sophie suggest that we have different attitudes toward women who exercise the power to choose whether a child lives or dies than toward men (or male gods) who exercise the same power. Medea's choice, Sophie's choice, and perhaps the choice of ordinary nameless women to have an abortion has a different quality, is taboo in a way that is different from the choice made by Abraham and Agamemnon. I wonder what would happen if men had the awesome capacity to become pregnant and nurture new life. Would women condemn them, based on *logos* principles alone, if they chose to end the lives of their unborn children? Or would they combine such principles with *agape*, empathy and compassion? In this culture,

needs and toward the imperfect mother who cannot protect her child from the dangers that exist in an indifferent universe?

It seems clear to me that we need a protective mechanism that is less destructive than this injunction limiting the rights and power of women. Instead of channeling energy into *assaulting* women for exercising the power to choose life or death for their unborn children, it seems to me that we could all profit from becoming aware of and restraining the power we have to injure and destroy others in a multitude of circumstances. I think of the many ways we have of symbolically wounding, or murdering, those we love and how we do so without even realizing it.

In this context I think about the recent game of Monopoly that I played with Ben and Becky. My connections to the game of Monopoly go back to childhood, when I played it endlessly with my best friend. I would go to her house early in the morning, more than an hour before we had to leave for school, and we would retrieve the game board from beneath her bed, where we had stored it the night before. Our games were very serious and lasted for days. Our absorption was intense; through experience we learned the ins and outs of investment strategy until we could sense exactly how much money we could safely place without overextending ourselves in "property improvement" (houses and hotels), and the best trades of property we could negotiate, and until we could even intuit whether a "Chance" or "Community Chest" card would be favorable or costly. We were evenly matched, both in the intelligence we brought to the game and in our capacity to learn from our experience. Consequently our games usually ended without a winner, arbitrarily terminated by mutual agreement. I do not know how many years our interest lasted; my memory is only of the intensity and single-mindedness of this interest and not of the chronological span of time.

It amazes me that I haven't played Monopoly at all for thirty years. My children have owned the game for at least four years and have occasionally played it, but never with the degree of focus I once devoted to it. In fact, despite my childhood pleasure in playing a whole variety of games

(Parcheesi, Scrabble, Sorry, Go to the Head of the Class, Clue, Solitaire and other card games, such as War), I never play games at all as an adult. Whatever I needed to master through games I mastered as a child and now no longer need them. I must have acquired the cognitive skills they develop and gained sufficient mastery of my competitive and assertive strivings. Nor do I now play games very often with my children; my guilt at not giving them enough quality time and attention is assuaged by the fact that the three of them are able to play the games among themselves whenever they choose. They do not often choose this activity, perhaps because we live in an age of computers and television, perhaps because they do not have the same need to master game skills that I had.

The incident I recall took place on our recent family trip to a rented house that made available a number of games, including Monopoly. After we returned from the trip, I recorded the experience in my journal, so haunting was its effect on me.

It is a gray, rainy day, and, unable to go to the beach or play outside, Ben and Becky set up the Monopoly game. I laugh to myself, thinking how unusual it is to see them cooperate with one another; cooperation for them is a state of relationship that always reflects an exactly equal degree of need on both their parts. After several relatively short games together, with my occasional interjections of advice and counsel, they ask me to play with them. For a long time I resist, preferring to read. But even when I finish my own book, I find myself still resistant to becoming involved in the game. This resistance puzzles me: Why would I have no interest in a game I so enjoyed as a child? Why would I refuse to spend time in this way with my children on a trip? On impulse, in this state of puzzlement, I agree to play with them.

It is amazing how the thirty-year gap disappears in a moment. I instantly recall all the rules, the names of the properties, even the rents, and recognize my favorites. My knowledge seems to reside in my body; my hands automatically move my marker the exact number of spaces without counting, find the correct amount of money without thought. And my old interest returns; I take great pleasure in my competence, my capacity to make judgments, investments, trades. I do not feel at all competitive with my children; in fact, I devote attention to instructing and advising them on their own moves, literally teaching them my skills. This new role is just as pleasurable as my own competence in the game.

My knack for the game compensates for any lack of luck, and my age and experience clearly put me in an altogether separate sphere from my seven-year-old son and eleven-year-old daughter, who so infrequently play the game. It is only about an hour until I acquire two sets of property on the third most expensive side of the four-sided board. In only another half an hour, I have put hotels on one set and three houses on the other, impoverishing myself in ready cash, but making myself rich in rental possibilities.

The inevitable moment of "murder" arrives soon. Ben lands on my highest rated property with a hotel. His rent is the astounding sum of $975. Ben looks at me, bewildered: "What do I do, Mommy?" Becky, who normally would volunteer herself as his executioner, fingers his small store of play money helplessly and says accusingly, "He doesn't have that much money, Mommy. He can't help it; he just doesn't have it." Both of them sit and stare at me in bewilderment, stare at the mother who at this moment they can no longer count upon to protect, provide, care for, and nourish them. I stare back, just as confused: I, too, do not know what to do.

Within moments the feelings connected to annihilating my own little boy in the once-favorite game mount. I cannot bear having defeated my son so abruptly, so unexpectedly. I cannot bear the stunned and bewildered looks of my children. I stand up and tell them, "I can't play this anymore. I can't stand feeling like this," and I walk away. I am aware that they try to continue playing without me, as if I had simply evaporated. Of course, it is impossible for them to continue in this way for very long, and they soon stop and abandon the game. Some time later Michael puts away the game; somehow the three of us cannot bring ourselves to return to the setting of the awesome moment when I vanquished my son.

We haven't talked about our game since, but I have filed the experience away both in my own memory and in my journal. Now it serves to remind me of the many ways in which we as parents symbolically murder our children in the seemingly trivial interactions of ordinary life, without even noticing.

Should I have behaved as a model of a good winner and taught my son to tolerate defeat, taught him that winning and losing are part of any game? Perhaps I conveyed to Becky and Ben that it is unbearable to be successful, to defeat others, that winning is intolerable because it elicits guilt that is too great to be borne. Maybe I left them with the sense that games are too serious, are not played just for fun. Others might think that my experience of the abortion left me with an unnecessary residue of sensitivity and that I am excessively or unnecessarily worried about hurting my children's feelings, but this explanation does not match my feelings.

I prefer to think of that appalling moment in terms of the way I felt it at the time and in terms of the way I saw my children respond: It was a moment in which I vanquished my son, causing shock and bewilderment in my children and in myself. I prefer to let this experience remind me that, while I cannot restore the life of my lost fourth child, I can remain aware of my potentially annihilating effect on my living children. I can be aware, and restrain, the murdering parent within myself.

I meditate again upon what a different world it would be if we could each become aware of and take responsibility for our capacity to annihilate others! In such a world we would be less likely to judge women for making the impossible choice between the life of an unborn child, her own life, and that of other family members. Perhaps in such a world we would be able to help women make the best possible choice and then help them shoulder whatever burden of sorrow might result from that choice. Perhaps we might even be able to honor them for their courage in the face of unavoidable loss.

Alone with these thoughts, I begin to cry. I am crying because I have become aware of yet another facet of the loss

of my unborn child. I wish now that my fourth child could
have been sacrificed with my love and tears, even with my
own hands, in the circle of a family or a community of
women, in the circle of a compassionate and loving community of men and women who might be able to perceive my
vulnerability as a mirror of their own, and not as it was, in a
cold and lonely hospital room with instruments of steel. I
wish now that I might then have mourned my loss openly, in
full view of my fellow sojourners, and seen my own sorrow
reflected in their compassionate regard for me and for the
child who could not be. My feelings would not have been less
painful, my grief would not have been diminished. But I
would not have been so alone.

ELEVEN

Exploring the Realm of the Feminine

The woman who . . . feels compelled to choose abortion, seldom experiences it lightly. Despite frequent rhetoric to the contrary, few women see abortion as easy birth control. Rather, it is a kind of amputation. Abortion removes something whose existence simultaneously threatens yet forms a new part of a woman's very selfhood. . . .

Such pain over the baby who might have been receives no ritual recognition in our culture. But in Japan a very different attitude prevails. Instead of demonizing abortion and stigmatizing women who choose it as does the Judeo-Christian tradition, Japanese Buddhism recognizes abortion as a deeply disturbing part of some women's lives. To help a woman acknowledge her anguish over choosing not to bear a child who might have been, common practice permits her to place a special statue at a shrine. This statue represents Jizo, a Buddhist bodhisattva especially dedicated to the care of children's souls. Such statues commemorating dead fetuses may range in size from a few inches to about a foot. They resemble abstract human forms lacking specific features. Rows and rows of them stand at shrines, rather like gravestones in a cemetery. Placing one of these figures in its appropriate setting allows a woman to acknowledge in ritual a painful experience that our own culture largely passes over in silence once the abortion has been performed.

—KATHRYN ALLEN RABUZZI
Motherself: A Mythic Analysis of Motherhood[1]

Over the next weeks my meditations continue. I realize that the legalization of abortion by the relatively recent *Roe v. Wade* Supreme Court decision has actually enabled complex psychological issues to be brought to the surface. When abortions were illegal, women who sought them had to devote all their time and attention to finding a way to arrange for one. Even now, for women who cannot easily afford an abortion, financial need occupies all the available psychological space, leaving no room for addressing the emotional and psychological issues that abortion raises. I hope that the more complicated issues are not pushed back underground by a change in the law, because I believe that grappling with them can lead to a greater understanding of the feminine realm so neglected in our patriarchal culture. I am convinced that all of us would reap the benefit of a greater understanding of feminine experience. Given the complicated set of feelings and responses I am now coping with, I sometimes wish that I had only had to worry about obtaining and paying for an abortion. But I remind myself when this wish overtakes me that although these worries might seem at first glance to be simpler concerns, psychologically they are not necessarily less painful. I know this from an old but very real set of personal encounters with women.

Memory carries me back more than twenty years. I remember Margo, a friend of the roommate I had during my first year in graduate school. Margo was the first woman I ever met who needed an abortion. Her primary concern was whether she could collect enough money from friends to be able to fly to Mexico for an abortion because she could not obtain one in the United States. We gave what we could—women who hardly knew her were willing to contribute—and off Margo went. She was fortunate and survived her experience with little apparent physical or psychological distress.

Thoughts of Margo remind me of Carolyn, a mutual acquaintance who was not so lucky. Carolyn, too, went to Mexico for her abortion but returned with an infection, for which she was afraid to seek treatment from a local doctor. I remember how anxious we all were as we tried to care for her ourselves, waiting to see whether she could recover on her own, without antibiotics. Young as we were, we still knew that an uncontrolled infection could mean death. Anxiety about life and death occupied all the psychological space we had and left no room in any of us for feelings of loss about her baby. Like Margo, Carolyn was fortunate; she was ill for a long time, but eventually recovered.

Thoughts of Carolyn take me to Katrin, who was then only nineteen years old, prominent in campus politics and thus extremely vulnerable to any negatively tinged public exposure. She became pregnant and she, too, had an illegal abortion in Mexico. I remember the horror we felt when she talked about her experience and shared her impression that, after she was given medication to relax her for the procedure, she was raped by the doctor. While she was still struggling to absorb the traumatic experience of the abortion and the rape, she, like Carolyn, developed an infection that eventually became serious enough to force her to seek medical attention from a local physician. The physician treated her, then reported her to the police. Subsequently she faced an investigation, which was not only personally painful and distressing but publicly humiliating as well.

The tangled knot of my memories continues to unravel. My thoughts turn to my relatively new friend, Alison, who is now an attractive woman in her early forties. She has a solid marriage and enjoys mothering her two adored adolescent children (to the extent that it is possible to enjoy parenting adolescents). When she learned about my unplanned fourth pregnancy, she confided in me a private part of her own past, dating back to her twenties, a time long before we had met each other. In listening to her, I was aware both of the gift she was giving me in opening this locked cupboard of her life and of my sadness that her experience had never been part of our intimate conversations before. Just as men and women often hesitate to talk about divorce, as if it implies failure and an incapacity to maintain an intimate relationship, a stigma is attached to abortion, a dark shadow of shame hovering over it, which keeps women isolated and alone with their experience, walled off from the comfort and support that could come from sharing.

On that day when our personal relationship deepened, Alison told me that when she left her family to go to college, three new experiences came, one after the other: She had her first serious boyfriend, her first sexual experience, and her first pregnancy. Certain that it was not the right time in her life for either marriage or motherhood, she had no doubt that she must have an abortion. On her own, through the college underground network, she found a doctor who referred her to a clinic in Mexico. All alone, she took a plane to the West Coast and then rode a bus for a full day to get to the clinic. She then underwent an abortion in a strange, dirty clinic, in a completely calm, dispassionate state, without any anxiety or fear. When it was over, she rested there for a short time and then took the next available bus north. On the way, the bus made a rest stop. She went into the white-tiled bathroom with the three private stalls separated by gray metal doors. Alone for the first time, she closed the metal door and leaned her head against it, cradling her head in her arms. Enormous relief washed over her, cleansing her of any physical discomfort. She did not experience then, she confided to me, nor has she yet experienced a single moment's regret about her choice. But she added, "I didn't have any children then, and I didn't understand the quality of attachment a mother instinctively feels toward her child. I know I could never have an abortion now without having the kind of feelings you're struggling with."

I wonder what has happened to Margo, to Carolyn, to Katrin? How have they absorbed their abortions into their adult lives? Have more complex thoughts and feelings surfaced for them, or have their abortions remained hidden in the recesses of their unconscious minds? Now that abortion has been legalized, we can begin to explore the psychological complexity of the experience for women, as well as for the men involved. Freedom to begin this exploration represents evolution toward a culture that balances the complementary masculine and feminine principles. But we have some distance to go before all the dimensions of the experience of abortion can be adequately addressed and forms created to help women (as well as men) manage the painful emotions and potential crises of soul that this experience can bring about.

I go to have lunch with Margaret, and we take up the abortion issue. Margaret puts forth her opinion, similar to the feeling Alison had shared with me, that age and stage of development make a difference in a woman's reaction to having an abortion. She tells me, "I think that because you were approaching midlife and had already borne living children, the abortion was more painful and had a different meaning to you than it would have to a younger woman."

"You know that I had an abortion when I was eighteen," she reminds me soberly, picking at her salad indifferently. "But I was completely undeveloped psychologically then. I was totally preoccupied with not wanting to have a baby at that point in my life. The unborn baby had no reality to me. I think a woman's response to an abortion is going to depend on her stage of life and her circumstances, as well as to her particular consciousness."

"I think you're right," I reply. "My own reaction certainly has to do with my own special psychological makeup. That's true for every woman. But I also know that young women can have powerful reactions to an abortion, too." I tell Margaret the story of the eighteen-year-old young woman who began therapy with me some years ago because she was having recurrent nightmares. The scene of her nightmares was always the same: the hospital in which she aborted the child that she and her boyfriend had conceived. Repeatedly in her dreams she relived the surgical procedure, experiencing over and over again the coldness of the hospital, the coldness of the instruments, the coldness of the doctor and nurses, whom she perceived to be judging her harshly, as if she had been mindlessly promiscuous rather than swept up in the throes of romantic love only to find herself saddled with responsibilities beyond her years. Once I could provide her with a reflection of her own distress and the support for her personal struggle that was unavailable to her from either her boyfriend or her parents, who were coping with their own anxieties, she was eventually able to work through her experience consciously, in my presence, rather than alone at night in frightening dreams. "Although age and stage of life do make a difference," I tell Margaret as I conclude my thoughts, "there are clearly some women at every age and stage of life who have trouble deciding to have an abortion. I think it's imperative to consider the meaning of abortion within the psychological context of each woman's life. Besides, women can have reactions about an abortion years later, even if they didn't have a particularly intense response to it at the time— particularly during life phases that are critical for women, such as when they give birth or have their last child or go through menopause." I think to myself about Liz and the difficulties she has been experiencing so many years later.

"I suppose so," Margaret says, sighing. "It's an impossible situation! And you're right about one thing—we're only beginning to find ways to work with these reactions in a positive way."

Only a few weeks after my lunch with Margaret, I have a consultation hour with Lee. She is a young woman therapist who has been seeing me weekly for consultation about her own psychotherapy practice. When she arrives for her scheduled appointment, I greet her with my usual smile but notice right away that she seems preoccupied. She sits down on the couch in my office and curls her legs up under her. Then, as if she is cold, she wraps around her shoulders the plaid blanket that I brought back years ago from a trip to Canada and keep folded at one end of the couch. Usually Lee sits in a businesslike position, legs crossed and notebook on her lap. What could possibly be going on, I wonder.

Abruptly Lee asks me, "Have you ever had an abortion?" Stunned by this unexpected and direct personal question, a complete deviation from our well-established and professional supervisory relationship, I almost blurt out, "Yes!" without hesitation. A long-entrenched habit of taking advantage of every opportunity to explore meanings rather than to foreclose possibilities with an impulsive response takes over; I manage to ask her why she is curious. She then tells me that she had an abortion three days ago. She had become pregnant early in a new and potentially permanent relationship with a man. Neither of them was ready to rush into parenthood or into marriage, and together they decided that an abortion was the most sensible choice. But, fond of children though not a parent herself, Lee did not find this decision easy to make. "I feel such pain, I don't know what to do!" she exclaims, breaking down and sobbing. "I even called my mother and told her! Actually I was surprised at how supportive she was. We usually fight a lot and can argue about anything, and yet I instinctively wanted to talk to her about this—and she really came through!"

Listening to Lee, I think about the profound moment of contact I had with my mother when we stood outside the Chinese restaurant and looked at each other. I think about the many mothers who accompany their teenage daughters to abortion clinics, knowing by virtue of their age and life experience the complexity of the experience their daughters are about to undergo. I picture these mothers struggling with their ambivalence about abortion and their wishes for a grandchild, nonetheless stoically supporting their daughters through the procedure. These mother-daughter contacts surely must have something to do with gaining access to the feminine bond that I had felt with my mother, and to the source of feminine wisdom that I talked about with my client Liz.

I think about the missed connections between other mothers and daughters, the painful ruptures that critical judgment, centered only in the rational *logos* principle, can create in the absence of the *agape* qualities of empathy and compassion. I recall how, at the beginning of my own unplanned pregnancy, Michael and I were virtually torn apart when we limited ourselves to this rational perspective, trying to find the "right" choice when none existed. I recall Dr. Ross's perception of the abortion: He objectified the pregnancy into a problem, saw the abortion as the appropriate solution, and then, like me, was bewildered and stunned by the intensity of my emotional reaction. I recapture memories of my father's warm, supportive voice, reassuring me that I had made the correct decision, and find myself swallowing yet again the lump that rises in my throat as the pain wells up anew. Michael, my father, Dr. Ross, I, even my women friends— all of us were conditioned to respond in the traditionally masculine mode of approaching complex moral issues from the perspective of rational principles. None of us had access to words with which we could articulate the psychological and emotional dimensions; we could not offer or receive feelings rooted in *agape*.

A new thought occurs to me: I wonder whether another dimension of the masculine principle with which we are so familiar is expressed in our conception of a hero and in our conviction that heroes overcome obstacles through their resolute and courageous action. The myth of the hero to which I refer is exemplified in the fairy tale we hear in childhood, where typically the prince wins the princess by meeting a series of difficult challenges. It seems to me that there is a problem, a lack of balance, reflected in these stories. The problem that I see is not that the heroes are men—this imbalance can be corrected by creating stories with female "heroes"— but that a corresponding and complementary myth of the *heroine* is absent. The myth of the heroine, as relevant for both men and women as is the myth of the hero, would be exemplified in the story of a woman (or man) who, instead of *acting* courageously to meet challenges that are imposed from without, simply *endures* with fortitude the challenges that life inevitably brings. Only now am I beginning to understand that the silent shouldering of sorrow requires as much courage as the taking of action. And just as women can follow the path of the traditionally male hero, so, too, can men hold firm and withstand sorrow.

Through the veil of these thoughts I hear Lee telling me

how empathically her mother listened to her: "My mother is such an extraverted person, full of energy, who likes to talk and be the center of attention. But she just sat and listened to me cry." I am glad for Lee that she was able to reach her mother on this feminine plane.

Today, rather than focusing on her cases, Lee and I continue talking about her abortion. During this hour I eventually tell her that I, too, had an abortion, and I refer her to Karen Ortman for some special counseling.

Some weeks later Lee reports back to me that she went to see Karen, just as I had, for a limited number of sessions until she reached a state of resolution about her choice and was able to identify the specific aspects of it that had triggered her despair.

For Lee, as for me, an abortion had led to a crisis of soul, though unlike mine, hers had been responded to immediately and effectively rather than allowed to spiral out of control. Such crises, I realize, are often felt as shameful, or seen as signs of weakness if not pathology in the person experiencing them. As a result, women do not dare to put intense experiences into words, words that could enable the experiences to be shared. More often than not, I imagine, experiences of abortion are locked away as quickly as possible, both in order that life can return to its ordinary, stable level and also because there is no other choice. Almost all other losses from death in this culture can be openly grieved, mourned in existing ritual forms. But soul-crises such as mine, if experienced within an empathic and compassionate human relationship, within a culture that makes room for them without judgment and condemnation, have the possibility of becoming opportunities for personal growth and transformation rather than dreadful experiences simply to be endured and survived.

I realize, as I ruminate about crises of soul, that abortion is only one trigger for a crisis of soul. There are others. I think of the many issues that arise from being female—miscarriage, having a child with birth defects, infertility, menopause, hysterectomy, ovarian cancer, mastectomy. Any one of these might precipitate a profound crisis for a woman (and men who are involved with women grappling with such crises may also be vulnerable to crises of soul). Even normal life transitions, such as having one's children grow up and leave home, can trigger a crisis of soul, the crisis that occurs when a *definition* former sense of self is irretrievably lost and a new one has not yet evolved. As women become increasingly able to take their life experiences seriously, I know we will begin to create forms that will mark, honor, and hold the feelings that events such as these evoke.

I meet my friend Judith at our favorite Japanese restaurant for lunch. Judith sits quietly for a moment once we have ordered our usual fare of teriyaki chicken and then takes a deep breath. "I've never told you this before, but I want to tell you now. Even though I didn't face the choice you had to make—an unplanned pregnancy—I had to face a situation that evoked the same kind of anguish. When I remarried, Rob and I wanted to have a child together, but I just couldn't conceive. Finally we went through endless fertility tests. They were horribly humiliating! And none of them revealed any physical problem, but I still didn't get pregnant. Coming to terms with my inability to have a biological child with Rob has been very hard for me. We so badly wanted to raise a child together; that experience cements a relationship in a special way; nothing else can come close to it. And Rob has had to accept the fact that he will never father a child of his own. I guess for men that issue corresponds to what a woman goes through when she's infertile. When I couldn't conceive a child, I wanted to adopt one, but Rob had already adopted my daughter from my first marriage and he didn't want to adopt another child, even though I pleaded with him to consider it."

Her voice trails off into silence, and she looks down at the shiny Formica tabletop. She has told her story so concisely, yet I can completely grasp the unspoken feelings that are silent companions to her words. My problem related to childbearing was caused by being too fertile; Judith's pain originated in being infertile for reasons unknown. Beneath this paradoxical set of opposites, our deep grief in this moment arising from our relation to childbearing brings us close to each other.

But I have not yet heard all of Judith's story. She looks up at me and continues: "You won't believe this, but just at this difficult time in my life, I found myself in the practically unbearable position of being the close friend of a woman— you don't know her, she's a friend of mine from high school who isn't married—who became pregnant unintentionally. She didn't want to have an abortion and finally made the decision to give birth to the baby but give it up for adoption. I ended up being available to her for emotional support all through her pregnancy, the birth, and even through the eventual adoption of her baby. The whole time I wanted so badly to adopt her baby myself. It was so hard to see that little baby, a really adorable boy, go to another family. I never told her that I would have given anything to be able to raise her child with Rob."

Judith stops then and looks down at the table again, while I sigh and think about how the strength and courage to bear emotional suffering that women have always had around such issues is often manifested in silent, solitary struggles. Silent and solitary, that is, until our culture develops that myth of the heroine to complement the well-known story of masculine heroes.

After lunch I drive Judith the short distance to her car, and we sit for a moment with the motor running, prolonging our time together. As I put the car into the parking gear and no longer need to watch where I am going, I glance over at my friend. I am shocked to see pain in her ordinarily calm face, even tears in her eyes. Responding to my look of concern, Judith tells me, "I was just thinking about my therapy with the male therapist I was seeing when the issue of infertility came up for me. I remember how I told him I was worried that I might not be able to get pregnant. He just shook his head and told me not to worry, that if I just relaxed, I would get pregnant. I must have realized at that very moment that he was shutting a door; I was not going to be able to move into the suffering I feel around my fertility, not with him. He couldn't appreciate the depth of my feeling. But the pain I feel now, sitting here, is for myself, for seeing how I've learned not to question, not to ask for a different response from men, not to break that sacred web. And it's the pain of knowing what I didn't realize at that time, that infertility is a special subject—it belongs to the realm of the feminine, and my male analyst was too grounded in the masculine to appreciate that. And I wasn't grounded enough in the feminine principle to know better."

We sit together in sadness for a moment and then hug good-bye.

I learn of another soul crisis arising from a friend's mastectomy. Madeline, a colleague whom I had not seen for a while, recently had a modified radical mastectomy (modified, perhaps, as a medical procedure, but nonetheless radical psychologically). She and I together find striking parallels in our different situations during a recent lunch that we schedule specifically to talk about our difficult times. Like me, Madeline found that she wanted to protect a space for herself to make the choices that were right for her rather than those that would make tasks easier for the physicians or that are more commonly chosen by other women. For example, with this guideline in mind, she chose not to give permission for an immediate breast removal if the initial biopsy indicated cancer cells. Separating the two procedures in this way gave her the vital time she needed to seek other opinions, to educate herself about the procedure, and to prepare psychologically for the removal of her breast.

Later she chose to look at her body only one week after the surgery, when her bandages were first unwrapped, even though her surgeon, whom she liked and respected, recommended that she wait another week so that the wound would have more time to heal, and so that, though he did not consciously realize it, she would be less likely to call upon him to soothe her distress. Is the mutilation of the female body yet another trigger for unthinkable anxiety, evocative of the murderous rage that the helpless child feels toward its all-powerful mother? In any case, Madeline found the sight of the scar less terrible than she had expected and was glad she had chosen to look at it. Her surgeon told her, as she looked at herself, that the majority of his patients accept his recommendation to wait before seeing themselves. Together Madeline and I recognize how much better she would have felt had he said to her, "Your wound will look much better one week from now. If you look at it now and feel upset, go right ahead and cry, and I'll be here with you." Or if he felt unable to be present in the face of distress, he might have said, "I just hate to see my patients cry, so I'm going to have my nurse, who's very good at that, come in and be with you. Take all the time you need; this is a big moment." But to respond in that way, he would have had to allow room for the feminine principle within himself.

While other women, upon hearing of Madeline's plight, came forward to share their own personal experiences with her, often in courageous ways, Madeline noted that they were able to find words to describe their physical trauma and recovery far more readily than they could articulate the course of their psychological responses. Some friends, not knowing what to say or how to put their feelings into words, avoided contact with her altogether. If they were unable to avoid seeing her at work or in social situations, they simply did not allude to this major event in her life at all. Just as we are only beginning to find words to describe the inner experience of a crisis of soul, both because ordinary language fails us and because we are still encumbered by shame, we are also only beginning to know how to respond in words to others who are in the midst of deep psychological turmoil.

I think of yet another example of soul crisis that many men and women face: widowhood. I have not yet come across an account of this experience by a widower, and until Lynn Caine wrote about her own experience in her book, *Widow*, the inner response of a woman to this experience had also not yet found its way into words or into a form, such as a book, that would be readily accessible to women at large. An older woman I know who has been a widow for some time said to me at a social gathering some months ago, "It's still terribly lonely, even though my husband has been gone for six years now. But I don't tell anyone about it. People don't really want to hear your problems, so if you tell them, they just stay away from you. Then the loneliness gets even worse." I had listened to her and thought to myself, what about the loneliness of being with people yet unable to say what you are in fact thinking and feeling. I can understand the fear that if we once yield to despair, we will be lost forever in a black hole from which we cannot emerge. When I was in the midst of my own worst pain, I could not imagine I would ever feel anything else. I could not have known then that the possibility of new life, a new path, would actually lead me out of the black hole of despair.

Well, I tell myself, women are not the only human beings to experience crises of soul. Such experiences, though they cannot begin to be articulated in words until men become freer to expose vulnerability, arise for men too. I think of the man, a client of mine, who is currently facing a difficult decision. His father is slowly dying of kidney failure as a result of a rather rare disease. For five years the father has survived on dialysis, but now is deteriorating physically to the point where he is having intermittent convulsions, severe pain, and occasional delusional episodes. His doctor has informed my client and the client's two siblings that they must decide whether or not their father should continue on dialysis. It is unclear whether their father will be lucid long enough to make such a decision himself, though the doctors cannot know for certain that he will not have a period of remission. My client is the oldest child and the only son. His younger sisters are relying upon him to lead the decision-making process. In a recent session with me, my client asks me how he can possibly make such a choice. "How will I live with any decision I make?" he asks. "If I choose to end the dialysis, even with the concurrence and support of my sisters, even with encouragement from the doctors, how will I endure the last days of my father's life, watching him be slowly poisoned? How will I survive with the memories of this experience in my mind? Will I be left to worry whether or not I made the right choice or whether my father might have recovered sufficiently to choose for himself? I never imagined in my wildest dreams that I'd ever have to take on this responsibility. I've always looked up to my dad; he's always been strong, and now our roles are reversed." Men, too, certainly require a firm holding environment for crises of soul and need both *logos* and *agape* principles operating in harmony to provide support and guidance.

My crisis over the abortion and tubal ligation, as well as Liz's and Lee's about their abortions, and Judith's around her infertility, or Madeline's response to her mastectomy, were all profound in their own way. It seems to me that solid grounding in both principles—cognitive, rational notions of right and wrong as well as empathy, compassion, and relatedness—is essential if such crises as these are to be worked with productively so that healing can occur and the positive transformative potential of the crisis realized.

Just as the feminine principle of *agape* has been subordinate to the *logos* principle in our culture, the vast realm of female experience has also been subordinate and unexplored, at least until recently as the feminist movement has taken hold. Without an affirmation of the importance of the realm of female experience, which we are only now beginning to explore, the sacred aspect of the feminine connection, through female biological function, to life and death will remain lost. Without a connection to the realm of feminine experience, women cannot know that their creativity need not be limited to creating new biological life, that they have within them the potential to gestate and give birth to new life on a psychological plane as well. Restoring the lost connection to my feminine heritage and marking my passage from a life phase of biological creativity to one of psychological or spiritual generativity is to be the final part of my quest.

TWELVE

Reconnecting to the Feminine Part I

we need a god who bleeds now
a god whose wounds are not
some small male vengeance
some pitiful concession to humility
a desert swept with dryin marrow in honor of the lord

we need a god who bleeds
spreads her lunar vulva & showers us in shades of scarlet
thick & warm like the breath of her
our mothers tearing to let us in
this place breaks open
like our mothers bleeding
the planet is heaving, mourning our ignorance
the moon tugs the seas
to hold her/ to hold her
embrace swelling hills/ i am
not wounded i am bleeding to life

we need a god who bleeds now
whose wounds are not the end of anything
                    —NTOZAKE SHANGE
                    "We Need a God Who Bleeds Now"[1]

On my own, I begin to do some reading and research and learn that other cultures that are less predominantly patriarchal in form do have rites of passage—rituals of initiation—for young women in puberty. As an outsider to these rituals, I find myself regarding them as not only foreign but as alarming and primitive at times. I cannot imagine enduring some of the ceremonial procedures that the young initiates manage to survive, such as fasting, wearing hot buckskin clothing in summer, running long distances, being painted with ochre. Yet there are other aspects of the ceremony that awaken a hunger in me: the public affirmation of the young girl's new status as woman, the presence of her father and other men in the community welcoming her into the next phase of life, the circle of women who lovingly adorn her in ceremonial clothing, the expression of satisfaction I picture on her face and of pride in the eyes of her parents. Above all, the simple beauty of the blessings and chants that honor womanhood evokes this yearning.

I discover the five-day ritual in which the Mescalero Apache Indians sing the girls of their tribe into puberty; they believe that this ritual, a reenactment of their creation myth, enhances fertility and accounts for the increase in the numbers of their tribe. Special male singers honor the young women; their status and power is enhanced rather than diminished by acknowledging the status and power of women. At the end of the five-day ritual, the girls are escorted to a runway that is surrounded by their fathers and male relatives. In turn, they step upon four crescent moons that are painted with colors that represent both the four directions and the stages of life. On the first such stepping-stone, which represents the onset of puberty, the following song is sung:

237

Now you are entering the world.
You become an adult with responsibilities.
Now you are entering the world.
Behold yourself
Walk in this world with honor and dignity.
Let no man speak of you in shame.
For you will become—
The mother of a nation.[2]

I come upon the Blessing Way ceremony of the Navaho
Indians. Unlike our culture, in which young girls feel shame
and a need to conceal their first period, the Navaho have
ceremonies that honor the first menstruation of young women
in the tribe:

A girl for whom it is the very first time—she still not being
united with a man so that children will be born— the very
first time that the blood flows through her she tells about
it:

"Blood has indeed flowed through me," she says as she
tells about it. "Now it is all right! You say that you have
become menstruant!" In this way, when she tells about it,
she at once comes to be called Menstruating for the First
Time. All right! Now it is this way: at once she is decorated. She is decorated with beads, she is decorated with
bracelets. A tanned skin is inquired about, the skin of a
deer which has not been killed with a gun, the skin of one
which has not been killed with an arrow. That is called
One Which is Not Arrow-marked. That is what they
inquire of each other about. . . . Even if it is small, even if
it is narrow, it is obtained.[3]

In addition to these alternative ways of welcoming young
girls into the stage of mature womanhood, I come upon the
ceremonies of other American Indian tribes in Arizona.[4] I
find that the Oglala Sioux, as part of their initiation of young
girls into womanhood, have Slow Buffalo's Prayer:

O you, White Swan, Power of the place where we always face, who control the path of the generations and of all that moves, we are about to purify a virgin, that her generations to come may walk in a sacred manner upon that path which You control. . . .

O Mother Earth, who gives forth fruit, and who is as a mother to the generations, this young virgin who is here today will be purified and made sacred; may she be like You, and may her children and her children's children walk the sacred path in the holy manner.[5]

I cannot help but wonder what it would have been like to have been able to rejoice publicly in the occurrence of my first period and to have been surrounded by an entire community of men and women welcoming me so proudly and naturally into my new status.

Closer to home, within my chosen professional field, I read the words of Esther Harding, a physician trained in London who went on to study under C. G. Jung and become a Jungian analyst. She wrote extensively on feminine psychology, capturing the essential feminine experience so accurately that her ideas have withstood the passage of time. My abortion and tubal-ligation experiences become magnifying lenses that amplify the meaning of her ideas. Her words are surprisingly matter of fact and ordinary, yet profoundly true:

For to women, life itself *is* cyclic. The life force ebbs and flows in her actual experience, not only in nightly and daily rhythm as it does for a man, but also in moon cycles. . . . In the course of one complete cycle, which most strangely corresponds to the moon's revolution, the woman's energy waxes, shines full and wanes again. These energy changes affect her, not only in her physical and sexual life but in her psychic life as well. Life in her ebbs and flows, so that she is dependent on her inner rhythm.[6]

I realize how accustomed I have become to ignoring and suppressing my feminine nature, as if the waxing and waning of

energy is indicative of membership in the weaker sex. I have
not wanted to lend weight to the notion pervading our culture
that because women function at a different pace and rhythm
during their "time of the month," they would be unreliable in
important elected political positions. I hardly ever allow myself a time of reduced energy output during a menstrual cycle;
instead I work to overcome any impulse to slow down and
retreat so that I can keep going according to my regular
schedule. Harding's affirmation that I have my own rhythm
as a woman, and the implication that this cyclic rhythm is not
merely acceptable but can even be conceived of as valuable,
startles me into action. With her encouragement that I need
not deny my personal female rhythm, I begin to experiment
by honoring it. Now when I have my period, I try to let
myself succumb to the internal force that slows me down;
instead of rushing to do errands and chores, I may curl up
with warm blankets and books or music. Instead of fighting
against the foggy sensation that leaves me feeling removed
from the clamor of activities going on around me, I allow it to
shroud me in a protective cushion. I find that my family and
friends easily acclimate to and survive my temporary with-
drawal; the errands can wait, and I even return to them with
renewed energy and spirit after a time of retreat.

I begin to use my new awareness in my work whenever the
opportunity arises, to help other women who are grappling
with such issues. Nancy, a woman who has been my client
for several years, finally decides to leave a bleak and loveless
marriage. After a time of grieving for the loss of her former
life, she tries to help her three children adjust to the change
and is finally able to turn her attention to her own future. At
forty Nancy is beginning to look forward to a new life in
which she can nurture herself. Exhilarated by this long-denied
sense of freedom, she decides rather impulsively to have a
tubal ligation and schedules an appointment only a few days
away. When she comes to her hour with me, she informs me
for the first time of her plan. Although the surgery is scheduled to take place in a matter of days, and although I do not
believe her choice is wrong for her, I encourage her to exam-

ine the meaning of the choice and to explore her sense of urgency. She tells me, "I want to be free! I'm determined to devote all my energy and attention to myself from now on. I've had to wait so long even to know my own needs, let alone to act on them, that I don't want to wait even one more minute!"

Gently I assure her that my intention is not to question her choice, that I only want to make room for the possibility that other feelings about having a tubal ligation might arise as well, such as feelings of loss for the fertility that has been part of her entire adult life. "Choosing to end her fertility is a big step for any woman to take, and I can imagine that you might have many different feelings about making this decision that will come to the surface. I want to make sure you leave enough time before the surgery so that there's room for them to come up."

We sit in silence for a minute while she considers my suggestion. In the interval I realize that I wish her to be able to approach the operation in a psychologically centered and self-aware position. Yet knowing she may not share them, I do not want to impose upon her the painful feelings that I grappled with in undergoing the same operation. Finally Nancy tells me, "I know you're encouraging me to take the time I need, but my mind is made up. I appreciate that you want me to be thoughtful, but I don't have any doubts at all, and I'm looking forward to the surgery."

When Nancy arrives for her hour the following week, she says, "You won't believe what happened to me! I came down with a bad cold the day after we met, and they made me postpone the operation. The doctor couldn't administer anesthesia to me when I had a virus. At first I was very disappointed, because I had geared myself up for the surgery and I didn't think I was that sick. I'd already arranged to take the time off from work, and a friend was all set to wait with me and take me home. Now I'd just have to go through the whole thing all over again. But afterward I began to feel a little relieved. I found that I did have some other feelings about the sterilization procedure and I was glad to have the time to talk them over with you, because they were pretty upsetting." Nancy proceeds to tell me about these feelings. "I actually pictured myself like Hester Prynne in *The Scarlet Letter*, only instead of an *A* for *adultery*, I would have an *S* for *sterile* written on my chest."

Eventually Nancy does reschedule the tubal ligation and goes through with the surgery, but this time with a wider range of conscious feeling about it. Afterward we both wonder whether catching that cold was her body's way of buying time so that she could let the full range of her feelings into her awareness.

Cheryl, another client, comes to see me in my office. She wants help with the rejecting feelings she is having toward her second child, who was born severely retarded. With her young husband's limited income, Cheryl is left by herself to take full-time care of an older daughter as well as this extremely difficult younger child, whose increasing physical size is making the essential daily caretaking even harder. At times she feels so angry at how burdened she is that she finds herself wishing her "defective" daughter would die. These thoughts terrify her far beyond the constant guilt and remorse with which she struggles. Filled with self-hatred because of her rejecting feelings toward her damaged child, she views the child's birth as her just punishment for her sexuality. Eventually she makes a decision to have a tubal ligation, even though she is only twenty-three; she feels that she could never risk having another child.

I can see that Cheryl's decision, while understandable, is fueled in part by the power of her self-hatred and that the tubal ligation carries a wish to mutilate herself. But such shadowy, dark feelings are not accessible to this young woman; she sees the sensible aspects of her choice and consciously experiences only her firm decision not to bear any more children. I find myself wishing I could find a way to help her value her body, to affirm her fertility even in the face of having produced a physically defective child. But I cannot undo the years of conditioning in a matter of weeks. This is psychological work that could take years, if not a lifetime.

Nevertheless I know that Cheryl likes to garden, and so I bring into my office a packet of bulbs, a pot, and a bag of soil. I explain that, by planting these bulbs, I thought we could mark together the ending of her biological fertility and the beginning of the channeling of her creative energy in a different direction. She is clearly pleased at this idea and tells me, "I never would have thought of doing anything like that! Thank you!" Together we carefully fill the pot with the dry soil. Completely self-assured and at home with this activity, she skillfully embeds the bulbs deep in the soil. For a moment she seems younger to me and carefree, as if the lines of worry that carve a permanent frown on her face have momentarily softened. Finally, while I watch her silently, thinking to myself how young she is to be carrying such a heavy burden of feelings, she sprinkles the mixture with life-giving water from the cracked yellow plastic watering pot that I have had in my office for years.

Without making a conscious link between my overt behavior and my newly discovered inner need for a connection to the long-submerged feminine principle, I begin instinctively to work toward providing this connection for my daughters, who are each rapidly approaching their adolescence and young womanhood. Now as an adult woman and as the mother of two daughters, I find myself urgently needing to welcome my daughters into womanhood in a different manner, one that will go beyond merely imparting practical or physiological information. It is a need too urgent to ignore; I know I must find some way to communicate to my daughters the larger female mystery of which menstruation is only one important part. Because I cannot pass this knowledge on to them in any form that I myself have experienced, I realize that I will have to create new rituals. The first step is to empower myself to act.

Not yet knowing exactly how I will accomplish this personally imperative task, I begin by letting Jill know, several weeks in advance of her thirteenth birthday, that I want to spend a few minutes alone with her sometime during that day. I decide that later I will intuitively know what to do with this time.

"Jill," I say casually, one morning when we are in the kitchen together buttering English muffins, "your thirteenth birthday is coming up soon. It's going to be on a Tuesday, so I know it'll be a busy day for you, what with school and everything. But it's an important birthday, and I want to plan to spend a few minutes alone with you sometime during that day. This is a special birthday! It marks your transition from being a child, a little girl, to being a young woman."

I wait a bit nervously for her response. I know that Jill has not yet needed to separate herself from me with the same fierce and stubborn resistance that already typifies her sister, Becky. Perhaps, I think, she won't need to fight me on this. I watch Jill turn her head toward me with an expression that manages to combine both irritation and fondness. "You would think of that!" she says, shaking her head.

Eventually Jill's birthday arrives. It is a cold, gray January day; the air is heavy with moisture following a winter storm. Without conscious effort or thought, a plan for a simple ritual to acknowledge her immanent fertility as well as the waning of my own has come to my mind. In fact, this experience of simply knowing what to do is quite amazing to me. Usually, in order for me to figure something out I have to think about it, plan in an effortful way, or investigate with thorough research. I enjoy the new experience of relying upon my intuition, or my unconscious, or perhaps some deeper stream of feminine consciousness to which I have somehow gained access for this moment.

We have planned to celebrate Jill's birthday at our favorite Chinese restaurant. Before dinner, I approach my lithe young daughter, who is relaxing in front of the television set with her younger sister. "Jill, will you come outside with me for a few minutes now? I want to do something special with you for your thirteenth birthday. You know, the idea I talked to you about a few weeks ago. Remember? You agreed to do it."

Without either answering me or hesitating, Jill unfolds herself from the couch in an unhurried fashion and leaves the room with me. I wonder whether she is being cooperative because she does not want Becky to know what we are doing or whether she somehow understands the importance to me of this occasion. As the two of us pass through the kitchen, I choose a ripe red apple—the most perfect I can find—from the fruit basket and bring a small kitchen knife with me. These are the only implements we will need.

"Let's go down the hill a bit," I say to Jill, who still has not spoken aloud. We go out through the back door into the cold air and proceed to pick our way carefully along the wooden steps that lead from the backyard down the steep hillside beyond our house. We have planted fruit trees on this hill-side, but now, in the heart of winter, they seem especially vulnerable with their naked trunks and thin, fragile branches. As I pass through them, with Jill a few feet behind me, they acquire a certain human presence, as if they are benevolent witnesses, or a silent cheering section, or guardians of our passage.

About halfway down the hill I see a wooden ledge that has somehow been spared a coating of mud. "We can sit on the edge of this retaining wall," I announce to Jill and make my way over to it, my shoes sinking into the water-softened earth. I sit down cautiously and make room for my daughter to sit next to me. Grimacing with distaste, she as fastidious as I in not wanting to get her shoes muddy, Jill gingerly tiptoes over to me and sits so close to me that our shoulders and legs are touching. We are both wearing blue jeans, and I look down at the neat row our four thighs create; our legs, nearly identical in size and shape, could be interchangeable. Jill has somehow grown up to be even taller than I am, metamorphosing gradually from the tiny female person that I can still close my eyes and see, lying on the hospital bed as I dress her to bring her home when she is only a few days old. Then she was only half the size of the new terrycloth jumpsuit I had carefully washed and folded for her, the little white one that had, appropriately, "Take me home!" embroidered in blue letters on the chest. In that tiny package, remarkably enough, were all the ingredients necessary to bring her to this state of womanhood today.

I speak only a few sentences aloud to Jill; words are to carry only one small but essential part of our ceremony. "Jill, I expect that you will begin to get your period sometime this coming year, and I want to welcome your fertility with you. Fertility is more than just a physical change in your body. It means that you are taking your place as a part of an awesome feminine mystery, a part of the cycle of birth, life, and death, a part of nature. To honor this coming of age, I'm going to split this ripe apple in half. Then we'll each bury one of the halves in this earth, the seeds consecrated to new growth, to your new stage of life, and the pulp to decay back into the earth, just as my fertility has passed away. I know that you've been worried about me this year and that I've been deeply upset. This transition has been very hard for me. Burying the apple will symbolize my transition in this womanly cycle as well as yours."

Carefully I use the knife to split the apple. This moment has a special emotional intensity to me. I have a heightened awareness of every aspect of the scene, as if Jill and I had been filmed not only in color but with a film capable of especially sharp, heightened images. The flesh of the apple I hold in my hands is moist and crisp. Every grain of its white flesh is visibly apparent, a contrast in color and texture to the shiny dark brown seeds that surround its core. I look at the two halves and then carefully hand one to my daughter. I keep the remaining half, and as a way of demonstrating to Jill how to proceed, I dig a shallow hole in the earth with a small trowel that I found and picked up from the ground on our way to our spot on the hill. I feel Jill watch me cover the apple with the soft mud. "Okay, it's your turn now," I say, and hand her the trowel.

Jill digs a small hole next to mine and puts her apple half into it. Then using the trowel, she carefully spoons the mud over it. Deep down I had known that Jill would cooperate, that she would listen to me and do as I asked. But I did not know that after we finished burying our apple halves, we would sit quietly with each other, linked by emotions that neither one of us anticipated or understood, visible only by the tears that have filled our eyes.

"Time to go back!" I say, acknowledging my leadership role, and I stand up, brushing grains of dirt off the back of my pants. But as we return home, I am the follower. Jill leads us back to the house, with the golden light from the kitchen warm and welcoming now that the sun has nearly set. Becky hears us come in and comes into the kitchen to ask, "Where were you?" I find myself unable to answer her, because I do not understand myself where Jill and I have in fact been. The realm of the feminine has not yet become clearly defined in my vocabulary.

Some months after this ceremony, which continues to be a source of profound satisfaction, a new idea that will serve to anchor me further to that feminine source-ground of wisdom I seek comes synchronistically into being. I am having one of my regular biweekly lunches with Judith, who is telling me about a talk she attended with a colleague whom I have never met.

"Morgan and I went to hear Helene Lindstrom give a talk on the position of women in ancient Greece. She told us about a particular ritual that they used to enact—it's not one that's commonly known. It's called the Thesmophoria, and it was a ritual celebration held in the autumn of the year. Not much is known about how it was carried out, but it had to do with the fertility cycle of women and the fertility of the earth. In other words, the ritual celebrated the sacred mystery of the seed in women and in the earth. The participants of the ritual were mature women who had gone through all those important female experiences—menstruation, defloration, pregnancy, childbirth, and menopause. They took nine full days to prepare for this ritual with different purification rites. Can you imagine it? Such an event would be unheard of in our time!"[7]

I can't keep myself from interrupting Judith, impelled by a memory that now makes sense to me. "You just reminded me of something! My friend's sister—an adult woman—was telling me a while ago that to celebrate her thirty-fifth birthday she was going to have a slumber party with her closest women friends! I'd always associated pajama parties with childhood, and it never would've occurred to me to have a slumber party as an adult. But when she told me about her plan, I felt such a pang of longing. I found myself both craving that lost intimacy with a group of women and also a bit afraid of it, as if it would mean leaving my family connections behind me. Maybe a slumber party is actually a faint echo of a former time when women regularly had such retreats and when the retreats were organized around the central experiences women share."

"That's an interesting idea," Judith responds. "I never thought about slumber parties that way. Maybe young girls today are actually keeping alive a kind of sisterhood that's lost to adult women in this culture. How did her slumber party work out? Has it happened yet?"

"Yes, it did. Actually it turned out to be wonderful. The women had such a good time that they decided to do it again and not even to wait for a birthday. In fact, they're planning to take a whole weekend away together next time. You know, the other part of it that was fascinating was how jealous all the men were. The husbands didn't like being left out and acted as if they were being abandoned. My friend's sister told me she cooked a special dinner for her husband that night, even though she wasn't going to be there to eat it! Afterward he wanted to hear about everything that happened and got upset when she couldn't tell him. It wasn't that she was deliberately keeping it secret from him or even that anything momentous had taken place—they played games and told jokes and ghost stories by the fireplace! It was more that she couldn't convey the feeling of closeness, the sense of being female, that they had shared." I pause for a minute and then add, "I wonder if I have unknowingly given up separate experiences with women because I don't want to hurt Michael! Maybe he's given up close relationships with men to protect me!"

"Well," Judith responds, "I think that being related to men and being busy with children does keep women apart from one another. Somehow, in some of the ancient cultures we're beginning to learn about, women seem to have preserved their sisterhood, their connection to each other."

Not wanting to dwell upon what I have lost, I shift the direction of our conversation. "I didn't mean to get you completely off the track of telling me about the Thesmophoria ritual. You were about to tell me what they did!"

"Oh, yes, the nine-day preparation. . . ." Judith retrieves the thread of her story. "The women would sleep alone, apart from the men, sometimes even on separate cots, basically in order to enter into their 'femaleness' in a total way. They even ate garlic cloves because the odor would repel their men! For each of the nine preparation days they gathered at dusk to build huts for sleeping during the ritual itself. Each woman had her own hut, which she lined with branches from fig trees. I know that figs were a fruit that had a special significance, but I can't remember exactly what Helene said about them. Anyway, inside the hut, each woman made a bed for herself out of grasses and leaves. There was a special plant, the lygos plant, that the women wove into the walls of the hut and into the bed. Lygos also went into a drink they sipped; some ingredient in it worked to bring on their periods. Somehow, through its influence, or maybe just in the course of time, they would all get their periods within a few days of one another. When they began to menstruate, they tied red bands around their arms, to indicate that they were now ready for the ritual—they were sacred. Then they began the festival itself, gathered together at their sacred field. No men were allowed, not even male animals. Do you really want to hear about it in this much detail?" Judith asks me, stopping abruptly.

"Yes!" I say, emphatically. Judith has no idea how interested I am in hearing about this ancient women's ritual. I have not told her about the ceremony that Jill and I so recently shared, a ceremony that was far simpler, yet just as profoundly connected to the same feminine source-ground. "It's remarkable that you remember all the details!"

"I know," Judith goes on. "I think the very idea of it

touches some buried need in me, because it's satisfying just to hear about it. Telling you about it gives me a chance to enjoy it again! Anyway, the festival took three days in all. On the first day the women go down into a chasm carrying newborn piglets. Later that day they climb back out of the chasm carrying heaps of rotted pig's flesh. Not much is known of what happened while they were down in that chasm, except that they killed the pigs. It's said that the piglets were intended as food for the great underground primal deity, the Snake. The Snake, a deity associated with women, represented the power in the earth, the fields, and in the bodies of women. Women, by virtue of their connection to the cycle of life through their childbearing capacity, are ineluctably bonded to the Snake. They honored the bond with the sacrifice of the pigs, a special reminder lest the women forget about the power of the Snake during the year, on those ordinary days when life goes along without great difficulty."

"What a different meaning they gave to the Snake than we do!" I exclaim, interrupting Judith's tale. "In the Old Testament the snake lured Eve into evil."

"I know," Judith responds, nodding. "In those times the Snake was a powerful deity, connected with nature; and with regeneration—snakes shed their skin as they grow; it was a positive force. I guess the association between the snake and disobedience to God's will must have come much later."

"Still, it seems kind of barbaric, sacrificing baby pigs to the Snake!" I can't help but add, nearly shuddering with revulsion.

"I know!" Judith agrees. "You'd think that it'd be horrifying to hear of animal sacrifice, but somehow the way Helene told the story, it wasn't at all horrifying. The women were acknowledging the impersonal force of nature, the repetitive alternation of life and death. Sacrificing the baby pigs helped the women to accept this natural force rather than struggle against it. If we had such a conscious ritual acknowledgment, even if we didn't actually sacrifice a living being, maybe we wouldn't need to struggle so hard against the natural processes of life and death; we wouldn't need to flee from it because we're so terrified of mortality. At any rate, it was quite an evening! After it was over, Morgan and I went out for coffee and we just couldn't get over it."

"You're so lucky to have had that contact with Helene!" I say to Judith, feeling envious.

"I know!" answers Judith. "She's a remarkable woman, way ahead of us in her interest in women's issues. I'd love to have more contact with her."

A new idea suddenly takes shape, full-blown in my mind. "Do you think she might be interested in meeting with a small group of women on a regular basis? Kind of like a study group?" I ask Judith.

"Gee, I don't really know. It wouldn't hurt to ask her. I'm sure Morgan would also be interested in being part of it. I know you haven't met Morgan either, but I think you'd appreciate knowing her! She'd also contribute a special perspective to a group. Well, why don't I call Helene and see. All that can happen is that she'll say no," Judith replies thoughtfully.

But Helene does not say no to Judith; in fact, she is happy to have a forum within which to present and explore her own ideas and experiences. In this way our small women's group begins. We first become a group by taking the time to tell each other our individual stories, our life histories, with the general aim of explaining, both to ourselves and to one another, how we have each arrived at a common and pivotal juncture in our lives. The paths of our separate and quite different outer lives have converged at an internal meeting ground: that of needing and actively seeking a connection to some firm, substantial, and nourishing feminine source of wisdom.

The differences we uncover among us are astonishing. We represent four different religions, chronological ages, personalities, places of origin, physical appearances, current family situations, and educational backgrounds, not to mention four different sets of specific past experiences and current attitudes toward life. Yet our hunger and need for a connection to the elusive but essential feminine source-ground unite us in an immediate shared bond that runs far deeper than our surface differences would have led us to believe could be possible. The bond continues to deepen and grow with the passage of time and as we share our respective knowledge and experiences with one another.

During the next two years of meetings with this group, I expand my understanding of women's history, in a variety of fields—anthropology, religion, sociology, philosophy, psychology. I am able to put some of this information directly to use with women clients who, like Nancy and Cheryl, are struggling with issues related to being female. Other information enriches me personally; through my studies I learn about the Goddess Demeter and her connection to grain, which amplifies my understanding of the word "müller" in my dream encounter with my fourth child. More generally I learn—and come to appreciate down to my very core—that recent archaeological finds indicate that there was a time in written history when cultures worshiped a female deity. Synchronistically, this proof of the existence of matriarchal cultures has occurred only in this century, in tandem with an awakening hunger in women for such roots.

To one meeting, Morgan brings a slide show she has put together for a graduate-school course she will teach on the emergence of the feminine principle in psychotherapy. The four of us gaze with rapt attention at images of the archetypal feminine, manifested in cave drawings and primitive sculptures from ancient Near Eastern cultures. To another meeting, Helene brings translations of ancient Sumerian poetry. The poems are signed by the name Enheduanna, a priestess from Sumerian culture, who was perhaps the first woman poet in written history. Helene tells us that Enheduanna was a high priestess in a culture that worshiped a goddess named Inanna, who, as She was absorbed into other cultures, later became known by the names Ishtar, Ashteroth, and Astarte.

I come to understand, through my own reading and through the presentations of Judith, Helene, and Morgan, that in the ancient time of a Mother Goddess, women were celebrated, revered, praised, and feared because in their physical bodies they symbolized or embodied all the great mysteries of our universe. The recurrent cycles of day and night, the waxing and waning of the moon, the alternation of rain and drought, the evolution from seed to grain, the birth and death of all living creatures, the inexplicably strange and rhythmic appearance of menstruation, the wondrous miracle of pregnancy and birth—all these mysteries were once embodied in the being of women, who were respected and revered.

The great Mother Goddess, known over centuries by different names was worshiped from the beginning of the Neolithic period (7000 B.C.) until the last Goddess temple was destroyed, in A.D. 500.[8] Imagining what human civilization was like nine thousand years ago is as difficult for me as conceptualizing the distance from the Milky Way to other galaxies in outer space. Our knowledge of long-gone eras is just as astonishingly recent and as hard-won as our understanding of the physical sciences. Since there are no written records to rely on, most of the information we have is derived from archaeological finds, artifacts that are still in the process of being retrieved from excavation sites in the Near East.

At one point during the years of our study group, I listen to a televised lecture by Stephen Jay Gould, a Harvard scholar and popular writer on evolution.[9] In discussing the unquestioned assumptions we bring to this subject, he states that evolution is not synonymous with progress; there is no reason to assume without question that our culture represents a higher form than those that came before. With that in mind, I think about ancient cultures with new respect. Perhaps we can learn from examining them what we have lost in ritual and tradition, rather than seeing only how we have surpassed them through our astonishing technological advances.

From one of the books I read, written by archaeologist Marija Gimbutas, I learn that although a female deity was worshiped in early cultures, myths were not polarized then into male and female. Instead there appears to have been a state of balance, of unity and harmony, between masculine and feminine power. Gimbutas points out that the male divinity, in the form of a male animal or young man, "affirmed and strengthened the forces of the creative and active female.

Neither is subordinate to the other; by complementing one another, their power is doubled."[10] It was upon this unified culture, in which masculine and feminine formed a strong and cohesive whole, that the masculine culture of the Indo-Europeans was superimposed. When two very different sets of mythical images collided, the result was complex: Sometimes masculine symbols replaced the existing feminine symbols; sometimes these symbols existed side by side in chaos rather than in harmony; sometimes images fused and lost their original meaning, and new complexes of symbols that we now see in Greek mythology developed. Those cultures may have managed to find a balance between the masculine and feminine principles, something that seems absent in our time and causes both men and women to develop psychologically in an uneven, one-sided manner. Perhaps a balance may yet be restored; perhaps it need not be lost irretrievably.

Though I value the blossoming of an entire new world of information through my women's group, my newly acquired knowledge is important to me in other ways as well. I know by now only too well that historical "facts" are controversial, subject, like scientific data, to interpretation. I know that the very existence of early matriarchal cultures, as well as of cultures in which women at least shared power equally with men, is currently a matter of debate. What matters to me more than the facts is the affirmation I find in them for the personal sense of loss I have come to feel for myself of images or symbols of women, of the feminine, that would have served to guide me through my own abortion and fertility crisis. I am determined to find such images for myself as well as for my son and daughters.

Eventually my younger daughter, Becky's, thirteenth birthday rolls around. I know there is a very good chance that she might refuse to participate in any ritual with me celebrating her coming of age. In relation to me, she has needed to be quite independent and autonomous, as if any closeness or similarity, no matter how trivial, would jeopardize the unfolding of her own separate self. Consequently, I know that any ceremony we share will have to be very brief; Becky will not sit with me for long, if she comes at all. And I know that the burying of fruit, which was so appropriate for Jill's depth, her steadiness, her solid center, and her Athena-like wisdom and inner strength, is not right for Becky.

I discover that the same unusual intuitive faculty that had come into play for Jill works again for Becky. I had known ever since Jill's ceremony that any ritual welcoming Becky into womanhood would have to include the physical act of throwing. Becky is a child of action, of quick impulse, of rapidly shifting moods. Her strength and determination derive from Artemis, Greek goddess of the hunt and the moon; her softer side comes from Hestia, Greek goddess of the hearth and temple.[11] But it is not until the morning of Becky's thirteenth birthday that I know what I must throw—not fruit but whole grain. Which whole grain? I wonder for a brief moment and then know instantly that it should be brown rice, with its hard outer shell and its soft center, so like my daughter.

Becky's birthday, like Jill's, happens to fall on a weekday. The only possible time that Becky and I can be alone together that day comes about through good luck—or perhaps benevolent feminine forces. Michael has left to pick up the traditional Chinese food from our favorite restaurant; Becky has too much homework to take the time to go out to eat and wants to have dinner at home. Jill is off at a late school meeting, and Ben is secluded in his room with the door shut. This is my chance. . . .

Becky has temporarily taken over the small room that serves as her father's study. Her own bedroom, which became flooded with water during a recent series of storms, is in a state of disrepair. We have taken up her rug and installed a fan to circulate the air. Her mildewed walls have been sprayed with chemicals. But Hestia, ancient goddess of the hearth who is so alive in Becky, has enabled her to create a new home for herself in her father's study. Her flannel-encased pillows provide comfort and support for her collection of stuffed animals; her shoes are arranged with precision in front of the closet; and her clothes are neatly suspended from hangers. The television set in the new bedroom more than adequately compensates her for the temporary loss of her familiar sanctuary. And Michael and I are enjoying her proximity to us; she is more accessible in this room than in her own bedroom, which is downstairs and feels farther away.

I knock on Becky's door and open it before she has a chance to tell me to go away. She is watching television instead of doing her homework.

"Becky!" I announce, my heart pounding more loudly than usual. "I need you to come outside with me for one minute. You can come when your program is over if you want." I have learned to speak in imperatives to her, as assertively as I can.

"It just started, Mom! Give me a break!" Becky protests.

"Well, come at the next commercial, then. You have to come. There is no choice about this," I insist in a firm, clear, no-nonsense voice.

Becky must sense the absolute, unyielding power in my words. It is apparent to both of us that right now, in contrast to our ordinary positions, I am the strongest. Simultaneously we hear a shift in the television broadcast as an advertising jingle bubbles into the room. Becky is caught! "I guess there's a commercial on right now," she says, her voice dragging with reluctance. She stands up slowly and makes her way to the door.

"Come on right now, then! Let's go," I say, trying to infuse an encouraging tone into my voice.

I have filled a small glass jam jar, which is etched with fruit designs, with kernels of raw brown rice, and I snatch it up from the kitchen counter as I propel Becky outdoors, my hand on her shoulder. It is a sunny, but cold and windy March afternoon, not at all like the gray, wet dusk of Jill's thirteenth birthday. We are enjoying an interlude of spring weather after the storms that have flooded Becky's bedroom. Good weather for planting.

Becky will not go beyond the wooden deck that is built out from our back door. She climbs up on the back of the wooden benches that line the edge of the deck. I smile to myself;

unintentionally Becky has chosen a perfect spot for our ceremony. We are high up, looking out from this vantage point over the hill below, the very hill that Jill and I had picked our way down two years ago. Becky and I are to remain at its peak.

My younger daughter hunches over, her head buried in her arms resting on a fence post. She has found a physical way to preserve the integrity of her separate self and yet remain with me. Her body forms a closed circle; she is a small sphere, but I know she will hear me if I speak. I also know that the clock is running. I have only one minute in which to choose my words and communicate the essential.

I walk over to her, place my hand on her back, and speak.

"Becky, you're thirteen today. This is the age that marks the beginning of young womanhood. If we practiced Judaism, you would have a bas mitzvah like your friend Debbie, and that could be the ritual that welcomed you into womanhood. But since this Jewish ritual isn't specifically about fertility, it's up to me to create a ritual for you. This year you're likely to get your period. I want you to know that fertility is something very special, even sacred. It's more than just a physical change in your body. As a woman, you will become part of the natural cycles of the earth, of nature. It's my job as your mother to acknowledge this change with you and to honor your passage from childhood into young womanhood."

I feel the muscles in Becky's back tense, and I speak more quickly. "I am going to throw a handful of whole grain—brown rice—into the earth in honor of your coming fertility." I pour a handful of rice into my right hand and, steadying myself, throw the grains as far as I can off our deck. I cannot see them fly through the air—they are too small—but I can hear each one land upon the dark green leaves of the bushes in a gentle rainfall of sound, strangely beautiful. I feel a sense of satisfaction, as if an invisible inner hole has been so perfectly filled no one would ever know it had been there.

Now I take a huge risk. Her refusal at this moment would devastate me. "Becky," I command, "it's your turn now. You must throw some rice, too."

I feel Becky pull away from me. I know she wants to refuse, and I can almost hear her voice saying, "No, I won't. I'm going back inside." Urgently I tell her, "It feels so *good* to throw it," and I reach for her arm. Still facing away from me, hunched over, she extends her small, strong limb—oh, how I yearn in that instant to touch once again the tiny arm of my littlest girl—and she opens her fist to accept the rice that I quickly pour into her hand. Without looking either at me or at the rice, she throws it out in front of her, and I listen with pleasure to another rainfall sound of grain landing on the strong green leaves.

I know I have no more time. Immediately I announce, "That's all there is, Becky. We're finished."

Wrenching free, Becky hurries inside and disappears into her makeshift room. I follow her more slowly, and by the time I arrive in the kitchen, I can hear the murmur of voices from her adopted room; Jill has come home and is in there talking to Becky. Then I hear the groan of our garage door lifting, and I hurry to open the back door for Michael. As he comes up the steps from the garage, I reach for the brown bags with the familiar and pungent smell of potstickers, egg rolls, fried rice, mu shu pork, and cashew chicken. I carry them into the kitchen where I begin to unpack them to set out on the table. In honor of Becky's thirteenth birthday, the table is set with a clean blue tablecloth instead of our usual vinyl placemats. In the middle of the table is our glass anniversary bowl. I have filled it with water, in which I have floated three rose-colored camellias from our front garden that have bloomed early in unseasonable hot weather. The goddess Hestia in Becky likes beautiful settings.

Later, as Michael and I clear away the remains of the birthday meal, I tell him how the brief ritual with Becky went. I am gratified by his genuine interest and support.

"It's really lovely how you're trying to give something special to Becky," he tells me as he attempts to stack the empty take-home cartons into one another so that they'll take up less room in the trash can.

"She wasn't too responsive," I tell Michael. "For all I know, I might have totally alienated her."

"I wouldn't worry about how negative she seemed," Michael says comfortingly. "You don't know how she felt inside, and even if she can't see your ritual as something positive now, I know she'll appreciate it later on. Seeing you do a ceremony for Jill and Becky makes me want to do one for Ben when he reaches thirteen. I wonder what we could do that would mark a rite of passage for him."

"Probably the pieces will fall into place once you decide to do it," I tell Michael. I do not have a more specific answer for him, but seeing Michael begin to empower himself is like watching myself in a mirror. Instead of passively living our lives within existing forms, regardless of whether they are satisfying or not, we are beginning to find ways to modify them or to invent new forms that will provide us with the guidance, support, and meaning we need.

Some weeks later when my women's group meets, I tell Helene, Judith, and Morgan about my ceremony with Becky, just as two years earlier I had recounted the way Jill and I had acknowledged our separate transitions in the life cycle of women. Bringing these celebrations to this special group gives them an affirmed reality. Helene, Judith, and Morgan appreciate the importance of such rituals, particularly those that focus attention on the special needs, so neglected in our culture, of women. They, too, have shared their own stories of ceremonies they created and enacted for different purposes, but all with the common purpose of providing special ways of marking and facilitating the significant life passages of women. As vulnerable human beings, we cannot control the inexorable flow of life passages, but we do have the power to acknowledge and celebrate them. Through the telling of our personal stories in the special place that our group has become, the four of us are increasingly able to recognize and appreciate the satisfying and powerful effect of such ceremonies.

I do not know yet that I am to be the recipient of such a ritual myself on the fifth anniversary of my abortion.

THIRTEEN

Reconnecting to the Feminine Part II

"The first step is generally falling into the dark place, and usually appears in a dubious or negative form—falling into something or being possessed by something . . . Even the worst things you fall into are an effort of initiation, for you are in something which belongs to you, and now you must get out of it."

—MARIE-LOUISE VON FRANZ
The Feminine in Fairy Tales[1]

"A ritual can be defined as an enactment of a myth. By participating in a ritual, you are actually experiencing a mythological life. And it's out of that participation that one can learn to live spiritually."

—JOSEPH CAMPBELL (WITH BILL MOYERS)
The Power of Myth[2]

In the same spontaneous manner that we began our group, a ritual for me comes into being; its purpose is to acknowledge and enclose my profound response to the abortion and the abrupt end of fertility. During one of our biweekly Japanese lunches Judith and I together plant the tiny seed that will gradually take hold and blossom, just as we first helped come to fruition the idea that became our women's group. I had been talking to Judith about my abortion and how difficult it continues to be for me at times, even though it happened nearly five years ago.

"You know," says Judith, "we've all been sharing the rituals we've created for so many different purposes in our group—the one that I had when my daughter left home and separated from the family, the one that Morgan did for her patient who had the miscarriage—why don't we plan a ritual for you!"

At first I am touched, pleased that Judith wants to offer me something special. "That's a lovely idea! Thank you!" I reply. But after the lunch, as I drive home alone, apprehension at the idea of yielding to an unknown experience and anxiety about being the center of attention begin to arise. I soon recognize that apprehension and anxiety are part and parcel of the process itself, necessary accompaniments to any experience that has the potential to break new ground. I do not want to allow these uncomfortable feelings to prevent the ritual from evolving.

I also recognize that my anxiety is related to a powerful message from the dominant culture. I can give specific words to this negative legacy: Rituals won't really help anything, they're just made up of words; your reaction to the abortion and tubal ligation was pathological; why don't you just go on with your ordinary life as other women do without needing such special attention? I am determined not to let these nega-

tive inner voices triumph, even if it will take all my courage
and an effort of will to forge ahead with them in tow.

When the day of the next women's-group meeting rolls
around, I wonder if Judith will remember to bring up the idea
that had come to her during our lunch. I do not want to be
the one to ask the group to create a ritual for me! After the
usual checking-in period, when we catch up on one another's
current pressing concerns, Helene announces that she has
some material she wants to share with us. I turn my attention
toward her with a mixture of relief and disappointment.

"I want to tell you about a chapter from this book called
Images of Women in Antiquity,"[3] Helene announces with enthu-
siasm. "It has to do with Hittite birth rituals that date back to
the seventeenth through thirteenth centuries B.C. These two
rituals are completely different from one another, yet they
were enacted in close proximity, in the area that today is
known as Turkey. They were transcribed on clay tablets, just
like the Sumerian stories of the goddess Inanna, but in the
Hittite cuneiform language. Both included incantations and
cleansing rituals, but one was conducted by women priestesses and the other by male priests. The differences between
them seem related to the fact that one was grounded in the
male principle and the other in the female principle."

Helene turns to Morgan, who is curled up in a chair across
from her. "This is a library book, but it isn't due for another
few weeks. I thought I'd give it to you to take home, because
I bet you could use this material in the class you're offering."

"Yes, that would be wonderful," replies Morgan. She is
about to begin the second series of her classes on the emergence of the feminine in psychotherapy.

"One word of caution," Helene adds. "I don't mean to
idealize the early culture with women priestesses and to deni-
grate the one with male priests. We can't assume that the lot
of women in matriarchal cultures was superior to ours in all
respects. Today we live longer, are healthier, have more
freedom and options, with all the benefits and problems that
this freedom brings. But I think we can examine the differences in these early cultures from our own perspective and

learn from the attitudes they had toward women—attitudes that we can see in the rituals they carried out."

The three of us then listen to Helene describe the two sets of rituals in detail. I cannot help but notice my fascination with a subject that would not have held my interest at all when I was in college. At that time, when I was less than twenty years old, I would probably have dutifully recorded and memorized the details in order to pass the final exam, but they would not have ignited the passionate interest they do today. "We should be going to college now," I whisper to Judith, who readily agrees as we laugh ruefully.

"In the ritual conducted by women," Helene explains, "pregnancy was dated from the last rising of the full moon before the cessation of the menses. The root of the word *pregnancy* in that language was the same one as for *moon* and *month*. In fact, the office of midwife had its origins in a Sumerian story from the twentieth century B.C., even earlier than the tablets. The ancient story goes, in one version, that the moon god became infatuated with a grazing cow, impregnated her, and then witnessed her pain while giving birth. Filled with compassion for the pain of the laboring mother, the moon god dispatched mother goddesses to help her."

"That story sounds a lot better to me than the one we have from the Bible," Judith says, intervening in Helene's narrative, "where Eve is punished for seeking knowledge and is cursed both with menstruation and painful childbirth forever after."

"You're absolutely right!" exclaims Helene. "At the birth itself, two types of women practitioners were present—a midwife and a wise woman. The midwife was the one who knew the internal organs and was skilled in giving birth incantations to absorb evil from the newborn baby. There were magic formulations to ensure the health of both the mother and the child. If the child was a boy, it was given the gift of a bow and arrow, and the midwife wished for a girl to be born in one year. If the child was a girl, it was given the gift of a distaff and spindle, and the midwife would wish, 'Let there be a boy born in one year.' "

"So girls and boys were of equal value," I comment.

"Yes, or at least there seems to have been a balance," Helene responds, "Then the midwife presented the child to the wise woman as if she, the midwife, had given birth. In a sense, you could say that the midwife took on the archetypal role of the birth goddess. For the birth itself, they took two stools—just ordinary ones that were used every day. The mother sat on one and the midwife on the other, facing her. They placed a cushion on the ground between them to catch the child. The wise woman did the ritual cleansing of the child in a wooden tub, as well as some substitution magic, in which they took a goat and placed parts of the goat on the corresponding parts of the child to remove all evil from the child. Afterward the goat was dismembered and burned."

"Ugh!" we all exclaim, shuddering.

Helene smiles sympathetically at us and continues talking. "In the second ritual, the one conducted by male priests, the priest had to purify a special birth stool, as well as any implements for the birth and the laboring woman herself, as if she were somehow unclean and needed purification. There was a special chamber, which had to be sealed right after it was cleansed. The priest was required, as part of the purification, to sacrifice a kid (goat) to the male gods. If any damage was done to the birth stool or to the vessels, the whole process had to be done all over again, with even more detailed cleansing rituals. It seemed to me that in contrast to the ritual conducted by women, the men distanced the women from the birth experience itself through such compulsive, repetitive cleansing. Oh—I almost forgot! In the cleansing ritual for the woman, the priest bound her hands in red wool. Then, after the birth, there was a big feast at the woman's house, where they roasted a lamb and dressed it in garments, with red wool on its feet! As if there might have been a correspondence between the image of women and the animal that was eaten. You really get a sense here of the important role that culture plays in how women see themselves."

The stark contrast in the two rituals that once coexisted so closely in time and space, now more than three thousand years ago, again brings home to me that complete absence in our time of any cultural form that would have acknowledged how dreadful a choice I had to make at my fourth pregnancy. I again find myself silently wishing that I were part of a culture that could accept the reality, without blaming and condemning women, that as long as women are able to become pregnant, pregnancies unplanned and unwanted (by either parent) will occur. I wish our culture could help women who are confronted with this impossible choice simply by having compassion and recognizing the complexity of the dilemma.

The thought of the repetitive purification rituals of the male priests makes me think of the gleaming, sterile hospital room where my unborn child was annihilated. My three living children were delivered in forbidding rooms filled with alarming mechanical devices. I was strapped onto an uninviting narrow metal table with stirrups for my legs, swathed in sterile gowns that left only a small square opening through which the baby could emerge. Fluid from my body went neatly onto disposable paper pads, which were quickly discarded and replaced. Even now, recalling these experiences, my wish is not to do away with modern scientific accoutrements—I know they help save lives—but rather to have some presence of the feminine included. My thoughts turn to a friend's story that I had heard some time ago of a very different birth that a good friend of hers had just experienced. That birth took place in a hospital's alternative birthing center. But what made the birth so unusual, such a contrast to my own, was not the setting but rather the singular feminine presence of a Chinese midwife, tiny and ageless, who calmly presided. She instructed the participants in helpful tasks, such as massaging the forehead of the birthing mother, and when it was necessary to make a decision regarding an episiotomy because the baby was large, she chose to massage the area with her skilled hands instead. Deftly she manipulated the baby through the birth canal and left unused the sterilized instruments that were ready in case they were needed. She provided the feminine presence I missed, yet within a context that offered the safeguards of a trained physician, emergency equipment, and the latest medical technology. This is a birth story with the masculine and feminine elements working together in the state of harmony and balance that characterized the ancient Middle Eastern cultures Gimbutas describes.

As I recall my friend's story, Judith speaks up. "That reminds me of our lunch, Sue, where we thought about doing a ritual for you!" Without waiting for me to respond, she goes on to explain to Helene and Morgan how the idea of creating a ritual for me had come up. Helene and Morgan are immediately interested and responsive, and we agree that I will bring my ideas for such a ritual to the next group.

Over the next two weeks I find that I am gradually able to create a ritual for myself by relying on that same intuitive faculty that had worked so well with Jill and Becky. Like a child's uncomplicated jigsaw puzzle, the pieces simply seem to fall into place of their own accord.

I know immediately that the first puzzle piece will have to acknowledge the reality and the permanence of the pain of my loss. My grief for my unborn fourth child, though perhaps different in quality than the grief I would have for any living child, is just as palpable. To acknowledge this subjectively substantial loss, I turn to a quotation from antiquity, a translation of an ancient Abyssinian noblewoman's statement, recorded by Leo Frobenius, a scholar of anthropology and myth. I had been taken with it the moment I first came across it while reading a collection of essays by Jung and Kerényi, though when I read the passage to Michael, Margaret, and her husband, Martin, at one of our frequent dinners together, a lively discussion had ensued.

Michael and Martin were very upset at being told they could not "know" the experience that women have of childbirth. After all, they insisted, men can be as attached to their children as women can. I had agreed with them that men can feel equally attached to children, but I had also persisted in speculating that the *bodily* experience of pregnancy, which only women can have, makes the loss of a child different for women than it is for men. Even if women do not actually bear children, having a physical body that has the capacity to do so must shape their psychological attitude, I had insisted. How, I had asked, shifting my perspective, does it feel to a man to father a child from sperm contained in bodily fluid that shoots forth with such power? I had tried to imagine what it would be like to exist in a body with the capability of showering fertile ground with my seed. Martin, Michael, Margaret, and I struggled to communicate our experiences across the gulf of our different genders, but found that we could not describe them in words. I had reached a similar impasse any number of times with Michael, when he would try unsuccessfully to make our mutually created fourth child as real to him as it was to me. I continued to be puzzled by Michael's and Martin's insistence during this dinner that men have attitudes toward children that are identical to those of women, despite the uniquely female physical experiences of pregnancy and childbirth. At the time, I had attributed it to the envy men may have of the mysterious ability of women to give birth, or to the resistance we may all have to the notion that certain experiences of the opposite sex must necessarily remain a mystery.

Even though the four of us never reached a resolution to our discussion, I continued to value the quotation because of its matter-of-fact acknowledgment that uniquely female physical experiences are special for women, just as uniquely male experiences have special significance for men. Reading the passage, I determined, could constitute the first part of the ritual:

How can a man know what a woman's life is? A woman's life is quite different from a man's. God has ordered it so. A man is the same from the time of his circumcision to the time of his withering. He is the same before he has sought out a woman for the first time, and afterwards. But the day when a woman enjoys her first love cuts her in two. She becomes another woman on that day. The man is the same after his first love as he was before. The woman is from the day of her first love another. That continues so all through life. The man spends a night by a woman and goes away. His life and body are always the same. The woman conceives. As a mother she is another person than the woman without child. She carries the fruit of the night for nine months in her body. Something grows. Something grows into her life that never again departs from it. She is a mother. She is and remains a mother even though her child dies, though all her children die. For at one time she carried the child under her heart. And it does not go out of her heart ever again. Not even when it is dead. All this the man does not know; he knows nothing. He does not know the difference before love and after love, before motherhood and after motherhood. He can know nothing. Only a woman can know and speak of that.[4]

Once the first piece of the ritual is in place, I know that the second part will have to acknowledge the psychological descent into despair I made after the abortion and tubal ligation. I find this part right away in my favorite story of the descent of the Sumerian goddess Inanna.[5] In the story, Inanna, a mature queen ruling the upperworld with her consort, Dumuzi, chooses to descend to the Great Below, or underworld, to visit her dark sister, Ereshkigal. After leaving all her worldly belongings behind, Inanna instructs her faithful servant, Ninshubur, to go to the gods for help if she does not return in three days. She then proceeds to the first gate of the underworld, where the gatekeeper, Neti, lets her in and goes to inform Ereshkigal that Inanna has arrived. Ereshkigal instructs Neti that Inanna must be stripped of all her precious possessions and enter the underworld completely naked. In accord with this demand, Inanna undresses and passes through each of the seven gates, after which she comes to Ereshkigal in the throne room. But rather than welcome Inanna with open arms, Ereshkigal fastens the "eyes of death" upon her, transforming Inanna into a corpse, and then hangs her from a hook in the wall. There Inanna remains, while Ninshubur, who awaits her return, finally turns to the gods for help. The first two male gods she beseeches for aid refuse to help her, but finally, Enki, god of wisdom, comes to her rescue. He fashions two odd creatures from ordinary dirt under his fingernails and sends them with the food and water of life to the underworld to rescue Inanna. He instructs them to echo Ereshkigal's laments—by this time Ereshkigal is groaning with labor pains—and tells them to ask for Inanna's corpse when Ereshkigal offers them a gift in return for their empathy. The creatures follow Enki's instructions; they echo Ereshkigal's moans and request in return the gift of Inanna's corpse. They then sprinkle the food and water of life on her corpse and revive her. Before Inanna is allowed to return to the upperworld, however, she is told that she must send someone else to take her place. Demons from the underworld, called *galla*, accompany her to the upperworld to make sure she carries out this mission. When Inanna returns to the upperworld, she finds everyone there is mourning her loss—everyone, that is, except Dumuzi, her consort, who is blithely enjoying his position of power as king. Witnessing this, Inanna fixes the "eyes of death" upon Dumuzi, intending to send him to the underworld in her place. Dumuzi flees in terror but is finally captured. Ultimately Dumuzi's sister, Geshtinanna, takes pity on him and agrees to share his fate. Geshtinanna and Dumuzi then resolve that each of them will spend half of each year in the underworld.

The story symbolically reflects my experience. Through a voluntary and consciously chosen descent into her own darkness, Inanna's consciousness is transformed. Only through the death of her innocent self that knows only the upperworld of light can Inanna continue with her own psychological development, progressing not toward an impossible state of perfection but toward wholeness, in which she faces both the light and the dark side inherent in her nature. Henceforth, she must live with both.

To find the second part of the ritual, I reread a copy of poetic renderings of the translations of these Sumerian myths that Helene gave us and select a portion of them to be read aloud in the ritual. Concerned that the ritual will be too long,

I choose only the small portion in which Inanna calls her chosen minister, Ninshubur, and instructs her to stay in the upperworld while she is down below:

> I am going down below
> when I reach that place
>   wail for me
>   cry in lamentation by the ruins
>   play a drum song
>   drum for me in the throne court
>   wander for me
>   wander through the houses of the gods
>
>   tear at your eyes
>   tear at your mouth
>   tear at that unspeakable place
>
>   wear rags for me
>   only rags[6]

As I read these simple words written by the priestess Enheduanna so long ago, at the very beginning of written history, I picture Ninshubur wailing in grief, tearing at her clothes, and remember my own anguish during the maelstrom, the time of that unforgettable internal storm. My inner wildness, which seemed so frightening then, so pathological, now takes on new meaning with my broadened understanding of the feminine. Now I am able to conceive of this anguish, the great roaring that once threatened even the physical confines of my being, as an integral, inevitable part of the vast underworld of grief. For grief comes with the pain of being human, of experiencing loss with the lidless eyes of human consciousness. No longer is the roaring wildness inside me a pathological, terrifying state; now it is a psychological state mirrored in nature, in the tempests, tornadoes, sandstorms, windstorms, and thundering that mere human beings cannot control, cannot defy, can only endure.

Suddenly exhausted even from my brief conjuring up of such turbulence, I decide that at this juncture in the ceremony there should be a cleansing, a simple purification ritual that will provide a sense of completion and calm following the experiences of loss and descent. For this purpose we can use a glass of water and a dish of salt, which we can mix together. Salt is a substance that draws out water, as I know only too well from helping Jill study osmosis for her biology class. Salt seems an appropriate substance to use symbolically to draw out pain and darkness. I decide to let Morgan, Helene, or Judith come up with an appropriate blessing.

After the completion ceremony, I know that the next part of my healing ritual should be a celebration of each stage of life that every female member of our species encounters, a celebration that will include all the potential and difficult choices around childbearing as a consequence of living in a female body. I select a piece I wrote a few months after the tubal ligation, when I felt joined to all women across time and space through our shared suffering. I wrote it late at night when I was alone and unable to sleep, while everyone else in my family floated safely in dreams, or so I imagined. I had gone to my typewriter without any conscious plan and a rather odd poem, almost a ritual chant, had simply emerged from me. I had never written any poetry or "nonprose" before, at least not since elementary-school days of composing limericks. Recording this poem or chant was a unique experience. I now thought that it might find a home in my ritual:

Honor and Remember Her

Girl-Child who explores the world in delight,
little bud upon the branch

> curious, playful, timid,
> brave,
> not yet knowing what is
>   to come
> learning, preparing

Honor and Remember Her!

New-Fertile Adolescent upon the brink,
ripening fruit upon the branch

> caught—concealing and displaying
> caught—embarrassed and proud
> caught—shy and bold

Honor and Remember Her!

Sexual Woman
ripe fruit upon the branch

> sensual, juicy, lusty,
> receptive, yielding, reaching

Honor and Remember Her!

Bountiful Woman bearing seed soon to sprout,
bud yet to become

> cradling her child, bearing her risk with
>   serenity,
> immersed

Honor and Remember Her!

Barren Woman, my friend too
bare branch upon the tree

> yearning for a bud
> shouldering the invisible heavy burden
>   of her loss

Honor and Remember Her!

Woman Alone
proud strong single branch upon the tree

> choosing to bear no fruit
> energy will flow elsewhere

Honor and Remember Her!

Woman Murderess who ends the life within
tears the budding fruit from her branch

> She has her reason
> Who can judge Her?
> Who claims to Know?

Honor and Remember Her!

Woman-Based Woman who seeks no Man,
exiled, outcast, separate branch upon the tree

> Not to be pitied!
> Not to be scorned!
> See, instead, Her special access
>   to Woman's World

Honor and Remember Her!

Woman aging, growing older, growing old,
branch withering upon the tree

> Still new life within.
> Wisdom flows within this withering branch,
> through the trunk,
> into the Earth,
> Not to be lost.

Honor and Remember Her!

I wonder to myself what it might be like to hear this piece read aloud, especially by women friends. I realize that I have never had the experience of hearing anything I have written read back to me. This form of mirroring, or reflecting back to me of myself—through hearing my own words spoken aloud— would undoubtedly be an unusual and powerful experience. Would the four of us take turns with each stanza, or would we read them aloud all together? No matter how we might organize the reading, I feel certain that our joint naming and hearing of each segment will, in and of itself, affirm the unique value and specialness of women, no matter what their stage of life or what choices they might be compelled to make connected to childbearing and sexuality.

After this portion of the ceremony, which I hope will honor all women, I realize that I wish to evoke an archetypal image of woman, one like our image of a male god, that will reflect the power, strength, and wholeness in each of us. For this section I choose one of my favorite poems from the book *Daughters of Copper Woman*, a recording of stories and poems from oral accounts entrusted to the author, Ann Cameron, by women who belong to a secret society of a tribe of Canadian Indians. The stories have been transmitted through a now-threatened oral tradition in a culture that has remained matrilinear and matriarchal. The story that contains the poem I select tells of Copper Woman, the wise old woman of the tribe, as she grows old and tired. She prepares to leave her family through death and, before departing, passes on to her daughter the feminine wisdom she has acquired during her long life, instructing her daughter to pass it on in turn to other women. The story ends with a poignant chant, containing a positive image both of woman and of death. I like the way the image in the poem contrasts with the frightening images of old women and of death that so pervade our culture; rather than abandoning those she leaves behind her, Copper Woman becomes a part of the entire cosmos, thus everpresent.[7]

With an image of wholeness for women in our minds and hearts, the substance of my healing ceremony will be complete. To conclude, we will share food and then formally end the ritual with a closing blessing. The food and blessing will facilitate our return to ordinary life from the sacred space we will have created together through the mingling of our combined feminine energies.

I bring my plan to our next group meeting. Only Morgan, Judith, and I are present because Helene is away on vacation. Most of our two hours is taken up with the question that Judith brings to us. Earlier in the day, she had gone to a surgeon to check a lump in her breast. Although the lump turned out to be a cyst, which the doctor was able to aspirate successfully, for the past two days Judith has had to live with the fear that the lump might be cancer.

"I have a question for you both," she announces. "It's more of a spiritual question than a pragmatic one, since I know how to handle finding a lump, that is, in terms of the procedure to follow. What's more of an unknown to me is the question of what attitude to have towards the impermanence of life. How to live with the awareness that one second you can be perfectly healthy and the next you can be dying of cancer. Just as with raising children, for eighteen years your child is with you and then she can step on a plane to go to college and be gone from you in an instant."

Together, Morgan and I share our responses to Judith, and the three of us meander through this realm together, finding, if not definitive answers to Judith's questions, at least a comfort in knowing that it is a question we share. I find myself marveling at the awareness of how comforting our mere presence in this group is for each of us. Judith's anxiety has lessened simply through our seeing and affirming her worries, even if we cannot do anything to change the reality of what she may have to face.

When there is a long lull in the discussion, I bring up my budding plan. "I've thought a lot about the idea of having a ritual in this group for me. While I'm anxious just thinking about it, I'd really like to go ahead with it if you're all willing. And I brought some ideas for it."

Morgan and Judith turn toward me with their full attention. I am touched by how conscientiously they search their belongings for pens and paper to take notes and realize all at once that my suffering has left me open to receiving such loving attention. I am no longer as insistent on being self-sufficient. When they are ready, I explain that I would like my ritual to have four parts: an acknowledgment of the reality and permanence of my loss; a recognition of my difficult but transformative descent into an underworld of pain; an appreciation and celebration of all women for their courageous efforts to bear the difficult life-and-death issues with which they struggle because of their capacity to bear children; and, finally, an evocation of archetypal images of wholeness for women. As Judith and Morgan diligently record my ideas, I go on to name the specific readings I have come up with.

"Well," Morgan says, "I have an idea of what you want. But I think that the three of us—Helene, Judith and me— need to get together without you. If there aren't any surprises, if you know exactly what will happen, you'll be too much in your head, in your thoughts, and it won't affect you in the profound way that rituals can. So, I don't want you to give us the readings you picked."

"I guess that's exactly what I'm afraid of, and why I want to plan the whole thing!" I laugh. "It isn't easy for me to give up control! But I'm determined to try."

Judith, who has been sitting quietly, says, "I think it would be nice if we each brought artifacts connected to the feminine that are important to us and put them out. I have that lovely carved wooden statue of Kuan Yin I showed you a few weeks ago."

"Yes, and that poster of Georgia O'Keeffe, the one where she is a remarkable crone, wise and staring straight out at the viewer," I add.

"We can include personal articles, too," Morgan comments. "When my class did a ritual for one of the members who was about to have her first baby, we created a powerful altar of objects. People brought remarkable artifacts. Our group is half the size, but I bet we can create just as effective an altar. But I really don't want to go into any more of the details now. Sue, you have to let Judith, Helene, and me plan it without you."

Morgan and Judith decide when to get together with Helene to map out the event while I watch them, listening, filled with gratitude as well as an excited and anxious sense of anticipation. I can sense that a shift in control has occurred; my women friends have taken over the planning of my ritual, and I have yielded to them, despite my anxiety.

I try my best to provide, in my work as a therapist, the safe holding environment of a relationship within which my patients can experience their own healing powers. I have tried to create ritual forms for my daughters and women friends within which they could experience the healing energy generated by our joint presence. Now for the first time I am going to have the opportunity to allow a group of women to weave together a special ceremony for me and to let myself be held by their loving arms.

I drive home from the meeting in silence, shutting off the car radio that is usually on whenever I am driving somewhere alone. I want to think about the idea of participating in a ritual without ordinary distractions. When I pull into our garage, I see that Michael's car is already there; he has come home early. Responding to the noise of my car, he opens the door and gives his familiar welcoming salute.

"They're really going to do it!" I announce before I am even all the way out of the car.

"Do what?" he inquires. "Who's going to do what?"

"My women's group!" I tell him, as I climb up the steps into the kitchen. "They're going to put together a ritual for me, to complete and to heal the experiences of the abortion and the tubal ligation!"

"Tell me about it," Michael says with genuine eagerness, and we go into our bedroom and shut the door in an attempt to create a temporary sanctuary away from the children. As I explain the familiar details I so recently presented in my group, I suddenly become aware of his expression as he listens intently and unself-consciously to me. His face is suffused with interest, concern, respect, and love. In this moment, with the prospect of the feminine ritual for me lying ahead, I think back to the time of my worst despair. Now I see not my own black pain and hopelessness but Michael's terror at the depth of the blackness and the prospect of losing me. I see the descent that he, too, was compelled to make as a result of the abortion and tubal ligation, and how long and hard he had to work in order to hold on to me. I see how he has struggled to carry me safely to the brink of a healing place and how happy he is that I have arrived here. In this moment, knowing even now how quickly it will dissolve into the ordinary irritations of everyday life, I understand the burden of love's incommunicability: How can I possibly convey to him these feelings?

With one part of my mind I continue telling Michael about my ideas for the ritual and explain how Morgan told me that I had to let them plan it, or nothing more than the routine carrying out of known procedures could take place. "I gave them my suggestions, but they're only going to honor my general ideas! The ritual is going to be a complete surprise!" With another part of my mind I continue to see the loving expression on his face and his delight in the healing ritual that will now come to pass for me.

The loving moment with Michael is short-lived indeed. Morgan gives me a detailed set of instructions, which I read carefully and then carry out diligently. As the date of the ritual draws near, I become inexplicably irritable and withdrawn from my family. I can only speculate that I am directing my anxiety about the coming ritual toward them, or that the knowledge that I am leaving them to have a completely separate and hopefully transformative experience pulls me away from them. Sadness at the memories of the abortion that are awakened like sleeping ghosts helps keep me apart. By the time the eve of the ritual arrives, I am filled with a mixture of excitement and dread but my family can hardly wait for the next day, when it will be over.

I ride in the backseat of Judith's car, lulled by the sound of Judith and Helene chatting together as we drive through late-afternoon traffic on our way to my ritual. The rich melodies of a Bach organ concerto fill the automobile, cushioning me from outer-world noise as well as the inner tension of anticipation. Following the instructions that Morgan sent me several weeks ago, I am wearing the same beige suit I wore to the first appointment with Dr. Rhodes to discuss my pregnancy and to the medical procedures that followed. Also in accord with my instructions, I am wearing no jewelry, not even a watch or my wedding ring; I am stripped as bare of adornments now as I was before both the abortion and tubal ligation. This time, instead of feeling barren and exposed, I picture the Sumerian goddess Inanna, who willingly removed her clothing and adornments at each of the seven gates of her voluntary journey to the underworld. On the seat beside me is a small bag that contains my wedding ring, a necklace with a charm that symbolizes each of my children, and a bracelet I have chosen for myself. My instructions told me to bring jewelry to adorn myself as a "woman-one-in-myself," though I have no idea how or when this adornment will occur. I have also brought a copy of the first draft of my written manuscript, the one that contains the burst of those raw and chaotic feelings I first needed to place outside myself through writing. Somewhere during the ritual that hovers mysteriously ahead, I know the manuscript will be destroyed; I have been instructed to bring something precious with me that I would be willing to sacrifice. The manuscript, which contains my personal world, my feelings for my lost child, my selfhood, is the most precious possession I can think of. I put my hand on the box that holds several hundred sheets of paper and contemplate the intensity of the emotional pain that I poured into the thousands of words covering them. Will I be able to let these sheets of paper go?

I turn my attention to the music and eventually realize that my mind has begun to wander, that I am no longer thinking about the ritual. The music has a coherent order to it, a form, which soothes me. I begin to feel relaxed and calm; I float in a pleasant limbo between the ordinary life I have now left behind and the new world of the feminine ritual that will soon occur. Dreamily I picture Michael's face when I first told him about the plans that Morgan, Helene, and Judith were making. I savor the love I see in it once again. Then his image changes, and I see his face taut with anxiety and pain as he regards me helplessly, unable to find words that can comfort me. This picture shifts again into the remembered image of Michael beaming with relief when he hurried into the recovery room to see me after the tubal-ligation surgery. Behind these shifting visions of his face, I conjure up the faces of my closest friends. There is Margaret, so vivid and full of passion in our discussion about whether all women who have abortions feel like murderers. There is Julia, sunlight and shadow dappled on her face in the patio restaurant when she tells me what it feels like to have anesthesia. There is Esther, frowning as she confides her dark feelings about her tubal-ligation surgery. I spend an especially long time smiling at the sight of Katherine when she was happily pregnant. Remembering the time she sat on my bed and drew me out of the Dead Zone after the tubal ligation, sensing again the pressure of her arms holding me as I sobbed when I was filled with dread facing that summer-vacation trip, I feel her love for me. Images of my clients and consultees come into focus and then recede. I know I will soon be crossing over a bridge constructed of the powerful bonds created from these human relationships, bonds that are surely as strong and solid as any natural or man-made element in the physical world, bonds that will be held together with the intricate struts I have created through my psychological explorations. I wonder what lies ahead of me on the other side of this bridge. . . .

After what seems like an endless journey, Judith stops the car and parks in front of Morgan's house. I have never been here before, and I am looking forward to seeing where Morgan lives. I climb out of the car, glad to stretch after the long ride, expecting to walk with Helene and Judith into the house. But instead Judith abruptly puts her hand on my shoulder to stop me and places a blindfold over my eyes. My heart gives an extra hard beat; what is she doing? I was not expecting this! In an authoritative voice—the voice of a priestess—Helene intones, "The ritual begins *now*."

EPILOGUE

Ordinary Life Moves On

They say that "time assuages,"
Time never did assuage;
An actual suffering strengthens,
As sinews do, with age.

Time is a test of trouble,
But not a remedy.
If such it prove, it prove too
There was no malady.

—Emily Dickinson[1]

As my ordinary life moves on in tandem and intertwined with the lives of my family and friends, the permanent place occupied by the abortion and tubal ligation continues to shift its position and meaning. Sometimes events in my life elicit feelings of grief at my loss that are as immediate as if it had just occurred. But I know that the making of meaning and the bearing of suffering are lifelong *processes*, not finite events that are accomplished once and for all. Some recent vicissitudes in these lifelong processes:

I talk with my son, Ben, after school. He is troubled by the intensity of the negative feelings that his older sisters, Jill and Becky, mercilessly direct his way. "The only family I have is you and Daddy!" he proclaims mournfully.

Michael and I begin to work hard to shift the entrenched family system that supports the polarization among our three children, while silently I wonder how my fourth baby, who would now be almost five years old, might have shifted this family constellation. Ben would have had a younger ally; there is no doubt in my mind that he would have adapted quickly to the role of adored older brother or that he would not be alone now to face the animosity of his sisters. At some deep place in my mind, I continue to track the development of my unborn child as if he or she were alive.

From time to time Ben continues to ask me, "Are you going to have another baby?" He has a keen yearning for a younger sibling. Even though I have explained to him many times that I cannot have babies anymore, at his age, when anything is still possible, when he contemplates a future in which he juggles the assorted professions of novelist, film producer, farmer, and actor, rotating his time equally among them, he cannot absorb the absolute and utter finality of the fact that our family is as large as it will ever be. And each time I reply to his question/wish, each time I explain to him this un-changeable reality, a pang of sorrow pierces my heart.

I sit in my office with Gayle, a woman who has come back to see me. Ten years ago we began what was to be a five-year psychotherapy relationship. At that time she was thirty-two years old, had been married to her husband for twelve years, and had two children. She sought psychotherapy for help with depression and a pervasive sense that her life lacked direction. During the five years we worked together, she made a number of changes, inner and outer, which included her pursuit of an interest in painting. She has returned to see me because, at age forty-two, she unexpectedly became preg-nant. Although she is not opposed to abortion on any philo-sophical, political, or religious ground, she believes that her child is fated to exist or such an unlikely pregnancy could not have occurred. Her conviction is so strong that, despite hav-ing grown children and wishing her years of mothering young children were behind her, and despite her husband's prefer-ence that she terminate the pregnancy (matching one side of her own feelings), she decides against abortion. Knowing that the pregnancy and birth would most likely be a problematic time for her and for her marital relationship, she arranged to meet with me in order to help herself work with the antici-pated difficulties. Gayle's pregnancy, though it proceeds well physically, remains an ongoing source of anguish because so much of her does not want to care for a baby again. She brings her negative feelings about the pregnancy and the unborn baby to me. I find myself in the odd position of being both diametrically opposite to and yet completely aligned with her at the same time. Every aspect of bearing a child that she dreads and dislikes, from feeling the changes in her body as the baby grows to anticipating the nighttime nursing and years of diapering once it is born, are aspects of mothering that I personally cherished and would give anything to have been able to experience one more time with my lost child. Yet I understand and empathize with her torment over feeling impelled to choose a course of action that was simultaneously right and not-right for her in essential ways, as well as with the suffering she must endure as a consequence. Shifting the structures of her life and redirecting her energy to make room for the baby are not simple changes for her to make. Both of us are relying upon a conviction that once her baby is born, she will love it just as fully as she does her older children.

Recently tragedy struck a family that Michael and I have known for more than twenty years. We met Norm and Corinne before we were married to each other, when they were newlyweds of just one year. The four of us proceeded through our lives on separate but parallel tracks, living through the early years of marriage when we were still free from the responsibilities of parenting and then through the pregnancies and births of each of our children. We stopped having regular contact with each other as we became engrossed in our separate careers and the multitude of activities related to our children. Nonetheless, the connection we had established early on held fast. When we received the stunning news that the older of their two sons had been hit by a car and killed, we were devastated too. They had faced the worst nightmare of any parent. Michael and I along with other friends of theirs were overwhelmed with a primitive terror as we shared, albeit briefly, their pain. Though psychological boundaries between our families were gradually reestablished, in the beginning it felt as if their loss had happened to us. I sat at the funeral service crying with everyone else; there was not one dry eye in the entire room. Sitting in the large room, I understood yet another underpinning of the horror of abortion. The death of a child, whether unborn or living, triggers an archetypal panic—a truncated life is a violation of the natural order and stability of the universe, a rupture of basic trust that we will endure, that we can rely upon proceeding in a linear direction from birth to death at a ripe old age, a momentary shattering of confidence in the existence of a future. My tears were shed not only for their lost son and for my lost child but for all of us who must shoulder, even temporarily, the fragmenting of our worlds.

From time to time Michael and I have conversations about the abortion. One example: "I was so worried about my

He reverses decision

And she must depend of the decision

physical well-being then," Michael reflects. "I don't have that apprehension now. Now I feel as if we really could have managed to raise that child."

"You can't know that for sure," I say, taking the position that is least likely for me. Usually I am the one who wishes we had made a different choice. "It may be that you feel more secure physically now just *because* you don't have the demands of four children. You'd be sixty years old with an adolescent! How would that feel?"

"I don't know," Michael responds solemnly. "Maybe I'd be happy to have an adolescent. Maybe that would have given my life more meaning than anything else. After all, what else really counts besides family? Loving connections to other human beings—that's what matters. You were the one who told me you read somewhere that no one who has retired ever looks back and wishes he had worked harder!"

I have no answer for Michael.

Other times we simply live with and share our regrets: Michael comments with sorrow, "I wish I could have understood how real that baby was to you. I can't believe how I abandoned you without even knowing it!" Or, when I realize how frightening my desperation must have been, I ask Michael, "How did you ever withstand my anguish?" When we vowed to be together for better or worse, neither of us could have imagined what worse might mean, and yet there is incalculable intimacy in sharing our deepest vulnerabilities and wounds.

We are also aware of experiences that our lives have been able to include because we did not have a fourth child: special times with Jill, Becky, and Ben because our energies were not needed to care for an infant; time for the two of us together and each of us alone; the prospect of having some time together alone after our children are grown.

As I approach menopause myself and live through this stage of life with my women friends, I sometimes feel deep sorrow about my tubal ligation. As I grumble about the hormonal shifts that cause symptoms of premenstrual tension or unexpected irregularities in my periods, I wonder (not without some anger) whether the blocking of my fallopian tubes might not be responsible for these problems. I have read, in fact, in a book written for women on the subject of premenstrual tension, that there is a correlation between tubal-ligation surgery and an imbalance in the production of progesterone, which could be the cause of the problems I have been experiencing. Each month when my period comes, I am reminded of the loss of the fertility that would normally be associated with menstruation. I miss the pride I used to feel each month in my female body and its awesome power to produce life. But I always remind myself that the temptation to replace my lost child by becoming pregnant again might well have been irresistible. I am not at all sure that I could have withstood the enormous pressure the temptation would have exerted. And if I had yielded to it, either consciously or unconsciously and become pregnant, I would only have been left to grieve anew for the death of my irreplaceable fourth baby.

There are days when I think back to the raging flames of my anger and disappointment with Dr. Ross for his inability to help me. Through enduring the heat of rage without channeling the feelings into action, I have learned that if it gets hot enough without being discharged, the fire can transform itself into a cooler but equally powerful understanding of the universality of human limitations and, eventually, into compassion. This, too, is a process and not a finite goal, one that recurs, though with lessening intensity, as understanding and awareness accrue.

I think of a recently aired public-television documentary called *Breaking Silence*, on the subject of incest and child abuse. A family in which two of three sisters were molested by their father was filmed. The sister who was not molested and one who was had a history of intense hostility toward each other. They were asked, in a meeting with a counselor, to look into each other's eyes. They complied, with resistance and hostility at first, but in less than a second they burst into tears and fell into each other's arms, filled with grief for the suffering they had each endured despite their very different connection to their father. I know that without allowing the initial burst of long-suppressed anger and disappointment toward Dr. Ross, I could not have arrived at the awareness of my own needs. Although I did not have a happy, mutually satisfying ending with Dr. Ross, I have been able to arrive at a sense of completion on my own.

I continue to have contact periodically with Karen Ortman. Six months after my final session with her, Karen called and told me, "I have good news to share with you! I've been accepted into graduate school in psychology! I'm actually going to go on and study to become a therapist!" I was delighted with her news. I knew that Karen, already educated in the school of her own life suffering, would have much to teach her professors and fellow students in a graduate program. She had already planned her master's thesis: a study of the effectiveness of short-term small-group sessions for women who have had abortions.

Sometime after our talk on the telephone, while browsing in a local bookstore, I unexpectedly came across Karen's name. I was thumbing through a stack of large soft-cover books near the cash register: *Yellow Pages for Women*. At the beginning, alphabetically under *A*, was the heading *Abortion*. Under a special section labeled *Counselors*, I noticed Karen's name. After her name, she had written a description of her qualifications. With characteristic honesty and openness, she had extended her hand to other women by writing, "I have had training in abortion counseling, but it is my own experience of an abortion that has been most important to me in learning how to help others."

Recently Karen sent me a copy of an article summarizing the results of a research study. In it I read that women who have both an abortion and a tubal ligation, either simultaneously or close together, experience more intense grief reactions than women who have had either an abortion or tubal ligation. Those women who must deal with both at once take a longer time to integrate and recover from them than if they had had either procedure alone. In return, I sent Karen a very poignant and thoughtful article written by a nurse who works

in a clinic where abortions are performed.[2] The author conveyed the psychological, emotional, and moral complexity of
her experience and observations in a clear, compassionate
manner. Karen mailed me a note thanking me and saying that
she planned to use the article in the training she would be
doing with counselors who will go on to work with women
who have abortions.

This note was soon followed by an announcement that
Karen had successfully passed the examinations for a Marriage, Family, and Counselor license and, in addition to her
part-time work at Planned Parenthood, had opened her own
office for private practice.

Reminders continue to surface of the imperative need for
feminine wisdom—centered in the *agape* principle—to encircle
and hold the profound suffering women must bear because of
the powerful drives of female biology. Recently, as only one
example, newspapers and magazines have been following the
painful saga of Baby M, product of a surrogate mother.
Regardless of the outcome of our judicial system's determination of custody, both the adoptive and biological mothers (as
well as the father and perhaps someday Baby M) will be left
with their separate pain. Our capacity to understand and aid
those individuals who must cope with emotional crises arising
from surrogate parenting and other new dilemmas has yet to
catch up with our technological possibilities.

Earlier this year I read an editorial column by journalist
Ellen Goodman on the complicated issue of transplanting
organs from anencephalic infants (babies born with a defective
brain who are doomed to die) to infants who need organs to
replace their own. The concept of harvesting organs from
dying infants, of prolonging the lives of these infants for this
purpose, is as abhorrent to me as it is to Ellen Goodman. Yet
to the young couple grieving the loss of their beloved baby,
offering the hope of life to another infant gives meaning to
their own baby's life and death. How can we honor the
guidelines that protect the rights of the infant yet allow the

parents the opportunity to wrest meaning from their tragic situation?

Anna Quindlen, in a *New York Times* editorial I read with interest, describes the soul-searching necessitated by her decision *not* to have an amniocentesis (a test to determine if an unborn baby is genetically normal) during her third pregnancy. Although I might have made a different choice in her situation, I did not feel critical of her decision; rather, I was glad that she had the option of choosing what was right for her. The following week I came upon a series of letters readers sent in response to her column; it generated such an unusually large number of letters that a representative sample was chosen for publication. I was struck by the diversity of the responses, as well as by the passion with which the readers communicated their feelings. Clearly many of us are touched to the core by the moral dilemmas modern life presents, and we grapple with their complexities in very different, but equally valid, ways.

I wonder how we will manage to make room for a wide range of acceptable choices as technology continues to provide new options—choices that differ as dramatically from one another as do the individuals who make them and yet are each "right" in the context of the situation of these individuals and their lives. We need the masculine *logos* principles to preserve the order and stability of our world and to provide guidelines and parameters that protect the rights and well-being of everyone concerned. To balance these vital principles, we must also have feminine *agape* principles that support individuals with empathy and compassion in their endeavor to live lives of equivalent integrity and meaning despite differing responses to complex moral dilemmas. Without *agape* in balance with *logos*, individuals who must confront such predicaments are left alone to negotiate uncharted territory without a map. In such uncharted realms the future cannot be seen clearly. Whatever direction one chooses eliminates some problems but creates others; making meaning of the inescapable suffering that results must necessarily take different forms. Individuals who must live through crises of soul need not remain alone if men and women can join together in circles strong enough to hold them securely and without judgment or fear so that th⸻ recover and heal. Such a healing circle i⸻ ⸻AMES Project Quilt: In 1987 a small ⸻gan creating quilt panels to commemo- ⸻l ones to AIDS. Their endeavor has ⸻e ongoing community arts project; the ⸻ for whom the separate panels were ⸻ies of those who made the panels are interwoven into a healing, unified entity.[3]

My newly acquired appreciation of the power and wisdom to be gained from exploring female experience in depth has led me to set myself some specific tasks for the future. One is to begin making room for the way in which Michael and I will welcome Ben into his young manhood at age thirteen. As I wish my daughters to value their feminine capacity for *agape*, I wish him to appreciate his special masculine *logos* potential. As I wish my daughters to develop the masculine *logos* principle within them, I wish Ben to balance this masculine side with his softer, feminine *agape* potential. Luckily for me and for Ben, Michael has been uncovering and appreciating this side of himself as a consequence of living through my psychological descent. With this head start, Ben should be well on his way to valuing not only his intellect, his capacity for rational thinking, his sense of right and wrong, but also his sensitivity to feeling, his receptivity, and his empathy: *logos* and *agape*, hand in hand, in balance and harmony, as in the moment when the moon rises and the sun sets. Michael and I will need our intuition to help us find a way to affirm the value of this inner balance in Ben's ritual. And I am well aware that we will also have to include in Ben's ritual some form of my "letting go" of him symbolically so that he can be free from the constraints that too strong a bond to his personal mother might entail.

Soon our older daughter, Jill, will be leaving home for college, embarking upon the first part of her life journey outside the parental umbrella under which we have sheltered

her so carefully. We know she has firm and deep roots; now
she needs wings that will carry her away. I hope that our
family will honor the significant leave-taking in a ceremonial
form, providing Jill with a memory that she will always have
with her. Letting go of Ben as a little boy and greeting him as
a young man, allowing Jill to soar away, followed in short
order by Becky, will not be easy passages for me. Attachment, not letting go, seems to be my forte. Although significant separations for me, both as a baby and as an adult, have
been catastrophic, I look upon the forthcoming separations
from my children as an opportunity for me to welcome the
beginning of something new in my relationships, as well as a
time to mourn the passing of the familiar.

Another task, which is less a task than an ongoing commitment, is to continue to lead my own life in a manner that
meets my needs to grow and develop as a separate person. I
do this not only for myself but also for my children. I want to
encourage them to let their unique selves unfold and not only
to react to and comply with the demands of our culture and
the needs of others. The best way I know to accomplish this
goal is to model this behavior for them.

However, I have discovered that this course of action does
not always yield the desired results right away. One day
when I was involved with the writing of my manuscript, I
arose at 6:00 A.M., paused briefly to throw on some ragged
running clothes, forgot to comb my hair, and proceeded
directly to the typewriter, where I became totally absorbed in
my project. Later Becky stayed nearby to help me organize a
rather formidable array of papers. Completely unaware of
how disheveled I appeared, I was taken aback to see myself
through Becky's eyes when she finally looked at me with
genuine concern and asked seriously, "Am I going to grow up
and be like you?" Not quite comprehending, I asked, "What
do you mean?" "Well," she replied, waving at my messy
clothes and hairdo, "what *you* have—is it inherited? Am I
going to get it?" I told her that I didn't know for sure if she
would and added what I realized right away was absolutely

true: "You know, what I have isn't bad at all, in the event you *do* get it!"

As is readily apparent from these vignettes, dark notes in a minor key continue to sound aloud along with brighter, clear ones. I expect that this mixture of harmonies will continue as long as I exist and as long as ordinary life, with its manifold vicissitudes, goes on. I hope that I will continue to listen to each of them, no matter whether they are melodious or discordant. The alternative of not listening would mean not living my life but merely existing physically, without the vitality and passion that *all* feelings, pleasant or unpleasant, bring. Perhaps this—listening to all the notes that sound in my life—is the hardest task of all that I have set for myself; each of us would understandably prefer to resist or flee from pain. This poem, a sort of haiku in spirit if not exactly in form, perhaps conveys most succinctly that image of my life—and one that is true of each human life. I am never able to sustain this image for long, but I know that I, like a butterfly, can alight upon it from moment to moment:

> My life began,
> a single note.
> Now a symphony sounds.

Acknowledgments

The following individuals were not only midwives for this manuscript, facilitating its passage into the world, but they were mothers to me in the finest meaning of the word, affirming that mothering energy need not be limited to women nor to biological procreation:

Kim Chernin helped me develop the rudimentary manuscript into its final book form. Despite the complexities of our separate lives, Kim managed to materialize in just the right way exactly when I needed her. She was consistently available and helpful from our first contact on the telephone when she happened to answer in person (a most rare occurrence), to her final reading of the last revision some five years later.

Diane Cleaver, whose exceptional talents as an agent are readily apparent even to a novice, took me under her wing. After reading the first version of *Soul Crisis*, she saw through to the vision of what the final draft needed to be. But she patiently held this vision and waited for me to arrive at it in my own manner and in my own time, while she persisted with unflagging energy in the task of finding it a home.

Alexia Dorszynski, senior editor at NAL, responded to the book and never distanced herself from the painful and frightening inner states I describe. She understood my vision of it without our needing to talk much about it, saw that it might be of use to others, and then calmly and respectfully helped me, a first-time author, anticipate the psychological tasks at each stage of the publishing process. Like all mothers on call twenty-four hours a day, Alexia gave me her home telephone number so I could reach her whenever I needed to. And Dodie Gerson Edmands brought both sensitivity and thoroughness to the task of copyediting.

Jane Lewin unstintingly applied her considerable skills as an editor and her capacity for critical thinking to the manuscript, pushing me to extend the borders of my ideas further than I thought I could.

Dorothy Witt and Ellen Siegelman, along with Jane, also served as editors; each in her own unique way balanced *logos* and *agape* principles by casting a firmly critical and questioning eye upon the text and lending a warm and supportive heart to me.

Mary Jo Spencer, in whose wise and empathic presence the manuscript and I both blossomed, provided invaluable support and encouragement during the ups and downs of the entire process.

Without naming each one individually to preserve privacy, but nonetheless with gratitude for their wide-ranging contributions which I know they will recognize, I thank everyone in my circle of friends, clients, and colleagues.

I thank my parents, husband, and children for all they have given me by being who they are, particularly for the ways they have been problems for me, without which I would not have grown and been able to write this book.

I especially thank my husband, who both fathered and mothered the manuscript and me; he nurtured the book with his full attention (from editing to collating pages) and protected me by taking over family responsibilities (with minimal grumbling) so I could accomplish the writing of it.

Without the en*courage*ment of all of you, I could not have broken personal and cultural taboos and made my story available to others. Persisting in the writing of this book has been an act of courage.

Notes

Prologue

1. Muriel Rukeyser, *The Speed of Darkness* (New York, Random House Publisher, 1968), p. 103.

Chapter One

1. Esther Harding, *The Way of All Women* (New York: Harper Colophon Books, 1970), pp. 171–72.
2. May Sarton, *Selected Poems of May Sarton* ed. by Serena Sue Hilsinger and Lois Brynes (New York: W. W. Norton and Company, 1978), p. 77.

Chapter Two

1. Esther Harding, *The Way of All Women* (New York: Harper Colophon Books, 1970), p. 167.
2. In Penelope Washbourn, *Seasons of Woman: Song, Poetry, Ritual, Prayer, Myth, Story* (San Francisco: Harper and Row, Publishers, 1979), p. 121.
3. Harry Guntrip, *Psychoanalytic Theory, Therapy, and the Self* (New York: Basic Books, 1973), p. 185.
4. In Edward C. Whitmont, *The Symbolic Quest* (Princeton: Princeton University Press, 1969), p. 172.

Chapter Three

1. Esther Harding, *Women's Mysteries: Ancient and Modern* (New York: Harper Colophon Books, 1971), p. 111.

Chapter Four

1. Esther Harding, *Women's Mysteries: Ancient and Modern* (New York: Harper Colophon Books, 1971), p. 111.

Chapter Five

1. Esther Harding, *Women's Mysteries: Ancient and Modern* (New York: Harper Colophon Books, 1971), pp. 66–67.
2. Susan Griffin, *Woman and Nature: The Roaring Inside Her* (New York: Harper and Row Publishers, Inc., 1978), p. 91.
3. *Ibid.*, p. 223.

Chapter Six

1. Esther Harding, *Women's Mysteries: Ancient and Modern* (New York: Harper Colophon Books, 1971), p. 69.
2. Rilke, *Selected Poems of Rainer Maria Rilke*, trans. by Robert Bly (New York: Harper and Row, Publishers, 1981), p. 55.
3. Morton Shane and Estelle Shane, "The End Phase of Analysis: Indicators, Functions, and Tasks of Termination, *Journal of the American Psychoanalytic Association*, (32, No.4, 1984), p. 757.
4. *Ibid.*, p. 739–40.
5. *Ibid.*, p. 740.
6. William Morris, ed., *The American Heritage Dictionary of the English Language* (Boston: Houghton Mifflin Company, 1980).
7. Nor Hall, *The Moon and the Virgin* (New York: Harper and Row, Publishers, 1980).
8. *Ibid.*, p. 88.

Chapter Seven

1. Emily Dickinson, *Selected Poems and Letters of Emily Dickinson*, ed. by Robert N. Linscott (New York; Doubleday Anchor Books, 1959), pp. 167–68.
Emily Dickinson wrote 1,775 poems. Only seven of these were published during her lifetime, and they were published

anonymously. Had she lived in a cultural milieu that valued the subjective experience of women, perhaps she might not have been deprived of public recognition during her lifetime.
2. Thornton Wilder, *The Woman of Andros* (New York: Albert and Charles Boni, 1930), p. 37.

Chapter Eight

1. Ginette Paris, *Pagan Meditations: The Worlds of Aprhodite, Artemis, and Hestia* (Dallas: Spring Publications, 1986), pp. 146–47.

Chapter Nine

1. Esther Harding, *The Way of All Women* (New York: Harper Colophon Books, 1970), pp. 186–87.
2. Anne Sexton, *The Complete Poems* (Boston: Houghton Mifflin Company, 1981), p. 464–65.
3. Pat Brady, *Rose Is Rose*, United Feature Syndicate, Inc., May 9, 1985.
4. See D. W. Winnicott, "Ego Integration in Child Development," *Maturational Processes and the Facilitating Environment*, (New York: International Universities Press, 1965), pp. 57–58.
5. Barbara G. Walker, *The Crone: Woman of Age, Wisdom, and Power* (San Francisco: Harper and Row, Publishers, 1985), p. 37.
6. Carolyn Kizer, *Yin* (New York: Boa Editions, Ltd., 1984), p. 16.
7. Marge Piercy, *My Mother's Body* (New York: Alfred A. Knopf, 1985), pp. 26–32.
8. May Sarton, *Selected Poems of May Sarton*, ed. by Serena Sue Hilsinger and Lois Brynes (New York: W. W. Norton and Company, 1978), p. 75.
9. Sexton, *The Awful Rowing Toward God* (Boston: Houghton Mifflin Company, 1975), pp. 356–57.

Chapter Ten

1. Esther Harding, *The Way of All Women* (New York: Harper Colophon Books, 1970), pp. 163, 166.

2. Ginette Paris, *Pagan Meditations; The Worlds of Aphrodite, Artemis, and Hestia* (Dallas: Spring Publications, 1986), pp. 146-47.

Chapter Eleven

1. Kathryn Allen Rubazzi, *Motherself: A Mythic Analysis of Motherhood* (Indianapolis: Indiana University Press, 1988), p. 117.

Chapter Twelve

1. Ntozake Shange, *A Daughter's Geography* (New York: St. Martin's Press, 1983), p. 51.
2. Claire R. Farrer, "Singing for Life: The Mescalero Apache Girls' Puberty Ceremony," in Louise Carus Mahdi, Steven Foster, and Meredith Little, eds., *Betwixt and Between* (Illinois: Open Court Publishing Company, 1987), pp. 239–64.
3. Penelope Washbourn, ed. *Seasons of Woman* (San Francisco: Harper and Row, 1979), p. 19.
4. Carolyn Niethammer, *Daughters of the Earth: The Lives and Legends of American Indian Women* (New York: Collier Books, 1977), pp. 37–55.
5. Original source is Joseph Epes Brown, editor, *The Sacred Pipe: Black Elk's Account of the Seven Rites of the Oglala Sioux*, (New York: Penguin Books, 1971), pp. 120-121. Penelope Washbourn, "Slow Buffalo's Prayer," p. 16.
6. Esther Harding, *Women's Mysteries, Ancient and Modern* (New York: Harper Colophon Books, 1971), p. 68.
7. This ritual is described in detail in Betty Meador, "The Thesmophoria: A Woman's Ritual," *Psychological Perspectives* 17, No. 1 (1986): 35–45.

Additional references may be found in: Judy Grahn, "From Sacred Blood to the Curse and Beyond," in *The Politics of Women's Spirituality* ed. by Charlene Spretnak, (New York: Anchor Books, 1982), pp. 269–70; and Kathryn Allen Rabuzzi, *Motherself, A Mythic Analysis of Motherhood* (Indianapolis: Indiana University Press, 1988), pp. 197–98.

8. Merlin Stone, *When God Was a Woman* (New York: Harcourt Brace Jovanovich, 1976). These dates are still in the process of being ascertained, so estimates vary depending upon the source.

9. This topic is also discussed in Stephen Jay Gould, *Time's Arrow, Time's Cycle* (Cambridge: Harvard University Press, 1987).

10. Marija Gimbutas, *The Goddesses and Gods of Old Europe* (Berkeley; University of California Press, 1982), p. 238.

11. See Jean Shinoda Bolen, *Goddesses in Everywoman* (San Francisco: Harper and Row Publishers, 1984).

Chapter Thirteen

1. Merie-Louise von Franz, *The Feminine in Fairy Tales* (Dallas: Spring Publications, 1972), p. 64.

2. Joseph Campbell (with Bill Moyers), *The Power of Myth*, ed. by Betty Sue Flowers (New York: Doubleday, 1988), p. 182.

3. Jackie Pringle, "Hittite Birth Rituals," in *Images of Women in Antiquity*, ed. by Averil Cameron and Amelie Kuhrt (Detroit: Wayne State University Press, 1983), pp. 128–41.

4. C. G. Jung and C. Kerényi, *Essays on a Science of Mythology* (Princeton: Princeton University Press, 1959), p. 101.

5. See Diane Wolkstein and Samuel Noah Kramer, *Inanna, Queen of Heaven and Earth* (New York: Harper and Row, Publishers, 1983).

6. These translations by Betty Meador are published in Judy Grahn, *The Queen of Swords* (Boston: Beacon Press, 1987), p. 151.

7. Anne Cameron, *Daughters of Copper Woman* (Vancouver: Press Gang Publishers, 1981), p. 54.

Epilogue

1. Emily Dickinson, *Selected Poems and Letters of Emily Dickinson*, ed. by Robert N. Linscott, (New York: Doubleday Anchor Books, 1959), pp. 157–58.

2. Sallie Tisdale, "We Do Abortions Here," *Harper's*, October 1986, pp. 66–70.
3. Cindy Ruskin, *The Quilt: Stories from the NAMES Project* (New York: Simon and Schuster, Inc., 1988).

Bibliography

Health Care

Boston Women's Health Collective. *The New Our Bodies, Ourselves*. New York: Simon and Schuster, Inc., 1984.

Budoff, Penny Wise M.D. *No More Hot Flashes and Other Good News*. New York: Warner Books, 1984.

Dalton, Katharina, M.D. *Once a Month*. Claremont, Ca.: Hunter House, Inc. 1979.

Demetrakopolos, Stephanie. *Listening to Our Bodies: The Rebirth of Feminine Wisdom*. Boston: Beacon Press, 1983.

Doress, Paula Brown, Diana Laskin Siegel, and the Midlife and Older Women Book Project. *Ourselves, Growing Older; Women Aging with Knowledge and Power*. New York: Simon and Schuster, Inc., 1987.

Greenwood, Sadja. *Menopause Naturally, Preparing for the Second Half of Life*. San Francisco: Volcano Press, 1984.

Lever, Judy, with Dr. Michael G. Brush. *Pre-Menstrual Tension*. New York: Bantam Books, 1981.

Poetry and Fiction

Cameron, Ann. *Daughters of Copper Woman*. Vancouver: Press Gang Publishers, 1981.

Carruthers, M., "The Re-vision of the Muse: Adrienne Rich, Audre Lorde, Judy Grahn, Olga Broumas," *The Hudson Review*, 1983, 36, no. 21 (293–322).

Dickinson, Emily, *The Complete Poems of Emily Dickinson*. Edited by Thomas H. Johnson. Boston: Little, Brown and Company, 1960.

――――. *Selected Poems and Letters of Emily Dickinson*. Edited by Robert N. Linscott. Garden City New York: Doubleday Anchor Books, 1959.

Grahn, Judy. *The Queen of Swords*. Boston: Beacon Press, 1987.

――――. *The Work of a Common Woman*. New York: The Crossing Press, 1978.

Griffin, Susan. *Unremembered Country*. Port Townsend, Washington: Copper Canyon Press, 1987.

――――. *Woman and Nature: The Roaring Inside Her*. New York: Harper and Row, Publishers, 1978.

Kizer, Carolyn. *Yin*. New York: BOA Editions Ltd., 1984.

Piercy, Marge. *My Mother's Body*. New York: Alfred A. Knopf, 1985.

Plath, Sylvia. *The Collected Poems*. New York: Harper and Row, Publishers, 1981.

Rainer Maria Rilke. *Selected Poems of Rainer Maria Rilke*. Translated by Robert Bly. New York: Harper and Row, Publishers, 1981.

Sappho. *Sappho, A New Translation*. Translated by Mary Barnard. Berkeley: University of California Press, 1958.

Sarton, May. *Selected Poems of May Sarton*. Edited by Serena Sue Hilsinger and Lois Byrnes. New York: W. W. Norton and Company, 1978.

Sexton, Anne. *The Complete Poems*. Boston: Houghton Mifflin Company, 1981.

Shange, Ntozake. *A Daughter's Geography*. New York: St. Martin's Press, 1983.

Washbourn, Penelope. *Seasons of Women*. San Francisco: Harper and Row, Publishers, 1979.

Wilder, Thornton. *The Woman of Andros*. New York: Albert and Charles Boni, 1930.

Wolkstein, Diane, and Samuel Noah Kramer. *Inanna, Queen of Heaven and Earth*. New York: Harper and Row Publishers, 1983.

Psychology

Bowlby, John. *Attachment, Loss, and Separation. Volumes 1, 2, and 3*. New York: Basic Books, 1982.
↳Gilligan, Carol. *In a Different Voice: Psychological Theory and Women's Development*. Cambridge: Harvard University Press, 1982.
Guntrip, Harry. *Psychoanalytic Theory, Therapy, and the Self*. New York: Basic Books, 1973.
Meador, Betty. "Transference/Countertransference Between Woman Analyst and the Wounded Girl Child." In *Chiron: A Review of Jungian Analysis*. Wilmette, Ill.: Chiron Publications, 1984, pp. 163–74.
Whitmont, Edward C. *The Symbolic Quest*. Princeton: Princeton University Press, 1969.
Winnicott, D. W. *Maturational Processes and the Facilitating Environment*. New York: International Universities Press, 1965.
Woodman, Marion. "Abandonment in the Creative Woman." In *Chiron: A Review of Jungian Analysis*. Wilmette, Ill.: Chiron Publications, 1985, pp. 23–46.

Women's Issues, History, Religion

Allen, Paula Gunn. *The Sacred Hoop*. Boston: Beacon Press, 1986.
Bachofen, J. J. *Myth, Religion, and Mother Right*. Princeton: Princeton University Press, 1973.
Bolen, Jean Shinoda. *Goddesses in Everywoman*. San Francisco: Harper and Row, Publishers, 1984.

Brown, Joseph Epes, ed. *The Sacred Pipe: Black Elk's Account of the Seven Rites of the Oglala Sioux.* New York: Penguin Books, 1971.

Budapest, Z. *The Holy Book of Women's Mysteries I, II, and III.* Los Angeles, Susan B. Anthony Coven, 1980.

Cameron, Averil, and Amelie Kuhrt, eds. *Images of Women in Antiquity.* Detroit: Wayne State University Press, 1983.

Campbell, Joseph, *The Power of Muth*, New York: Doubleday, 1988.

Chernin, Kim. *Reinventing Eve: Modern Woman in Search of Herself*, New York: Times Books, 1987.

Chodorow, Nancy. *The Reproduction of Mothering; Psychoanalysis and the Sociology of Gender.* Berkeley: University of California Press, 1978.

Christ, Carol, and Judith Plaskow, eds., *Womanspirit Rising.* San Francisco: Harper and Row, Publishers, 1979.

Daly, Mary. *Beyond God the Father.* Boston: Beacon Press, 1973.

Eisler, Riane. *The Chalice and the Blade.* San Francisco: Harper and Row, Publishers, 1987.

von Franz, Marie-Louise, *The Feminine in Fairy Tales*, Dallas: Spring Publications, 1972.

Fraser, Antonia. *The Weaker Vessel.* New York: Alfred A. Knopf, 1984.

French, Marilyn. *Beyond Power.* New York: Summit Books, 1985.

Friedrich, Paul. *The Meaning of Aphrodite.* Chicago: University of Chicago Press, 1978.

Gimbutas, Maria. *The Goddesses and Gods of Old Europe.* Berkeley; University of California Press, 1982.

Gleason, Judith. *OYA, In Praise of the Goddess.* Boston: Shambhala Press, 1987.

Gould, Stephen Jay. *Time's Arrow, Time's Cycle.* Cambridge: Harvard University Press, 1987.

Grahn, Judy. *The Highest Apple*. San Francisco: Spinsters Ink, 1985.

——. "From Sacred Blood to the Curse and Beyond," in *The Politics of Women's Spirituality*. Edited by Charlene Spretnak. Garden City New York: Anchor Books, 1982, pp. 265–79.

Hall, Nor. *The Moon and the Virgin*. New York: Harper and Row, Publishers, 1980.

Harding, Esther. *The Way of All Women*. New York: Harper Colophon Books, 1970.

——. *Women's Mysteries: Ancient and Modern*. New York: Harper Colophon Books, 1971.

Harrison, Jane Ellen. *Prolegomena to the Study of Greek Religion*. London: Merlin Press, 1962.

Herrera, Hayden. *Frida: A Biography of Frida Kahlo*. New York: Harper and Row, Publishers, 1983.

Iglehart, Hallie. *Womanspirit*. San Francisco: Harper and Row, Publishers, 1983.

Koltuv, Barbara Black. *The Book of Lilith*. York Beach, Maine: Nicolas-Hays, Inc., 1986.

Lauter, Estella, and Carol Schreier Rupprecht, eds. *Feminist Archetypal Theory*. Knoxville: University of Tennessee Press, 1985.

Lefkowitz, Mary R., and Maureen B. Fant, eds. *Women's Life in Greece and Rome*. Baltimore, Md.: Johns Hopkins Press, 1982.

Lerner, Gerda. *The Creation of Patriarchy*. Oxford Eng.: Oxford University Press, 1986.

Lincoln, Bruce. *Emerging From the Chrysalis: Studies in Rituals of Women's Initiation*. Cambridge: Harvard University Press, 1981.

Luker, Kristin. *Taking Chances: Abortion and the Decision Not to Contracept*. Berkeley: University of California Press, 1975.

Mahdi, Louise Carus, and Steven Foster and Meredith Little, eds. *Betwixt and Between: Patterns of Masculine and Feminine Initiation*. La Salle, Ill: Open Court Publishing, 1987.

Mariechild, Diane. *Motherwit*. New York: The Crossing Press, 1981.

Meador, Betty. "The Thesmophoria: A Woman's Ritual," *Psychological Perspectives*. vol. 17, no. 1 (1986): 35–45.

Niethammer, Carolyn. *Daughters of the Earth: The Lives and Legends of American Indian Women*. New York: Collier Books, 1977.

Pagels, Elaine. *The Gnostic Gospels*. New York: Vintage Books, 1981.

Paris, Ginette. *Pagan Meditations: The Worlds of Aphrodite, Artemis, and Hestia*. Dallas: Spring Publications, 1986.

Patai, Rafael. *The Hebrew Goddess*. New York: Avon Books, 1978.

Philips, John A. *Eve: The History of an Idea*. San Francisco: Harper and Row, Publishers, 1984.

Pomeroy, Sarah. *Goddesses, Whores, Wives, and Slaves: Women in Classical Antiquity*. New York: Schocken Books, 1975.

Rabuzzi, Kathryn Allen. *Motherself: A Mythic Analysis of Motherhood*. Indianapolis: Indiana University Press, 1988.

Rodman, Hyman, and Betty Sarvis and Joy Bonar. *The Abortion Question*. New York: Columbia University Press, 1987.

Shuttle, Penelope, and Peter Redgrave. *The Wise Wound: Eve's Curse and Everywoman*. New York: Richard Marek Publishers, 1978.

Spretnak, Charlene. *Lost Goddesses of Early Greece*. Boston: Beacon Press, 1978.

———, ed. *The Politics of Women's Spirituality: Essays on the Rise of Spiritual Power Within the Feminist Movement*, Garden City, New York: Doubleday Anchor Books, 1982.

Starhawk. *Dreaming the Dark*. Boston: Beacon Press, 1982.

———. *The Spiral Dance*. San Francisco: Harper and Row, Publishers, 1979.

Stone, Merlin. *Ancient Mirrors of Womanhood*. Boston: Beacon Press, 1979.

————. *When God Was a Woman*. New York: Harcourt Brace Jovanovich, 1976.

Teish, Luisa. *Jambalaya*. San Francisco: Harper and Row, Publishers, 1985.

Teubal, Sarah. *Sarah the Priestess*. Athens, Ohio: Swallow Press, 1984.

Walker, Barbara G. *The Crone: Woman of Age, Wisdom, and Power*. San Francisco: Harper and Row, Publishers, 1985.

————. *The Woman's Encyclopedia of Myths and Secrets*. San Francisco: Harper and Row, Publishers, 1983.

Washbourn, Penelope. *Becoming Woman*. San Francisco: Harper and Row Publishers, 1977.

Weigle, Marta. *Spiders and Spinsters: Women and Mythology*. Albuquerque: University of New Mexico Press, 1982.

Index

Candace Dwyer → Louisville — LEXINGTON